SAGE was founded in 1965 by Sara Miller McCune to support the dissemination of usable knowledge by publishing innovative and high-quality research and teaching content. Today, we publish over 900 journals, including those of more than 400 learned societies, more than 800 new books per year, and a growing range of library products including archives, data, case studies, reports, and video. SAGE remains majority-owned by our founder, and after Sara's lifetime will become owned by a charitable trust that secures our continued independence.

Los Angeles | London | New Delhi | Singapore | Washington DC | Melbourne

Decision-making in Foreign Policy & INDIA– CHINA BILATERAL RELATIONS

Decision-making in Foreign Policy & INDIA–CHINA BILATERAL RELATIONS

RAVIPRASAD NARAYANAN

Los Angeles | London | New Delhi
Singapore | Washington DC | Melbourne

Copyright © Raviprasad Narayanan, 2022

All rights reserved. No part of this book may be reproduced or utilized in any form or by any means, electronic or mechanical, including photocopying, recording, or by any information storage or retrieval system, without permission in writing from the publisher.

First published in 2022 by

SAGE Publications India Pvt Ltd
B1/I-1 Mohan Cooperative Industrial Area
Mathura Road, New Delhi 110 044, India
www.sagepub.in

SAGE Publications Inc
2455 Teller Road
Thousand Oaks, California 91320, USA

SAGE Publications Ltd
1 Oliver's Yard, 55 City Road
London EC1Y 1SP, United Kingdom

SAGE Publications Asia-Pacific Pte Ltd
18 Cross Street #10-10/11/12
China Square Central
Singapore 048423

Published by Vivek Mehra for SAGE Publications India Pvt Ltd. Typeset in 10.5/13 pt Adobe Caslon Pro by AG Infographics, Delhi.

Library of Congress Control Number: 2021946564

ISBN: 978-93-5479-236-6 (HB)

SAGE Team: Amrita Dutta, Shipra Pant and Rajinder Kaur

To Bharati and Tara

Thank you for choosing a SAGE product!
If you have any comment, observation or feedback,
I would like to personally hear from you.

Please write to me at **contactceo@sagepub.in**

Vivek Mehra, Managing Director and CEO, SAGE India.

Bulk Sales

SAGE India offers special discounts
for purchase of books in bulk.
We also make available special imprints
and excerpts from our books on demand.

For orders and enquiries, write to us at

Marketing Department
SAGE Publications India Pvt Ltd
B1/I-1, Mohan Cooperative Industrial Area
Mathura Road, Post Bag 7
New Delhi 110044, India

E-mail us at **marketing@sagepub.in**

Subscribe to our mailing list
Write to **marketing@sagepub.in**

This book is also available as an e-book.

Contents

List of Abbreviations ix
Preface xiii
Acknowledgements xv

Introduction 1

Part I: Theory

1 Foreign Policy Decision-making (FPDM) Institutions in China 23

2 FPDM and India–China Relations: Identifying Decision-making Themes 61

Part II: Praxis

3 The India-China Bilateral and the Significance of Environmental Diplomacy 109

4 China, India and the United States: Wary Trio? 151

5 New Variable for India in Its Tenuous Relations with China: Taiwan 177

6 Studying Risks of India Being Marginalized Within Its Own Geographical Sphere 201

7 Conclusion 226

Bibliography 234
About the Author 254
Index 255

List of Abbreviations

AGGG	Advisory Group on Greenhouse Gases
AIIB	Asian Infrastructure Investment Bank
AOSIS	Alliance of Small Island States
APP	Asia-Pacific Partnership on Clean Development and Climate
ARF	ASEAN Regional Forum
ASEAN	Association of Southeast Asian Nations
ASEM	Asia-Europe Meeting
BIMSTEC	Bay of Bengal Initiative for Multi-Sectoral Technical and Economic Cooperation
BISTEC	Bangladesh, India, Sri Lanka and Thailand Economic Cooperation
BJP	Bharatiya Janata Party
CAATSA	Countering America's Adversaries Through Sanctions Act
CAS	Chinese Academy of Sciences
CBM	Confidence-building measures
CCP	Chinese Communist Party
CDM	Clean Development Mechanism
CDU	Christian Democratic Union
CHOGM	Commonwealth Heads of Government Meeting
CMC	Central Military Commission
CMCGO	Central Military Commission General Office
CMP	Common Minimum Program
CPC	Communist Party of China
CPEC	China–Pakistan Economic Corridor
CPENR	Commission for the Protection of Environmental and Natural Resources
CPS	Central Party School
CWC	Central Water Commission

DMK	Dravida Munnetra Kazhagam
DPP	Democratic People's Party
DRC	Development Research Center
EAC	East Asian Community
EAS	East Asia Summit
ECFA	Economic Cooperation Framework Agreement
ELM	Expert Level Mechanism
ENR	Enrichment and reprocessing equipment and technology
EPB	Environmental Protection Bureau
FALSG	Foreign Affairs Leading Small Group
FASG	Foreign Affairs Small Group
FPDM	Foreign policy decision-making
GATE	Graduate Aptitude Test in Engineering
GHG	Greenhouse gas
GRE	Graduate Record Examinations
ICWA	Indian Council of World Affairs
IDP	Internally displaced people
INC	Indian National Congress
IOC	Indian Oil Corporation
IONS	Indian Ocean Naval Symposium
IOR	Indian Ocean Region
IR	International relations
ITA	India–Taipei Association
ITER	International Thermonuclear Experimental Reactor
JWG	Joint working group
KMT	Kuomintang
LAC	Line of Actual Control
LDC	Least developed country
LTTE	Liberation Tigers of Tamil Eelam
MEA	Ministry of External Affairs
MEP	Ministry of Environmental Protection
MKC	Mekong River Commission
MoCOM	Ministry of Commerce
MOE	Ministry of Education
MSRI	Maritime Silk Route Initiative
NAM	Non-Aligned Movement

NATO	North Atlantic Treaty Organization
NCCC	National Coordination Committee on Climate Change
NDA	National Democratic Alliance
NDB	New Development Bank
NDRC	National Development and Reform Commission
NDU	National Defence University
NGOs	Non-governmental organizations
NICs	Newly industrialized countries
NPC	National People's Congress
NPT	Nuclear Non-proliferation Treaty
NSG	Nuclear Suppliers Group
OBOR	One Belt One Road
OPEC	Organization of the Petroleum Exporting Countries
PLA	People's Liberation Army
PRC	People's Republic of China
ROC	Republic of China
SAARC	South Asian Association for Regional Cooperation
SCO	Shanghai Cooperation Organisation
SDP	Social Democratic Party
SEPA	State Environmental Protection Agency
SEZ	Special Economic Zone
SLPP	Sri Lanka Podujana Peramuna
SOP	Standard operating procedure
TALSG	Taiwan Affairs Leading Study Group
TECC	Taipei Economic and Cultural Center
TPP	Trans-Pacific Partnership
UNCLOS	United Nations Convention on the Law of the Sea
UNFCCC	United Nations Framework Convention on Climate Change
UNHCE	United Nations Conference on the Human Environment
UNSC	United Nations Security Council
UPA	United Progressive Alliance
USSR	Union of Soviet Socialist Republics
WHO	World Health Organization
WTO	World Trade Organization

Preface

China and India pose many a conundrum.

The world's largest countries in terms of population with potential to emerge as leaders in global economic sphere display an element of civilizational continuum. This continuum predates the Westphalian construct of nation and its attributes.

Multifaceted expressions in foreign policy decision-making (FPDM) are detailed in the book. When it comes to respective foreign policies of the two countries, their political ideologies make for contrasts, with one country dominated by a single political entity, while the other is democracy exhibiting multi-linguistic, multicultural, multiple democratic expressions with provincial slants, making political system resonating with multiple voices. Categorizing the centrality of FPDM as being intrinsic to external relations, China and India are evolving new methodologies enriching FPDM and how are decisions arrived at. Studies on foreign policymaking in China and decisions arrived at are more, in comparison to similar studies on India.

It appears that both countries have decision-making processes highly centralized with strong and, yet, subtle differences. While China has institutional flexibilities evidenced by its single-party state 'tolerating' views calling for greater economic diplomacy as one of its FPDM structural pillars, India differs with its limited innovative flexibilities in an over-centralized realm of FPDM, where generalists prevail over domain specialists.

The book has two sections—Theory and Praxis. These sections explain different theoretical frameworks influencing decision-makers with instances of the two countries and their decision-making regarding other countries and issues with global impact. With cooperation and possible conflict in the bilateral, the book is an effort attempting to introduce a fresh perspective to FPDM.

Acknowledgements

A book on FPDM with China and India is made possible when minds meet, express views, articulate opinions, with contrary views and helpful corrections in arguments being laid out. For this book to be published, it is owing to many people who think, read, reflect and critique the encouraging necessity for China–India relations to be explored beyond the official.

The early idea for writing a book on FPDM came to me while reading a book on policymaking in China, where economic decentralization accompanied the haloed 'Open Door' policy of the late 1970s. It was a revelation to read about how provinces in China had the flexibility to attract investment from abroad. Provinces on the southern and eastern coasts made the most of this, with Beijing, not placing obstacles. Thinking about how India, despite its relatively open economy since 1991, had seemingly run into self-imposed obstacles, the logical trajectory pointed in the direction of foreign policy. To read, acquaint oneself with the why, how, where, who and when required unstinting support of many academics and institutions.

I begin by acknowledging the epistemic community globally. My colleagues at Center for East Asian Studies, School of International Studies and Jawaharlal Nehru University have been a constant source of encouragement. I thank faculty members Alka Acharya, Srikanth Kondapalli, Dolla Varaprasad, Srabani Roy Choudhury, Ritu Agarwal, Jitendra Uttam, Sandip Mishra and Sudhakar Vaddi who are an inspiration. My profound expression of thanks goes to my erstwhile colleagues at the Institute of International Relations, National Chengchi University, Taipei, Taiwan. Cheng Tuan-Yao, Ding Shu-Fan, Liu Fu-Kuo, Yuan I, Tang Shao-Cheng, Yan Chen-Shen, Kan Yi-Hua, Hsiao Hsiu-An, Lu Chien-Yi, Wu Der Yuan, Chen Mumin of National Chung Hsing University; Fang Tien-Sze of National Tsing Hua University; Wu Yu Shan of Academia Sinica; Shen Ming-Shih, Alan Yang Hao, Liao You Te who are mentors and friends with academic insights second to none. Liu Zongyi, Wang Weihua, Chen Dongxiao, Yu Xintian and Wang Dehua in China are academic experts from whom learning China's positions on India were illustrative of views on FPDM in universities and think tanks at Beijing and Shanghai. The Asian Scholarship Foundation, Bangkok, and the Japan Institute of International Relations, Tokyo, augmented my research by providing scholarships to research topics on China.

Libraries are repositories of more than books by the coalescing of minds pursuing higher degrees, detailed information on various subjects and applying thematic perspectives with purpose. To read and understand the intricacies of FPDM, several libraries provided scholastic encouragement with a quietude reflecting in this book. My deepest appreciation is for several libraries with extremely helpful administration facilitating the quest of delving into what one has chosen as academic fount. Libraries at Institute of International Relations, National Chengchi University and Academia Sinica in Taipei, Shanghai Institutes of International Relations, Shanghai Academy of Social Sciences and Shanghai Library merit attention for being exemplars of accessing knowledge resources beyond boundaries and restrictions. The Institute for Defence Studies and Analyses (now Manohar Parrikar Institute for Defence Studies and Analyses) and Institute of Chinese Studies (ICS) in New Delhi have wonderful libraries and reading material. When in Taipei, how can one not mention Eslite, a private bookstore, where enthusiastic readers are sitting on the floor, reading, writing notes, checking stationery and, of course, buying books.

The years of researching FPDM and making notes of what one is reading have motivated me as a constant. This book is to all mentioned, who have become a template to me of academic rigour, institutional adaptability, scholastic profundity and seamless complementarities.

The acknowledgement has to confess that this book would not have happened without encouragement from Amrita Dutta, commissioning editor at SAGE. Thank you, Amrita.

Introduction

The study of contemporary foreign policies of China and India has produced well-researched and topical extrapolations. Detailed explanations on the bilateral, multi-faceted aspects characterizing a multi-hued relationship make for an evaluation of latest trends typifying Asia's two largest countries. The FPDM of the two countries deserves attention for being considered, not congruent with their respective worldviews, encouraging exasperation globally and locally.

Beyond statistical templates and wide-ranging disparate commentaries, a deeper ingress into bilateral foreign policy decisions the two countries are making, is wanting. There is China's FPDM being a field of interest to scholars and policymakers, leaving these very aspects regarding India deficient. This book is an attempt to critically decipher, delineate and deconstruct respective contemporary foreign policies of the two countries through their decision-making processes, structures and personalities.

Foreign Policy Decision-making and International Relations Discourse

The introductory chapter is to examine factors deciding the contours of foreign policy and diplomacy. In the realm of foreign policy, ideology is of seminal importance. It is rare that international or domestic political factors constrain policymakers to such a degree that they are left with no room for choice between alternative courses of action. Decision-makers' views of political reality, whether simple and intuitive or highly complex and formally articulated, structure their environment for choice, inform their consideration of various courses of action and provide rationalization for the choices that are made. An ideology here, may be defined as a more or less coherent and systematic body of ideas that helps to explain the nature of social reality and provides a programme of action for changing that reality in order to achieve certain desired social goods and values.[1]

Since problems are disparate, international relations (IR) approaches the objective through a variety of disciplines. Ideally, in order to be an effective discipline, IR must rest upon a set of value-free assumptions. Perhaps the most important determinant that also could be viewed as an assumption, is the existence, and legitimacy of nation-states as appropriate units of analysis and action. Subsumed under the 'nation-state' are social, cultural, economic, political elements and their associated valves. In making this assumption, IR imposes cognitive structures on various actors and cultural domains that sometimes look inappropriate.

The discipline of IR—the formulation and execution of foreign policy and the study thereof—has developed around congeries of problems, primarily historical and created. These problems arise from differences—political, economic, social, and equally important, if at times overlooked, ethnic, geographical and ecological—many of which actually constitute contradictions posing many a predilection to policy and decision-makers. Broadly, there are five major schools which dominate FPDM interpretation and analysis, and which to varying degrees extend their influence over current interpretations and analyses of IR. They are as follows.

The Classical School

Classical theories of foreign policymaking argue 'rational choice' being a driver of choices made by a nation-state as an actor in the international system. This aspect of 'rational choice' exemplifies achieving comprehensive results satisfying domestic actors/interests and international systemic processes.

While focusing on determinants leading to the study of policymaking, a choice is to be made between the 'external setting' and 'internal setting'. The external setting includes the state's geopolitical position within the global system and regional balance of power as well as its relationship with relevant individual powers.

As for the internal setting, two crucially important determinants are state's military and economic capabilities, which set limits to what the government can do. The internal setting also includes the domestic systemic environment and the structure of the political system in which the decision-makers must operate. In sum, they believe the objective constitutes the critical determinants.[2] Also, within this classical school some theorists diverge from the traditional political analyses that reify or personify nation-states as the basic actors. Instead of directing attention to metaphysical abstractions of the state, the government or broadly labelled institutions—the Executive—narrow the subjects of their inquiry from a larger collectivity to a smaller unit of identifiable persons responsible for making decisions. As Richard Snyder et al. had said, a basic methodological choice for decision-makers is to define the state 'whose authoritative acts are, for all intents and purposes, the acts of the state'.[3]

Apart from the above, scholars, who assign perception a central place in foreign policymaking, regard the world as viewed subjectively by policymakers to be more important than objective reality.[4] In line with this classical school in the study of foreign policy, there are three traditional schools that for some time dominated the study of contemporary Chinese foreign policymaking: the traditional/historical, the Maoist/communist ideology and the realist/rational actor.[5]

The Traditional/Historical

The Traditional/Historical School of scholarship, represented by eminent China scholars such as the late John K. Fairbank, emphasize China's uniqueness—historical and societal.[6] As most of its proponents were historians, it argues that China's foreign policy behaviour can only be understood on the basis of its historical and cultural legacy of the past. The foreign policy under the communist regime represents a continuation of the practice of traditional Sinocentrism, according to which the world as perceived by Chinese rulers is not one based on the concept of sovereign equality of nation/states, but one structured in hierarchical terms. Under such a world system as perceived by the Chinese rulers, China—the 'Middle Kingdom'—is the pre-eminent power that maintains a suzerain-tributary relationship with the rest of the world.

The Realist/Rational Actor

The realist/rational actor school focuses its attention on the objective 'operational environment'.[7] Allen Whiting in his *China Crosses the Yalu: The Decision to Enter the Korean War* is able to reconstruct the events that led to China's policymaking deciding to intervene in the Korean War. By carefully analysing US intelligence information and sifting through Beijing's public pronouncements at the time, Whiting concludes that China's action was largely reactive, for the purpose of self-defence. Aggressive communist ideology or the traditional behaviour to pacify its periphery, were a feint with realism in mainstream western theories on IR being a guide to making and implementing foreign policy. Given the operational environment, the realist/rational actor school argues, Chinese foreign policy can be viewed in traditional western paradigms of balance of power, national interests, and domestic, economic, military and systemic constraints.

Yet another sub-branch to emerge from the realist school is the factional model which places greater emphasis on the influences of some dynastic domestic variables like factionalism in China's power elite in the formulation of its foreign policies.[8]

A supposition of the classical school assumes that policymakers strive to be consistent, to make optimal choices in narrowly constrained neatly defined situations, and to rank and maximize values by choosing the most efficient alternative. It assumes that objectives, rationale, options available and likely consequences of each alternative choice, before making policy, are normative.

The Institutional School

The Institutional School came to the forefront owing to inadequacies found in the realist/rational actor model to explain foreign policy behaviours of nation-states. The Institutional School offers two frames of reference: the 'Organizational Process model' and the 'Bureaucratic Politics model'.[9]

The Organizational Process model envisages government behaviour less as a matter of deliberate choice and more as independent outputs of several large, key organizations, only partly co-ordinated by government leaders. The behaviour of these organizations is primarily determined by the standard or routine operating procedures with only gradual, incremental deviations. This model was most exemplary during Cold War decades, with growing resonance of an organizational temperament influencing foreign policy—debates, think tanks and writings.

The Bureaucratic Politics model, on the other hand, hypothesizes intense competition among decision-making units, and foreign policies are the result of bargaining among the different components of a bureaucracy. At times, the players are guided less by conceptions of national, or even bureaucratic and personal goals. The outcome thus depends not on the rational justification for the policy or on routine organizational procedure, but on the relative power and skill of the bargainers.[10] A Weberian process in other words, creates, manages, divides, confuses and flummoxes observers and practitioners alike.

The Maoist/Communist Ideology

The traditional/historical school that emphasizes China's uniqueness is challenged by the Maoist/communist ideology school of the early 1950s, coinciding with the onset of the politics of the Cold War and American military involvement in Asia. The historical and cultural legacy of the past, the ideology school argues, is less relevant than the principles of orthodox Marxism–Leninism and its Chinese derivative—Maoism—in understanding contemporary Chinese foreign policy behaviour. It suggests that China interacts with the rest of the world based largely on the ideological belief of its elite as personified in Mao Zedong, some of whose ideas often appear antithetical to Chinese tradition.[11]

A number of paradigms have been developed in an attempt to capture the essence of the Chinese politics and economic system. They range from bureaucratic authoritarianism, which emphasizes the rigidity of central control and party-dominated bureaucratic hierarchy, to fragmented authoritarianism that focuses on the centrifugal effects of the bureaucratic interactive bargaining process with the power elite and lower level components of the system.[12]

In conclusion, the Institutional School believes that the rational actor model under the Classical School does not completely capture the whole picture of decision-making and all the forces that influence policy formulation. It points to organizational processes and bureaucratically based politics as significant factors affecting the final policy outcome.

Chinese Foreign Policy Framework

At this stage, it is important to briefly examine the main theoretical frameworks that have influenced the course of Chinese foreign policy.

For the Chinese leadership, a foreign policy position is a unified, theoretically articulated, comprehensive design for dealing with the global system. Such a position begins with an analysis of the international situation. Then, on the basis of that analysis, the position prescribes a strategy for dealing with the principal problems that the analysis has identified. It is a paradigm or logically integrated mode of foreign relations containing prescriptions for both political strategic policies and international economic relations.

In terms of this particular interpretation, a foreign policy position requires that the components of political-strategic policy and international economic policy be compatible and synchronized.

An official survey of Chinese diplomacy in its first four decades, offers a periodization similar to those of some western studies. Corresponding to the four phases into which it divides the PRC's diplomatic history, four theoretical guidelines of Chinese foreign policy can be discerned.[13]

Two Camps

From the founding of the People's Republic to the late 1950s, China's foreign relations were characterized by allying with the Soviet Union. The official Chinese survey describes the foreign policy during this period as 'three great strategic decisions' laid down by Mao.[14] These three decisions are: (a) 'to set up a separate kitchen' (to make a fresh start)—that is, 'to refuse to recognize the diplomatic relations with other countries established by the Guomindang (GMD) government, but to establish instead new relations with foreign countries on a new basis'; (b) 'to clean up the room before sending invitations to the guests' meaning, 'not to be in a hurry to establish diplomatic relations with them' (the imperialist camp headed by the United States), but 'to get rid of all imperialist forces from China which could otherwise still have some influence'; and (c) 'to lean to one side' (the socialist camp headed by the Soviet Union). A theoretical foundation of these policies had been written by Mao in his, *On the People's Democratic Dictatorship*, and his five articles criticising the USA's *China White Paper*. In August 1949, the Truman administration had published the *China White Paper*, explaining past US policy toward China based upon the principle that only Chinese forces could resolve the final outcome of their civil war.

Intermediate Zone

Put forward by Mao in the 1940s, the 'intermediate zone' and other related concepts highlighted the role of the national liberation movement, and the role of the Chinese revolution in particular, in contributing to the international communist movement. How to evaluate the importance of the national liberation movement in fighting against the imperialist block headed by the United States became a central issue in the Sino–Soviet ideological dispute. But the model had emphasized self-reliance in domestic construction. They disputed, split and finally engaged in armed conflict with the Soviets, whom they called 'revisionists' and 'social imperialists'. Sino-American relations remained hostile and frozen, and Mao personally called for 'the people of the world to unite and defeat American imperialism and all its lackeys'. The global revolution theory was best manifested in a series of polemical articles written by the Chinese communists in 1963 and 1964, and was further radicalized during the initial period of the Cultural Revolution.

Three Worlds

From the early 1970s to the early 1980s, the Chinese leadership redefined its international strategies and their theoretical foundation. Beijing gradually moderated its attacks on the United States and improved relations, with the western world, resumed and expanded commercial transactions with foreign countries, and supported established governments in Asia, Africa and Latin America in their demands for a new international economic order. Identifying the Soviet Union as the gravest threat to China's security, Beijing sought to establish an 'international united front against Soviet hegemonism'. The theoretical milestone of this period was the lengthy *Renmin Ribao* (People's Daily) article in October 1977 [Chairman Mao's Theory of the Differentiation of the Three Worlds is a Major Contribution to Marxism–Leninism].[15] Publication of this article after Mao's demise could be construed as representative of factional tussles within the CPC with Hua Guofeng and Deng Xiaoping jostling for leadership. The basic tenets of this theory had already been elucidated by Deng Xiaoping in 1974.[16]

Peace and Development

From 1982 onward, Beijing assumed a more balanced position between the United States and the Soviet Union, and reasserted its solidarity and co-operation with what it defined as the Third World. The conceptual framework of Chinese leaders in adjusting foreign policy was reflected in Premier Zhao Ziyang's detailed survey of China's foreign relations at the Sixth National People's Congress (NPC) in June 1983.[17] Deng Xiaoping was the general architect of this adjustment. He singled out peace and economic development as the 'two really great issues confronting the world today'; noting that peace involved East-West relations and development involved North-South relations. China would be truly non-aligned and oppose hegemony. In North–South relations, China supported dialogue and South–South cooperation.[18]

A view shared by China watchers is that, 'no theoretical formulations have emerged from the post-Mao leadership to provide an alternative framework for foreign policy.[19] But since the early 1980s, significant, revisions with theoretical and conceptual implications have been made in Chinese foreign policy statements and international studies. And they are consistent with China's domestic reform and ideological reorientation. As Zhao Ziyang had said in 1986, 'our domestic and foreign policies are an organic whole'.[20]

Chinese Approaches to IR Theory

Numerous definitions of 'theory' can be found in Western political science and IR studies.[21] Most have at least one thing in common: a political theory may be a proposition (or a set of propositions) that tries to explain social reality. This aspect of 'social reality' was exemplified in northern Europe with Social Democratic parties advocating issues pertaining to human rights becoming accepted norm in their respective foreign policies. Some political scientists may agree to include part of the works of normative thinkers and of 'policy scientists' in the general boundary of IR Theory, while some others may believe that normative works and policy-oriented studies can well benefit from scientific theory but they are not part of it. A Western IR theory may not necessarily provide prescriptions or remedies leading to a better foreign policy or to desirable changes in international reality. In the next paragraphs, a brief review of literature introduces us to nuances of FPDM by China.

By contrast, under strong influence of Leninism, 'Mao Zedong Thought' and now Xi Jinping Thought, all social science theories in the PRC are expected by the leadership to contribute to the building of socialism. No distinction is actually made between those applied theories leading to the formulation of policy and social science theories with only descriptive, predictive and explanatory power.

According to a standard Chinese definition, a theory is a system of concepts and principles, or a systematic rational knowledge; a scientific theory is established on the basis of social practice, and has been proved and verified by social practice, and is a correct reflection of the essence and laws of objective things.[22] The significance of a scientific theory lies in its ability to guide human behaviour.

Quoting Lenin's remarks that 'practice is higher than theoretical knowledge', Mao Zedong observed that Marxist philosophy wants to 'actively... change the world' and 'the importance of theory precisely ... because it can guide action'.[23] In the Chinese context, a theory is not much different from a doctrine, an ideology or a set of propositions serving as a guiding principle for action. In Chinese Communist vocabulary, 'theoretical work' can be inferred to be 'ideological work', and theory is more closely identified with practice than with reality.[24] Theories without immediate relevance to policymaking or implementation are often referred to as empty and useless.

Therefore, IR theory, as understood by China, is not only an explanatory tool or a prism through which world affairs are observed, and more importantly, a guide for international action and foreign policy. In recent years, Chinese IR scholars have found themselves dissatisfied with many existing theoretical notions and have made efforts to formulate new theories.[25] At the same time, however, the Chinese conception of theory as defined above has hardly been challenged. When a senior Chinese IR researcher, Chen Zongjin, called for more theoretical ideas, he explained that 'without a deepening of theory, there would be no clear-cut decision or understanding of policy'.

IR theorists since Thucydides have noted the critical importance of perceptions influencing a nation's foreign policies. Stephen Levine ['Perception and Ideology in Chinese Foreign Policy', in *Chinese Foreign Policy*, ed. Robinson and Shambaugh (1994)] examines the roles, perceptions and ideology in particular—play in Chinese foreign policy.

In his work on China's opening to the outside world—*The Experience with Foreign Capitalism*, Robert Kleinberg develops a starting point for China's economic diplomacy. Beginning in 1978, China acknowledged the need for external development assistance by shifting its status from aid giver to aid recipient within the framework of the United Nations Development Programme (UNDP). Subsequent revisions in China's long-standing policy of self-reliance opened the way for significantly higher levels of trade (foreign), and acceptance of foreign investment, loans and credits from both bilateral and multilateral sources, Harold K. Jacobson and Michael Oksenberg in their book titled *China's Participation in the IMF, the World Bank and GATT – Towards a Global Economic Order* outline the process that China adopted in becoming a member recipient of the KIEO's.

One important outgrowth of the Open Door Policy in the 1980s was China's formal entry into the World Bank group—the International Monetary Fund (IMF), the International Bank for Reconstruction and Development (IBRD) or World Bank, and its affiliated agencies, the International Development Association (IDA) and the International Finance Corporations (IFC). In 1983, China was granted observer status in the General Agreement on Tariffs and Trade (GATT), and in 1986 it formally applied for full membership. In 1986, China joined the Asian Development Bank. Samuel S. Kim, *China and the World* (1989); *China In and Out of the Changing World Order* (1991) asserts in his works the important role international organizations have had in shaping the domestic agenda in China.

The interlinkages forged over the past four decades, as part of its economic diplomacy, are in a large way responsible due to the vision of globalization and regionalization that is gradually taking shape, is the perception of Denis F. Simon and Hong Pyong Lee in their book *Globalization and Regionalization of China's Economy* who examine this aspect. To qualify the intricacies involved in establishing an interrelationship between IR theory and the study of Chinese foreign policy, Allen Whiting (1994) juxtaposes the current posturing with future trends.

The shift in favour of economic aspects to diplomacy and its strategic corollaries were bound to alter established mechanisms that co-coordinated foreign policy. Gao Shanquan and Chi Fulin in *Theory and Reality of Transition to a Market Economy* trace the emergence in the past two decades of symmetry between the rapidly expanding foreign economic relations, and a reformist leadership that has seen the creation of several new central institutions. These include the Foreign Investment Commission, which manages the introduction of foreign investment; the State Import and Export Commission which makes policies concerning technology imports and new trading arrangements; and the General Administration of Customs, which was to formulate preferential customs policies as well as the MOFERT (Ministry of Foreign Economic Relations and Trade) and CITIC (China International Trust and Investment Company), which was to facilitate joint ventures.

The 'Open Door' policy once introduced, found further echo in the objective of transforming China into a 'socialist market economy'. The role of the various decision-making bodies that constitute the highest level of governance in China have been favourable to the promotion of the reform process by creating space for function. To encourage greater entrepreneurship, as a whole body of available literature proves, the reforms split the tasks involved in foreign trade. The non-governmental, China Council for the Promotion of International Trade (CCPIT), also plays a key role in arranging trade negotiations between China and potential trading partners, mounting trade expositions and providing consultancy services.

The most visible elucidation of China's strategic economic diplomacy was first seen in Southeast Asia. Southeast Asia as a vehicle to promote trade and investment has in the ASEAN an example of what a regional economic alliance can achieve, despite the recent setbacks. Zhao Quanshang in his article 'Achieving Maximum Advantage, Rigidity and Flexibility in Chinese Foreign Policy' (*American Asian Review*, Spring 1995) and Chiao Siow-Yue and Cheng Bifan in their book *ASEAN-China Economic Relations-Trends and Patterns*, establish that regarding ASEAN, there used to be little complementarity between China and the developing countries of Southeast Asia, and thus little scope for Chinese involvement in the region. Post-1978 saw the establishment of diplomatic ties between the Southeast Asian nations and China. This has been followed by an engagement with commercial interests dominating other issues. In the coming years as the ASEAN economies renew their development programmes, there is bound to be an expansion in the economic sphere, irrespective of existing contentious issues. The growing regional cooperation would be sustained by competition that would provide the necessity to minimize and resolve competition-based disputes, and to stress the importance of international economic institutions.

The expansion of China's foreign economic relations has prompted the emergence of an intermediary layer of quasi-state institutions mediating between the state and foreign capital. Xi Jinping's efforts at promoting Maritime Silk Road Initiative (MSRI), One Road One Belt (OBOR), New Development Bank (NDB), Asian Infrastructure Investment Bank (AIIB) are a continuity of sorts, with more capital and strategic calculations at play. The rise of such quasi-state institutions has accompanied the ebb and flow of decentralization policies. Whilst these quasi state institutions are supposed to operate like business entities, there is a need for further research to find out how much they relate to subordinate companies and enterprise according to economic rather than administrative principles. The rise of the quasi-state institutions reveals the emergence of a more entrepreneurial state. Quasi-state institutions allow for greater maneuverability than other state organs as is evidenced in the work *States Versus Markets in the World System* by Peter Evans, Dietrich Reuschmeyer and Evelyn Stephens.

Harry Harding, Steven Goldstein, David Shambaugh, Barry Naughton, and others involved in examining various facets of China's foreign policy represent a whole body of texts and interpretation upon which this proposal thesis draws its essential understanding.

The introduction of the 'reform and opening to the outside world' policy in the PRC in the late 1970s and 1980s has also resulted in a more flexible political and academic environment, which has enabled Chinese scholars to conduct their studies in more creative and critical ways. Simultaneously, the release of many previously unavailable documentary sources detailing the working of the Communist Party of China (CPC) makes it possible for scholars to base their studies on a more comprehensive documentary foundation.

It has however to be borne in mind that the publication of works of the CPC leaders was not designed for scholarly interests, rather it was aimed to guide the revolutionary mass movement in the early decades, into the orbit set up by the party. Thus, the criteria for selecting the works of Party leaders followed the Party's needs.

This book strives to tease out India's FPDM by explaining in detail the instances of cooperation, competition and misinterpretations in the bilateral with China. Unlike China, decision-making processes in India when it comes to foreign policymaking have not merited attention globally. By explaining a multi-spectral bilateral, chapters in this book decipher China–India bilateral, beyond the main obstacle—boundary dispute.

Chapterization

The book is comprised of two parts with six chapters, apart from the introduction and conclusion. The first part, **Theory**, explains FPDM as an important and intrinsic realm in making foreign policy. The second part, **Praxis**, describes in detail the cooperation, competition, conflictual stratagem of the two countries in their foreign strategic policies. The chapters are:

Part I: Theory

Chapter 1: Foreign Policy Decision-making (FPDM) Institutions in China

What are the institutions in China deciding foreign policy is a facet of who debates, frames, makes, implements the country's foreign policy. A one-party state, with the CPC at the helm since 1949, the country's foreign policy has evolved over the decades to become the most studied actor of international politics. This chapter elucidates on the inner domains of FPDM in China.

Chapter 2: FPDM and India–China Relations: Identifying Decision-making Themes

This chapter examines the evolution of China and India foreign policy and diplomacy. Tracing the origin and successful implementation of multi-layered diplomacy as determinants of bilateral foreign policy since the nuclear tests of 1998 by India, the main thrust of the chapter is to identify themes of IR decision-making within their respective frameworks. The year 1998 is chosen as nuclear tests conducted by India in the month of May was a 'demonstrator' with many concomitants.

Part II: Praxis

Chapter 3: The India–China Bilateral and the Significance of Environmental Diplomacy

The significance of China–India cooperation in global environmental cooperation at the Copenhagen Conference in 2009 was but an indicator of the criticality of the issue for both countries. This chapter emphasizes cooperative aspects of environmental diplomacy between China and India on Climate Change at the global level and the looming prospect of hydro-politics over the waters of the Brahmaputra as a significant bilateral/regional environmental concern.

Chapter 4: China, India and the United States: Wary Trio?

Policy choices with strong underpinnings of a rationale determined by domestic episteme made by a country help decipher continuities and discontinuities in foreign policymaking. The choices made in foreign policymaking reveal the imprint of internal political agendas and institutional arrangements that manage foreign policy. This chapter examines China, India and United States as being three countries exhibiting their global outreach in starkly different ways. An attempt is made to knit perennial wavering complementarities amongst the three countries, matched by an undercurrent of arriving at a compact on various issues.

Chapter 5: New Variable for India in Its Tenuous Relations with China: Taiwan

China–India relations are central to Asia and rest of the world. Bilateral relations the two countries perforce conduct are determined by a template, where apprehensions and inadequate political-institutional institutions exist between respective foreign policymaking establishments. The last couple of years have witnessed intensified mutual distrust in the bilateral with Taiwan as a new dynamic variable for India in its tenuous relations with its larger northern neighbour, that covets the island as 'unfinished business' since the civil war years of 1930s and 1940s when the CPC and GMD (*Kuomintang [KMT]*) fought on the basis of ideological differences. This chapter strives to capture the intricacies of China–India relations by adopting a slant where critique is continuum.

Chapter 6: Studying Risks of India Being Marginalized Within Its Own Geographical Sphere

For long a marginal sphere in geopolitics, South Asia is now witnessing the beginnings of a rivalry that are altering the strategic landscape of the region. The growing rivalry between China and India in the region has a powerful underlying message for India—it risks being marginalized within its own geographical sphere by China. China's strategy of 'Go West' and OBOR merges and almost clashes with India's 'Look East' strategy and the uncertainties and ambiguities buried in the rhetoric on both sides generates ample insecurities. The image of South Asian security has for long been dominated by the dyadic rivalry between India and Pakistan. Events in the subcontinent since the nuclear tests of 1998 have evolved in such a manner that India finds more flexibility in articulating a security framework that resonates more beyond the region, while the region opens up to inducements—strategic and economic—from China.

Chapter 7: Conclusion

A critical evaluation of FPDM by India and China is a motivating vehicle knitting the two countries. China with its adherence to ideology in political terms has succeeded in achieving economic progress that contrasts with a political orientation constantly becoming a rhetoric divorced from pronouncements made by its founder—Mao Zedong. A different exemplar is India, with its continuity as expressing and practicing a political temperament where democracy has established itself all through the country with its linguistic, geographical, ethnic, religious and social diversities.

Notes

1. Walter Carlsnaes, *Ideology and Foreign Policy: Problems of Comparative Conceptualisation* (New York, NY: Basil Blackwell, 1987), 149–65.
2. Richard C. Snyder, et. al. (eds.), *Foreign Policy Decision-Making* (New York, NY: The Free Press, 1963), 70.
3. Snyder, *Foreign Policy Decision-Making*, 72.
4. See Juliet Kaarbo, 'A Foreign Policy Analysis Perspective on the Domestic Politics Turn in IR Theory', *International Studies Review* 17, no. 2 (June 2015): 189–216.
5. A survey on the study of Chinese foreign policy was conducted by Yu Binyin, 'The Study of Chinese Foreign Policy: Problems and Prospects', *World Politics* 46 (January 1994). Also, Samuel S. Kim, 'China and the World in Theory and Practice', in *China and the World: Chinese Foreign Relations in the Post-Cold War Era* ed. Kim (Boulder: Westview Press, 1994); and James Rosenau, 'China in a Bifurcated World: Competing Theoretical Perspectives' in *Chinese Foreign Policy: Theory and Practice*, ed. T.W. Robinson and D. Shambaugh (New York, NY: Oxford University Press, 1993).
6. A selected number of works in this School include: John K. Fairbank, ed., *The Chinese World Order* (Cambridge: Harvard University Press, 1968) and 'China's Foreign Policy in Historical Perspective', *Foreign Affairs*, 47 (April 1969); C.P. Fitzgerald, *The Chinese View of Their Place in the World* (London: Faber and Faber, 1967); Chih-Yu Shih, *China's Just World: The Morality of Chinese Foreign Policy* (Boulder: Lynne Rienner, 1992); Mark Mancall, *China at the Centre: 300 Years of Foreign Policy* (New York: Free Press, 1984); 'The Persistence Of Tradition in Chinese Foreign Policy', *Annals of the American Academy of Political and Social Sciences*, 349 (September 1963); Morris Rossabi, *China Among Equals: The Middle Kingdom and its Neighbours* (Berkeley: University of California Press, 1983); J. Crammer Byng, 'The Chinese View of Their Place in the World: A Historical Perspective', *The China Quarterly* no. 53 (January–March 1973); Michael H. Hunt, 'Chinese Foreign Relations in Historical Perspective' in *China's Foreign Relations in1980s*, ed. Harry Harding (New Haven: Yale University Press, 1984).
7. Some works of this school: Allen S. Whiting, *China Crosses the Yalu: The Decision to Enter the Korean War* (Stanford: Stanford University Press, 1960); *The Chinese Calculus of Deterrence* (Ann Arbor: University of Michigan Press, 1975); 'The Use of Force in Foreign Policy by the People's Republic of China', *Annals of The American Academy of Political and Social Sciences*, 402 (July 1972); Jonathan Pollack, 'Perception and Action in Chinese Foreign Policy:

The Quemoy Decision' (PhD dissertation, University of Michigan, 1976); Michael Yahuda, *China's Role in World Affairs* (New York, NY: St. Martin's Press, 1978); MelGurtov and Byong-moo Hwang, *China Under Threat: The Politics of Strategy and Diplomacy* (Baltimore, MD: John Hopkins University Press, 1980).

8. Works in this regard include: Andrew Nathan's, 'A Factionalism Model for CCP Politics', *China Quarterly* no.53 (January–March 1973); Allen Whiting, *Chinese Domestic Politics and Foreign Policy in the 1970s* (Ann Arbor: Centre for Chinese Studies, 1979); John Garver, *China's Decision for Rapprochement with the United States* (Boulder: Westview Press, 1982); Jonathan D. Pollack, *The Sino-Soviet Rivalry and Chinese Security Debate* (Santa Monica: Rand Corporation, R-2907-AE October 1982).
9. Graham T. Ellison, *Essence of Decision* (Boston: Little Brown and Company, 1971), 34.
10. Ellison, *Essence of Decision*, 36.
11. Among works of this School: Benjamin I. Schwartz, *Communism and China: Ideology in Flux* (Cambridge: Harvard University Press, 1968), 'China and the West in the Thought of Mao Tse-Tung', in *China in Crisis*, Vol. 1, ed. Ping-Ti Ho and Tang Tsou (Chicago University Press: Chicago, 1968); Harold C. Hinton, *China's Turbulent Quest* (Bloomington: Indiana University Press, 1972); John Gittings, *The World and China, 1922-1972* (New York: Harper and Row, 1974); Greg O'Leary, *The Shaping of Chinese Foreign Policy* (Berkeley: University of California Press, 1970); J. D. Armstrong, *Revolutionary Diplomacy: Chinese Foreign Policy and the United Front Doctrine* (Berkeley, CA: University of California Press, 1977).
12. For a brief discussion of these and other paradigms, see Carol Lee Hamrin and Suisheng Zhao, 'Introduction: Core Issues in Understanding the Decision Process' in *Decision-Making in Deng China*, eds. Hamrin and Zhao (Armonk: M.E. Sharpe, 1995); Kenneth G. Lieberthal, 'Introduction: The "Fragmented Authoritarian" Model and its Limitations', in *Bureaucracy, Politics and Decision-Making in Post-Mao China*, ed. Lieberthal and David M. Lampton (Berkeley: University of California Press, 1996).
13. Michael Yahuda, *Towards the End of Isolationism: China's Foreign Policy After Mao* (London: Macmillan, 1983), 25–43.
14. Wang Jisi, 'International Relations Theory and the Study of Chinese Foreign Policy: A Chinese Perspective', in *Chinese Foreign Policy: Theory and Practice*, eds. T.W. Robinson and D. Shambaugh (New York: Oxford University Press, 1993), 482–83.
15. Excerpts of this article in English can be seen in King C. Chen, ed., *China and The Three Worlds: A Foreign Policy Reader* (While Plains, NY: M. E. Sharpe, 1979).
16. Chairman of Chinese delegation Teng Hsiao-ping's (Deng Xiaoping) speech at Special Session of the UN General Assembly, *Peking Review*, 16 (19 April 1974): 6–11.

17. Zhao Ziyang, 'Report on the Work of the Government', *Beijing Review*, 26–27 (4 July 1983).
18. Deng Xiaoping, 'Safeguard World Peace and Ensure Domestic Development', 29 May 1984; 'Peace and Development are the Two Outstanding Issues in the World Today', 4 March 1985, in *Deng Xiaoping, Fundamental Issues in Present-Day China* (Oxford: Pergamon Press, 1987), 46–47 & 97–99.
19. Allen S. Whiting, 'Foreign Policy of China' in *Foreign Policy in World Politics*, ed. Ray C. Macridis (Englewood Cliffs, NJ: Prentice Hall, 1985), 262.
20. Zhao Ziyang, 'Report on The Seventh Five-Year Plan', *Beijing Review*, 29/16 (21 April 1986): 28.
21. Stanley Hoffman has defined contemporary theory of IR, 'a systematic study of Observable phenomena that tries to discover the principal variables, to explain behaviour, and to reveal the characteristic types of relations among national units'. (Stanley Hoffman, 'Theory and International Relations' in *International Politics and Foreign Policy*, ed. James N. Rosenau (New York: Free Press, 1969), 30.

    Kenneth Waltz argues that theories are not merely collections of laws, but statements that *explain them*. 'A Theory, though related to the world about which explanations are wanted always remains distinct from that world. "Reality" will be congruent neither with a theory nor with a model that may represent it'. [Kenneth N. Waltz, *Theory of International Politics* (Reading, MA: Addison-Wesley Publishing Co., 1979), 1–17].
22. Ci Hai (Shanghai: Shanghai Dictionary Publishing House, 1979), 2766.
23. '"On Practice" in Mao Zedong', *Four Essays on Philosophy* (Beijing: Foreign Languages Press, 1966), 4 & 14.
24. Albert Feuerwerker, 'Chinese History and the Foreign Relations of Contemporary China', *The Annals* 402 (July 1972): 1–11.
25. Yong Deng, 'The Chinese Conception of National Interests in International Relations', *China Quarterly* (1998), 308–29. It is said that, former Chinese President, Jiang Zemin had encouraged scholars in major universities and think tanks to come up with more independent, in depth analyses of foreign affairs in the spirit of 'having multiple voices internally, while speaking in one voice externally'.

Part I

Theory

CHAPTER 1

Foreign Policy Decision-making (FPDM) Institutions in China

Introduction

Foreign policy decision-making (FPDM) in China is more than a hierarchical process. It comprises various groups and clusters, exclusively from within the Communist Party of China (CPC). These groups are not static, revealing tendencies to morph into becoming 'cliques' or 'factional' posturing on a particular issue. The General Secretary of the CPC is aware of dissensus on fractious issues, where his word, may or may not be, final. This chapter explains a few perceivable intra-CPC variables playing significant roles in China's FPDM.

'Groupthink' in Strategic Policymaking—
The Foreign Affairs Leading Study Group

Since Mao's time, there have existed informal clusters of 'small advisory and coordination groups' within the CPC, the government bureaucracy and the political policymaking process. These groups could be termed as precursors to contemporary think tanks.

Groups are a valuable part of any decision-making process.[1] Decisions made by groups are typically better than those made by individuals as there is a greater pool of available knowledge, identification of alternative options/courses of action, critical review of each course of option/action, a shared risk by group members in arriving at a decision as also the consensus arrived at after the due process of deliberation that is binding on members of the group.[2] A group decision approach argues that 'multiple policy makers' with the resources and initiative to 'pursue their own' policy goals emerge as 'central stakeholders' of the policy process.[3] Being a tightly knit group, the members are collectively entrusted with the task of arriving at a decision to do so, ensuring a strong element of coordination. Within a Chinese context, these informal groups had the brief to direct research agendas, advice the leadership and act as a 'facilitator' between various organizations in the political structure. These 'leading groups' (*lingdao xiaozu*), in the words of Alice Miller 'are directly subordinate to the Party Secretariat and report to the Politburo and its Standing Committee'.[4] Perhaps the most important of these groups is the party Secretariat's Foreign Affairs Small Group (FASG). The FASG is also known as the Foreign Affairs Leading Small Group (FALSG). The FALSG became 'essentially an advisory rather than a decision-making body'[5] during the 1980s.

In the opinion of Doak Barnett, FALSG was 'to exchange views, to study problems and to communicate'—significantly, it did not have the power/authority to decide. The FALSG is considered a mechanism of the party more than the government. A former Chinese diplomat, Lu Ning, however, holds a different view. For Lu Ning, the FALSG was of greater significance to China's policymaking process—and in the hierarchy comes after the Politburo and the Standing Committee. The FALSG as a group comprises important party and government officials including the President, the Premier who heads the State Council, state councillors and ministers of 'important' ministries—foreign affairs, commerce, state security and also 'specialists' from think tanks and academia.[6] Since the FALSG comprises and 'assembles' most of the key government and party leaders and who are best informed regarding China's foreign policy, its importance is not to be undervalued. Lu Ning's ranking of the FALSG could perhaps be attributed to Jiang Zemin's heading the FALSG for the first time in 1996 and its role in the Taiwan Straits crisis of that year.[7] Earlier, it was Li Peng, who as premier had headed the FALSG for eight years from 1988.

Several characteristics and values of the FALSG are as follows:

1. As a sufficiently small group, every member of the group is aware and knows (professionally/personally/through shared experience) other members.
2. An overriding motivation or goal (ideology during the Maoist era) unifies members of the group.
3. Informal interaction to exchange views and discuss stratagem.
4. Group behaviour circumscribes individual opinion and hence a more balanced outcome.
5. A small informal group with shared values and perhaps similar social dimensions is easier to handle than larger and socially unbalanced groups.

A significant development was the setting up of a National Security Leading Group (*Guojia Anquan Lingdao Xiaozu*) in 2000 to coordinate foreign policymaking. Under Hu Jintao's leadership, the levels of policymaking included multiple players—the Politburo, leading small groups, ministries, think tanks and even public opinion, according to a study by Lai Hongyi.[8] The Central Committee Organization Department of the CPC is another 'think tank' located within the recesses of the vast CPC bureaucracy. It came into prominence following the release of a 308-page document titled *Studies of Contradictions Within the People Under New Conditions*—that starkly documented the causes and effects of rising social inequality, skewed regional development patterns and the rise in collective actions (protests) against authority.[9]

With the coming into being of specialized think tanks, the policy process has become more diversified. Diversification apart, it is well known that policymakers in Beijing while considering inputs from think tanks have to consciously perform their role in 'protecting' CPC's hold on power.

Military/Defence Think Tanks

For a system whose policymaking is still considered opaque, the Chinese military—the People's Liberation Army (PLA)—has a fairly disproportionate share of think tanks. Most military research, analysis and intelligence prior to the reform period were coloured by ideological polemic and falling short of rational analysis. PLA-related think tanks and research organizations are classified into intelligence analysis,[10] weapons research and arms control,[11] exchanges[12] and research (scientific and non-scientific). Most PLA-affiliated think tanks in the last decade have set up crisis management groups within think tanks to address a range of multiple issues—Korean peninsula, terror scenarios as also pandemics. Reports produced by PLA research units for internal consumption (*neibu*) are routed through the Central Military Commission General Office (CMCGO) where they are evaluated, summarized and distributed upwards through vertical internal channels to top defence, foreign policy and national security policy organs.[13] To lend more credence to the policymaking process and make it more interactive, military strategists often attend, on an informal basis, various internal discussion meetings and report preparation conferences convened by civilian research institutes and departments.[14] Views generated by military think tanks are given due importance in the overall scheme of things and their views comprise one of the several reports considered by the final decision-makers in Beijing.[15]

Examples of PLA think tanks include the Academy of Military Sciences (*Zhongguo Junshi Kexue*/AMS) that approaches studies and concepts related to the future of warfare and security from a theoretical perspective, and the National Defence University (NDU), which has the mandate of educating the senior officer corps on current security issues.[16] Among the significant contributions from the AMS have been Gen. Li Jijun's writings[17] on 'asymmetric warfare' and Col. Huang Shuofeng extrapolating the concept of 'comprehensive national power' (CNP) into Chinese academic and public discourse, later accepted by the Chinese leadership.[18]

Within the apex policymaking circles in Beijing, the voice of the PLA remains powerful but has to compete with other alternative proposals from other bureaucracies, 'civilian' think tanks, universities and experts. It has to be stated that the leadership in China would not want the PLA to assume a much larger influence than what it already has. Perhaps, the maximum influence the PLA exercised over the polity was during the early days of the Cultural Revolution—a phase repugnant to the leadership today.

The 'Establishment Intellectual' in China

Intellectuals have always enjoyed special social status in Chinese history as the carrier of 'Chinese culture' and 'assistants to the ruler of the country'.[19] Intellectuals have been defined by their inclination to speak truth to power and thus seek to humanize the power.

The politically forced marginalized existence of intellectuals in China came to a close with the initiation of the reform era. To give intellectual legitimacy to the reform process, Deng Xiaoping rehabilitated intellectuals within the socialist firmament and equated them with the working class.[20] Intellectuals were defined by the CPC as producers of 'mental products' (ideology).[21] A prime reason for CPC's change in attitude towards intellectuals and think tanks stemmed from the Open Door policy initiated in 1978. Chinese leaders began to re-evaluate the abilities of professionals and specialists and placed particular emphasis on the restoration of think tanks in order to facilitate the progress of the 'Four Modernisations' programme.[22] It could be argued that for the post-Mao leadership, the Four Modernisations were to be a conduit with which it reached out and established rapport with intellectuals and thereby the people. An additional stimulus provided by the Open Door policy was the beginning of a new tradition—the seeking of policy-oriented advice and analysis by leaders and bureaucrats.[23]

By encouraging discussion and suggestions within party forums, Deng Xiaoping was assiduously cultivating a constituency for change within the party over the hardliners. In this manner, the approach of Deng Xiaoping differed from that of his predecessors. Deng Xiaoping's political style was to build coalitions in broad agreement with a particular course of action. The political context to Deng's attempt to establish a systematic and professional policy formulation process was also in order to legitimize his personal authority.[24] To his credit, Deng Xiaoping initiated the need for institutional procedures that would in the long-term separate the government from the party. Both Hu Yaobang and Zhao Ziyang justified Deng's policy towards intellectuals and argued that intellectuals and experts could solve the economic and social problems resulting from the reform programme and also provide a new foundation from which China's foreign and strategic policy can be articulated. From a libertarian perspective, the 'expert' plays a crucial role by 'engaging' with the problems posed by the government, systematizes and analyzes these problems through the development of specialized fields of knowledge, and proposes and enacts measures to bring about solutions to these problems.[25] Thus, since the early 1980s intellectuals and think tanks have been viewed as instruments of a more participative and inclusive process of policymaking.[26]

Currently, most intellectuals enjoy a privileged status and occupy powerful positions within policymaking circles. As party members, they also have a career that is relatively flexible and allows them to migrate from think tanks to universities to even diplomatic assignments. For want of any other term, these 'privileged' groups of people in China are called 'establishment intellectuals'.[27] These 'establishment intellectuals' prefer to lay stress on the need for the establishment of transparent institutions of governance—something which the CPC lays great stress on. The 'establishment intellectuals' in China are akin to Antonio Gramsci's 'organic intellectuals' who serve as the 'thinking and leading elements of a social group, and give their own class an awareness of its function in all economic, social and political fields'.[28]

Studies on intellectuals, think tanks and the Chinese state is a field of enquiry that is constantly evolving. A review of existing literature reveals some clear approaches. Peter Moody puts across the argument that there needs to be division made between 'establishment' and 'non-establishment' intellectuals.[29] Doak Barnett argues that the reform period has witnessed the emergence of a more 'systematic regularized and rationalized' policymaking process.[30] For Merle Goldman, the categorization and distinction of an intellectual in China lies with the 'sense of responsibility' that goes with being part of the establishment.[31] Taking Goldman's argument further, for Michel Bonnic and

Yves Chevrier, it is the 'legitimacy' aspect given by intellectuals (who are part of the establishment) to the state, which encourages a deeper engagement.[32] Adding to the wealth of literature on 'establishment intellectuals' is Shiping Hua's observation that the categories adopted by Peter Moody and Merle Goldman in their analyses 'may not be able to explain the situation in which establishment intellectuals seem to always go beyond the boundaries set by their party patrons' since Deng's reform took hold.[33] Reflecting the most perceptible 'division' amongst Chinese intellectuals is Zhidong Hao's distinction of the existence of 'in-institution' and 'out-institution' groups, depending on whether they work primarily within the state sector or out of it. This institutional boundary implies no anticipation that 'out-institution' intellectuals are 'autonomous humanists' who might otherwise work in an independent sphere of civil society.[34]

In the reform period, the emergence of policy advisory groupings and organizations in the words of Ding Xueliang is reflective of 'the lack of rigidity over ideology [that] has spurred informal intellectual networks, salons, study groups, non-official journals and think tanks'.[35] The emergence of this network of semi-autonomous organizations in the early 1980s was possible due to the 'protection' provided by the reformist faction to begin with. The emergence of 'establishment intellectuals' and their increasing profile in the reform years has undoubtedly been the positive consequence of a less intense political climate that has allowed the forging of new relationships between Chinese intellectuals and the state. The social and economic changes in the reform period have encouraged intellectuals to explore more possibilities in asserting their professional autonomy and intellectual independence. This has translated into Chinese intellectuals being conditioned to the existence of a wider world of academia where ideas and thoughts can be cross-fertilized.[36] The positive aspect of this development according to Shiping Hua is that 'establishment intellectuals are going through a process of reforming themselves' from being seen as 'merely the tools of the ruler' to a stage where they are considered 'independent' and speak for society.[37]

However, there are rules. 'Among the rules of the political game that influences Chinese intellectual life, the most important is what one might call the "within-establishment principle"—an unwritten Party requirement that publicly expressed views (in particular, non-conformist views) must be made "public" through proper Party–State channels and proper procedure'.[38]

Briefly, China's 'establishment intellectuals' are:

1. those who fulfil the tag 'intellectual' and are employed with official, quasi-official think tanks, research institutes or universities;
2. experts on social, economic, political, strategic and technical issues;
3. those who take part in the government process of policymaking by contributing through formal and informal channels of communication;
4. part of officially sponsored associations or the vast policymaking bureaucracy.
5. members of the CPC who wish to rise up the political ladder by contributing to policymaking.

As an all-encompassing term, 'intellectuals' in China today are academics (*xuezhe*), readers (*dushuren*), professors (*jiaoshou*), writers (*zuojia*), experts (*zhuanjia*) and the growing tribe of media stars (*meiti xing*).

Functions of Chinese Strategic Policymaking Think Tanks

The growth and increasing professionalization of the think tank community in China is perhaps reflective of the widening degree of interactions that researchers, policymakers and specialists have. As the system constantly evolves towards a greater level of participation and consensus building in policymaking, the functions performed by a think tank become vital. Some of these are as follows:

Policy Advocates

The political culture in China is accommodative of think tanks as long as they have their respective channels of 'official sanction' and 'patronage'. In the early days of reform, think tanks were 'used' by political leaders to advance their policies and positions. In a system where 'establishment intellectuals' are the norm, it is not surprising to note that think tanks become firm advocates and propagate CPC's *Weltanschauung* on every possible subject. Even in a political culture like China's, academic debates do not take place in a vacuum but are conducted by a group of people (party elites no doubt) who have various needs or are under various pressures with various motivations.

After nearly three decades of reform, a few 'establishment intellectuals' have managed to attract a wider audience. In response to western academic debates on the impact of reform on the Chinese political system, think tanks in China are generating 'alternate' views known for their 'Chinese characteristics' echoing the need for political stability as a precondition for economic progress as also tempered by the lacunae in understanding the nuances of democracy that led to the failure of the Tiananmen 1989 movement.

In the words of a prominent exiled intellectual Yan Jiaqi, the CPC represents a 'continuing despotic system characterized by a lack of legal limits on absolute power'.[39] For Pan Wei, a professor at Beijing University, existing definitions and versions of democracy have ended up mythologizing democracy—in the sense, it is made out to be the panacea for all evils.[40] The periodic elections of top leaders by electorates do not find favour with Pan Wei, as they (the elections) authorize a few with the power to rule, as opposed to a system where supreme power lies with the 'rule of law' that regulates government instead of creating one from time to time. Pan Wei's critique of democracy draws comparison with Chen Duxiu and Li Dazhao, two of the most influential May Fourth[41] intellectuals who concluded that established western liberal democracies failed to act according to the values they proclaimed and hence gravitated towards socialism with its promise of 'real democracy'.[42]

As 'policy advocates' to a system that in political terms is yet to be considered 'open', think tanks in China do go through a process that questions their very credibility. In order to make the most of a relatively tranquil phase in China's contemporary period, think tanks go to great lengths, so as to not appear as being 'agents of change'. By driving up an ambitious agenda for change, think tanks are apprehensive that should the limited and constrained 'window of opportunity' open to them be closed, it is wiser, to be not seen as fomenting an antithesis to the state and its agendas. The professional competence of think tanks in China as a consequence is in a unique way swayed by not only official agendas but also 'officially' endorsed outcomes. Resultantly, scholars and think tanks have to walk a 'tightrope' between policy analyses, policy advocacy and not offend the powers.

An instance of think tanks in China becoming policy advocates was during the early days of the reform period. It is known that conflicting views amongst the leadership on contentious issues generate policy debates with respect to the nature of an issue, policy priority, setting goals and choosing means. During the political divergence of views and policies between Hua Guofeng's 'whatever'[43] faction and Deng Xiaoping's 'practice' faction in 1978, Hu Yaobang persuaded and convinced intellectual circles to promote Deng Xiaoping's pragmatic approach and therefore legitimize Deng's leadership as also his new approach over the 'whatever' line promoted by Hua Guofeng.[44] This instance of a political factional battle and the roping in of intellectuals by one faction, in the words of Lucian Pye, are a consequence of the issues at stake, and are often 'the putative policy alternatives or the power positions of the factions or some combination of these'.[45]

The ideology and loyalty of the individual scholar in China is bound to the overarching construct of the CPC that effectively monitors the 'intellectual segment' through its vast administrative and at times 'coercive' apparatus. 'Autonomy' and politically free 'independence' for the intellectual in China thus remains in the words of Goldman, Cheek and Hamrin, 'intermittent and conditional'.[46] As a result, acting as a policy advocate seems an appropriate way for think tanks or influential scholars to preserve their own social interests and political privileges. It could be inferred that the relations between leaders and think tanks are based on a kind of instrumental orientation in which both leaders and intellectuals acknowledge the reciprocal benefits between them. To actively participate in the policymaking and advising process, scholars of think tanks and research institutes are required to recognize their 'limits' in terms of the official line set by the CPC.

Policy Interpretation

When 'strategic' foreign policy decisions are made by the central leadership, they often consist of no more than a vague concept, basic policy orientation, broad policy guideline, or long-term policy goal—in effect the 'basic bones' of policy. It is consequently up to the Ministry of Foreign Affairs (MFA) to make tactical policy choices and work out detailed plans for the realization of the leadership's policy goals. At this stage, strategic think tanks in Beijing, Shanghai and other places are approached by the MFA to prepare recommendations and policy outlines that agree, disagree or provide alternatives to the stated objectives of the leadership. As policy interpreters and 'input feeders', think tanks don a role in tracking and shaping the eventual contours of a stated policy.

China's 'independent foreign policy of peace' and 'new security doctrine' are significant themes that constantly get explained and refined to suit the country's interests. Ostensibly, these themes under which it would make decisions on international issues are based on independent judgements of their individual merits. In terms of policy 'spelling out' the subsequent interpretation and implementation of these themes is done by the MFA and government-sponsored think tanks.

As a case in point, since Hu Yaobang first announced China's new foreign policy in 1982, it has evolved several times over and currently reads as follows:

> China unswervingly pursues an independent foreign policy of peace. The fundamental goals of this policy are to preserve China's independence, sovereignty and territorial integrity, create a favorable international environment for China's reform and opening up and modernization construction, maintain world peace and propel common development. [47]

The absence of 'socialist rhetoric' and the promotion of economic reforms as a means to national salvation in defining China's 'independent foreign policy' are prominent indicators of the influences generated by the reform process.

China's 'new security concept'[48] enunciated first in 1996 provides another instance of a central precept in strategic policy that has undergone several revisions and accommodates the concerns of the time. Briefly, the 'new security concept' revolves around the core principles of ensuring political, economic, technological, military and social/human security.[49] The 'new security concept' also put forward the Chinese position that 'security would be based not on military alliances and arms build-ups, but rather on the principles of mutual trust and securing common interests'.[50] Beijing's active participation in multilateral initiatives and organizations since the mid-1990s follows this policy precept. New ideas advocating a leading role for China in multilateral initiatives are seen by the leadership as being 'desirable' in the 'national interest'.

If the language of the operational precepts of Chinese foreign policy is to read balanced and pragmatic, it is due to the efforts of the many suggestions and interpretations received from various strategic policy think tanks.

Policy Control

It was Karl Deutsch who had said, '[T]o understand and describe in full detail the political process even in a single country may well take the work of a lifetime'.[51] Making policies with respect to sensitive countries and sensitive issues in China is still the prerogative of the central leadership. However, with a plethora of issues and multiplicity of tasks, it is almost impossible for the central leadership to micromanage the intricate details of each situation and make decisions accordingly. A system that has been put into place to manage and control sensitive policy decisions has involved a long, gradual and incremental process that collates and arrives at a predicated position. With significant guidance and latitude given by the MFA, strategic policy think tanks are part of the process involved in calibrating the finer nuances of China's policy on sensitive issues.[52] A case in point here is China's policy choices over the contentious issue of Taiwan as also the security situation on the Korean peninsula. The range of options that China exercises over Taiwan and North Korea is far more today when contrasted with the ideological rigidity of the past and the central role played by the supreme leader in the past decades. With a limited consensual process emerging (parallel to leadership changes in the CPC) the influence of think tanks cannot be understated in the entire exercise.

Another instance of 'official mentoring' of research by think tanks relates to the issue of 'nationalism'. In China, the leadership and the political system it represents advocates the use of social science in the service of modernization. Part of this 'modernization' project is the need for effort on the part of the academic world 'helping to build a modern nation–state and attaining higher levels of prosperity and welfare'.[53] It is presumed that without the 'nation'[54] as a main framework of research, academic enquiry is without basis. Some statist and Marxist views presume the Chinese nation to be a product of administrative politics, characterized by the universal applicability of the dialectics of struggle and unification.[55] Hence, studies on national identity, the national economic, social and cultural strengths as also the rich history of the nation are realms of academic enquiry that would contribute to stimulating national development.

Information Filters

To a large extent, political actors in China (the CPC) are unable to gain access to comprehensive information and are unable to define a problem without the advice, recommendations and expertise of specialists. Clearly, it is difficult for leaders themselves to scrutinize every detail of an issue or problem, and this means that the information filter function of think tanks is extremely important. Chinese think tanks perform their role as 'information filters' in the absence of competition from private competitors and a relative monopoly over access to information sources.

For Ming Shen-Chai and Shaun Breslin, the function of being an information filter for the leadership (or client) is 'to conduct the preliminary task of removing repetitive, unworthy information in order to make a short list of essential reference materials on aspects of either international or domestic affairs'.[56] During the Maoist period, the primary and visible 'information filter' was Xinhua News Agency which used to publish the 'Reference News' (*Cankao Xiaoxi*), a daily newspaper with several pages which was for 'official and internal dissemination only' (*neibu*) and the 'Reference Sources' (*Cankao Ziliao*), a magazine of around 100 pages that was 'limited' reading material for middle- and high-ranking party officials.[57]

The flip side of 'information filtering' is the overwhelming presence of prominent institutions of the state involved in monopolizing and administering the 'intellectual sphere'—filters in another way. In China, these include, the Chinese Academy of Social Sciences (CASS); the Chinese Academy of Sciences (CAS); the China education and Research Network; the Central Propaganda Department of the CPC; the General Bureau of Radio, Film and Television; the Ministry of Culture; the Ministry of Public Security; the Ministry of Radio, Film and Television; the Ministry of State Security; the State Press and Publications Administrations, and other entities located within bureaucracies.[58] Participating in a guided process of filtering information for the state apparatus has been termed as the prevalence of the 'social mesosphere theory' by Wang Ying.[59] For an authoritarian government, the existence of think tanks and social organizations has double attributes. On the one hand, they are potential 'subversive actors' and 'enemies' as they display traits of collective behaviour. On the other hand, they could perform an 'instrumental role' by providing and generating public goods to society and thus share a few responsibilities with the state.

Introducers of New Ideas

Before the reforms were initiated in the late 1970s, with the exception of think tanks affiliated to the military and foreign ministry, most policymaking units and Chinese intellectuals were under the control of the Ministry of Education (MOE). The MOE decided on educational policies, running local institutions, designing curriculum, budgets salary scales, welfare, etc. This very 'supra-ministry' role of the MOE stifled creativity. With the coming of age of think tanks and their contributions to policy, new ideas and suggestions have an audience. An instance here is the Working Group for Reform of the Political System that existed from September 1986 to November 1987 and functioned as a 'think group' to Zhao Ziyang. Since intellectuals in

China have to constantly evaluate the political environment and their personal proximity to 'patrons' in the party hierarchy, Zhao Ziyang's 'encouragement of intellectual thought' led to the emergence of several research centres and think tanks that offered various methodologies on initiating not only economic reform but also political reform.

This proliferation of think tanks and advisory groups also reflected Zhao Ziyang's creation of a support group as also his policy intents.[60] Among these included the Economic Research Center (ERC), the Technical Economic Research Center (TERC) (later the Economic, Technical and Social Development Research Center—ETSDRC), the Development Research Center (DRC), and the Center for International Studies (CIS).[61] It was during this 'liberal wave' in China the first non-official think tank—the Social and Economic Research Institute (later shut down after the 'Tiananmen Incident') was established by Chen Ziming in Beijing in 1986.[62]

Although the official line limits their intellectual argument or analysis, intellectuals can still offer their suggestions and try to inject new ideas into the dynamics of foreign policy assessment. For instance, international relations (IR) emerged in the 1980s as an 'autonomous academic discipline' in China. 'Political inhibitions' and 'ideological constraints' that had prevailed earlier could not prevent the emergence of this field in the 1980s. That decade witnessed 'less critical thinking' on the generating of Chinese perspectives about IR and foreign policy as society was 'learning' after the lost decade that preceded the 1980s with the irrational excesses of the Cultural Revolution. For Wang Chaohua, the 1980s were a 'time of assimilation' and the 1990s of 'exploration' and creative tension'.[63] It is well known that China today hosts one of the world's largest 'epistemic communities' in terms of numbers of students, faculty, research centres, policy analysts and practitioners.[64] The extensive and intense debate that followed Zheng Bijian's 'China's peaceful rise' at the Bo'ao Forum for Asia in 2003 by the domestic and international 'epistemic communities' is perhaps an illustration of how far intellectuals influence and participate in debates in China. A grave limitation however of Chinese efforts in the direction of contributing to IR theory has been the 'sacrosanct' quality bestowed to the 'ethically correct home nation'.

Descriptions of the world in Hobbesian terms and the promotion of national interest as a survival mechanism bring forth a contradiction when the motherland is presented as an exception to otherwise selfish international behaviour.[65] Two goals motivate China's nascent IR epistemic community—first to influence foreign policymaking (issues and structures) by assuming IR as a cognitive body of thought,[66] and second to bring about the intellectual creation of an IR theory with Chinese characteristics[67]—dominated as the field is with exclusively western theoretical approaches.

Although experts and policy practitioners in China cannot confront the government regarding the course of a particular policy, they can gingerly feel around and sound out 'options' thereby, influencing a policy shift or 'course correction'. For instance, some experts specializing on the Taiwan issue have discussed the possibility and applicability of a 'confederation of great China' unofficially. For these pragmatists, the political reality across the Taiwan Straits being what it is, the idea of 'confederalism' offers a better way to solve the Taiwan issue than the formula of 'one country, two systems'. Another stream of thought on Taiwan is that under Hu Jintao Beijing has adopted a policy of *budu buwu* ('no independence, no war') aimed at maintaining the 'status quo' and putting aside *tongyi* ('unification'). This approach according to Sujian Guo and Shiping Hua is in contrast to Jiang Zemin's *jitong* ('hasty unification').[68] Officially though, China disagrees with these 'ideas' and sticks to the 'one-China' core principle.

This is an indication that these experts can provide new ideas to leaders and introduce new dynamics into the policymaking process, even if their opinions differ from the official line. It may be surmised that some researchers discuss new ideas which are slightly different from the official tone because they have close links with specific political leaders (*hou tai*). Therefore, think tanks could act as introducers of new ideas.

Think Development of Horizontal Linkages

It could be argued that strategic policymaking in China is still 'stovepiped' into vertical hierarchies or systems and research products transferred upward, not downward. Nevertheless, horizontal relationships and mechanisms have matured.⁶⁹ Think tanks perform the role of establishing 'policy networks' and there are horizontal initiatives in China that bring together civilian and military policy practitioners and enthusiasts. The Cross-Strait Relations Research Centre (CSRRC) and the China Arms Control and Disarmament Association (CACDA) are two such examples. Apart from the CACDA horizontal initiatives also include programmes launched in universities. Beijing University has a Program on Arms Control and Disarmament Studies, and so does Tsinghua University at its Institute of International Studies. As part of the American Studies Center (ASC) at the Fudan University in Shanghai is the Program on Arms Control and Regional Security. These programmes provide academic instruction and highlight research on arms control and national security. These programmes at China's most prestigious universities provide an 'interface' among scholars, practitioners, theoreticians, and the generally well-informed elite government officials.

The CSRRC 'organizes the writing of research reports, commissions research projects, holds various types of academic seminars, promotes academic exchanges, and edits and publishes collections of relevant research papers'.⁷⁰ The research conducted is channelized to the Central Committee as well as state organs, military departments, social science research institutes and universities. The CACDA aims 'to push forward the international arms control and disarmament process, to carry out research projects concerning arms control, disarmament and international security, to promote exchanges between domestic and foreign institutions and individual experts in this regard and to hold seminars on arms control'.⁷¹

Strategic Policymaking Think Tanks in China—Looking up...to the State

The role and influence of strategic and non-strategic policy think tanks on policymaking in China has been documented from the mid-1950s. This was the period when CPC leaders re-evaluated the role of intellectuals and acknowledged their positive contribution to China's modernization programme. However, their attitude towards intellectuals turned hostile during the 'Hundred Flowers'[72] movement, the anti-Rightist campaign,[73] the Socialist Education/Four Clean Ups Campaign[74] and the fallacy that was the GPCR.[75]

This chapter argues that the current trend involving the participation of think tanks in the policymaking process, to a large extent, has been effected by the changing perception of the Chinese political elite who are diverse from their predecessors such as Mao Zedong, Zhou Enlai, and Deng Xiaoping. To improve 'professionalization' and 'transparency' in the functioning of the government, the leadership in China has more or less de-emphasized ideology and stopped mentioning altogether the necessity of 'class struggle' in a socialist state. In other words, in the post-Mao period, Chinese leaders have recognized that the lack of institutionalization in the political system has been the decisive factor in China's economic and social backwardness and the consequent decline in strategic influence. It could also be argued that the 'newer generation' of leaders are functioning in an environment of lesser ideological concerns and lacking a 'personality centric' approach to politics that has created conditions and the space for opinions generated by think tanks to proliferate.

Since the reform process commenced in 1978, Beijing's policy process has changed several times over and become more informed, rational, participatory and sophisticated. The role of think tanks in this transformation is undeniable.[76] China's think tanks are willing to consider or even accept foreign ideas and methods although some of these concepts are in contradiction with official ideology transmitted by the political leadership. Think tanks in China inhabit a two-way process where they 'thrive' on official patronage and also facilitate the 'patrons' with a new avenue of not just scholarly freedom but a 'sounding board' where the possibilities of fine-tuning the weaknesses of the system could be discussed. To cite an instance, in December 2004, several prominent security policymaking think tanks in China and their counterparts in Europe established the EU–China Think Tank Round Table to discuss issues of mutual and contemporary concern. The discussions involved even 'controversial' issues such as European perceptions on human rights in China to the arms embargo imposed following the Tiananmen Square demonstrations in 1989.

The importance of this coming together of think tanks can be gauged by the fact that it was addressed by none other than Premier Wen Jiabao and the EU Trade Commissioner Peter Mandelson on the eve of the EU–China summit.[77]

As the following indicates, think tanks are representative of the articulations and postures adopted by the political elite which exist at different levels.

To Chen Mumin, political elite in China play a seminal role in FPDM. There are three levels, with first-level comprising members of the Politburo Standing Committee, Central Leading Small Group on Foreign Affairs (now renamed by Xi Jinping as Central Foreign Commission (2018) and senior PLA commanders with powers to abrogate, ratify and veto foreign security policies adopted, frame guidelines and objectives with emphasis on executing policy decisions adopted. The second level comprises members who are high-ranking officials of central bureaucracies, along with strategic analysts from think tanks and scholars with linkages to party and state leaders. They are to transform concepts into tactical policies and supervize the implementation of foreign security policies by drafting new policy choices and ideas for decision-makers to consider. The third level of political elite includes medium-ranking bureaucrats, journalists from state-controlled media who interpret official policies, discuss foreign policy and articulate views on national security.

The exponential growth of information sources (the Internet, online databases and academic interaction) and platforms for micro-level analyses have enabled strategic policymaking think tanks in China to provide their expertise to leaders in a more focused manner. From the CPC Central Committee's perception, a highly sophisticated policy process is in the interests of the leadership and the 'feeders' of policy inputs have to be aware of the issues happening around the world. Chinese establishment intellectuals working for research institutes have more opportunities than ever before to interact with the outside world. Particular ministries like the MFA regularly invite scholars to discuss policy issues with the leadership including individual Politburo members. A trend since 1980s has witnessed Chinese think tanks increasing their academic contacts with their Western counterparts by exchanging perspectives and ideas. Reflecting this academic 'openness', some leading think tanks have posted on their websites, institutional links they have developed over the years with other think tanks, primarily in the West.

Whether through the distribution of reports for restricted CPC circles or via research openly published as special papers, journals and books, policymaking think tanks are increasingly making their mark. In the words of Margaret Sleeboom, much of 'Chinese academic research tends to focus on how to pick the 'useful' from foreign cultures and the "excellent" from the national past'.[78] A crucial feature of contemporary intellectual discourse in China is the importance of theoretical approaches. A case in point has been the inclusion of the phrases 'harmonious society' and 'harmonious world' in describing an ideal-type in IR.[79] To the mainly Chinese audience/readership, Habermas, Rawls and Giddens are alternative approaches to resolve 'practical issues' of the day.[80] Moreover, the manner in which they are approaching their task is markedly strategic: focused on the provision of comprehensive, forward-looking and solution-based answers to China's contemporary foreign policy challenges. There are of course, occasional 'hard hitting' opinion pieces that lament the state of policymaking in China, but these tend to be exceptions rather than the rule.[81]

Despite the shift in bureaucratic temperament and increasing professionalization, there exist strong vestiges of a patron–client relationship in the functioning of policy think tanks. In other words 'political clientalism' is a feature of state–intellectual relations in China. For intellectuals who carry out political policy relevant research, the 'political choices' that are available in the limited and highly controlled 'public space' is inhibited by the 'rules and norms of the party–state'.[82] The 'invisible hand' of ideological constraints does inhibit research in China. This is despite the fact that what passes for political ideology today is a watered-down version of a 'socialist ideal' long given up by the CPC. In the early decades of the PRC, ideology reached out to every aspect of society and ended up colouring ultimate decision-making, even on security affairs. More than official ideology or the lack of it, intellectuals in China are at many levels hesitant to express their freewheeling views.[83] Expressing opinions that go beyond the 'official script' are sure to invite a swift response from the state. For instance, the *Freezing Point* (*Bing dian*), a supplement to the *Chinese Youth* newspaper was closed on a directive from the Propaganda Department of the CPC after an article (Modernization and History Textbooks) by Yuan Weishi, Professor at Sun Yat Sen University, criticized textbooks in the PRC for not basing arguments on facts and for sticking to an outdated and xenophobic way of interpreting post-1840 Chinese history.[84]

Occasionally, scholars known for their liberal inclinations are 'allowed' to get their controversial point of view published in journals and newspapers far away from the political center such as the *Nanfang Zhoumo* ('Nanfang Daily Weekend Edition') published from Guangzhou.[85] The *Minzhu Zhongguo* ('Democratic China') is an online forum where pro-democracy intellectuals are able to express their views. Other relatively 'open' journals and newspapers include the literary journal *Dushu* ('Reading') and *World Economic Herald* newspaper. The Chinese state is aware that although the eventual 'project' of reforms is to redeem the CPC's legitimacy by radically transforming the economy, the very process of transformation and success has spurred debates regarding the regime's weakened authority.

While there is a growing influence of 'official' think tanks on the policymaking process, these very think tanks are known for their 'dependence' and 'reliability' on official statements and policy pronouncements that are accepted without any hint or display of criticism. Also, there is hardly any introspection on the internal policy processes that lead to the taking/adoption of a particular policy. The glaring shortcoming of most Chinese think tanks is that they perform 'regime enhancing' functions rather than being 'regime critical'.[86] Putting it starkly, He Qinglian notes that 'most Chinese scholars today are willing to tailor their research to placate the regime, and adopt a cynical and perfunctory attitude towards sensitive political and social issues'.[87] From an elite perspective, it could be argued that China's think tanks are to be 'regarded as tools of the dominant class for producing the prevailing values as a basis for theorizing the official ideology and maintaining the political regime'.[88]

In the history of the People's Republic, there have been instances of political campaigns (as mentioned earlier) against the intellectual 'class' and the historical memories of these campaigns made intellectuals aware of the fragile benevolence of the state as also its brutal retribution if the 'official line' was transgressed.[89] The reality therefore, remains that the relationship fostered between the state and intellectuals in China has shades of 'tension' built into it. An instance of this tension is the relationship between the CASS—China's foremost 'think tank' which is subsumed within the State Council—and the government. From the government's viewpoint, the CASS was considered 'unreliable' after many of its personnel were found to be 'sympathetic' and also involved in the demonstrations at Tiananmen in 1989.[90] Following the 'Tiananmen incident' research tasks at the CASS are drawn up after consultation with the Central Committee of the CPC, its Propaganda Department and the CASS leadership, who in any case are high-ranking party cadres. For Merle Goldman, this 'tension' is a 'conflict' between the CPC and Chinese intellectuals who had a sincere (and hence idealistic) commitment to the 'humanitarian aspirations of Marxism' and insisted on the 'right to define Communism in their own way'.[91] Thus, the 'expert' is as vital to the Chinese leadership as in any other political culture. While in liberal systems, an 'expert' can create for himself/herself an autonomous sphere between the government and the individual, in China this 'autonomous sphere' for the 'expert' is conditioned by loyalty to the party and its political programme.

While the final policy is the outcome of decisions taken at the 'highest levels', the existence of an increasing diversity of viewpoints within the system is suggestive of the existence of a less authoritarian political temperament.[92] In established democracies, civil society emphasizes freedom of association, competition among diverse social organizations, and a social field independent of the state.[93] In China, the state dominates in the distribution of power between state and society, so that it controls 'all of the public sphere' and monopolizes resources for collective action.[94]

Chinese policymaking influenced by think tanks is not without its 'self-serving tendencies' and 'institutional lines of thinking'. As Margaret Sleeboom-Faulkner has pointed out, taking the nation–state as an 'unproblematic framework of applied research implies that national behaviour and identity can be treated as controllable units. The end result is that it distorts the final outcome by neglecting the 'local' and 'specific'; subordinating the 'universal' to the 'national'; and, representing the *Weltanschauung* of an 'exclusive elite interest group' ignoring others.[95]

A perception shared by some scholars is that the growing role of think tanks in policymaking in China is indicative of the emergence of a nascent civil society. It would perhaps be premature and hazardous to describe think tanks in China functioning as agents of a 'new civil society' as the very legitimacy of think tanks in China comes from the space provided to them by the state. On their part think tanks would not want to be branded as being at the forefront of a 'new civil society' as that could lead to the unravelling of the present 'arrangement'. Think tanks in China, especially so in the case of strategic policymaking institutes, are 'embedded' within the system. If the profile of think tanks and their contributions to the 'policymaking elite' have increased and are more relevant it is to be attributed to the increasing professionalization of the processes that lead to decision-making. The relatively smooth leadership transitions (Deng Xiaoping to Jiang Zemin, Jiang Zemin to Hu Jintao and Hu Jintao to Xi Jinping), routinization of bureaucratic work, a less constricting (if not absent) ideological milieu, and the plurality of information sources for the average citizen as well as policymakers, has led to a change in the manner in which think tanks function.[96]

It is indeed a welcome development in China of the emergence of independent think tanks in the last decade, but their numbers are small and the influence they wield is limited.[97] These independent expressions of ideas and thoughts from think tanks without any official affiliation are more to be considered a forum for intellectuals of all hues to informally discuss contentious issues. On their part, independent think tanks welcome and encourage retired government officials to contribute their experience and expertise in the functioning of think tanks as also to expand their influence within policymaking circles. Within the Chinese system, it gives immense leverage to an independent think tank to boast of having several retired senior government officials on its board of governors.

The transformation of the decision-making process in China to include other participants has allowed for different models of 'policy agenda setting' to emerge.[98] The policy agenda and its implementation are of immense value to a centrifugal force like the CPC. While defining the limits of a 'debate', the CPC lays emphasis on the plurality of views generated within defined boundaries. From the viewpoint of the leadership, the state has created a dense web of economic and social organizations in order to channel interest articulation and regularize the flow of information between the state and key groups in society—intellectuals in particular.[99]

Intellectual and political elites are certainly a privileged section in China today and it is a moot point whether their thinking does influence other actors within society or not. The idealist notions of this 'new social spectrum' emerging at the forefront of a political renaissance in China, for now, seems difficult to comprehend, as the CPC with its unique political culture has not yet permitted the academic fraternity including think tanks to create a value-neutral position for themselves. On the part of the intellectuals and political elites in China who are located within the CPC and its extensive patronage system, it appears that there is a need to 'marshalling China's material and ideational power resources to build a superior new socialist political civilization'.[100] It could be argued that from the point of view of the state, that the role of intellectuals and their responsibility towards society fulfils the Confucian ideal of the scholar serving society through official channels. This invokes images from China's past where the 'scholar' in an individual is recognized by the bureaucracy (through imperial examinations) and the 'will of the emperor' is exercised through 'scholar bureaucrats'.

The increasing profile of think tanks has no doubt provided policymakers with more options in the exercise of a decision. Yet, there remain sub-system tensions between the bureaucracy and academicians with residual notions of each other.[101] What the thinks tanks can do is to conceptualize and suggest strategies. Bureaucracies, on the other hand, are better at providing detailed information on specific problems—usually statistical and hence opaque. Bureaucrats largely perceive academicians and specialists to be a hindrance and representative of an idealistic temper while think tanks and universities lament the bureaucrats' inability to conceptualize the system and its requirements.

Finally, China's deepening involvement with the outside world in the reform era has increased the need for specialized analyses to guide the formulation of Chinese foreign and national security policy. As Chinese leaders and officials grapple with a range of complicated foreign policy issues, they have shown increasing willingness to turn towards policy think tanks, research institutes and universities for assistance.

Conclusion

Following Beijing's adoption of the 'Open Door Policy' in 1978 and the influence it effected in the adoption of a 'Foreign Policy of Peace'—the constant reiteration of 'peace and development' as also 'adherence to the Five Principles of Peaceful Coexistence' have become the cornerstones of Chinese FPDM. With the hierarchy of the CPC dominated by 'technocrats' and 'legalists', the role of the 'revolutionary elite' has come to a close. Reflecting the professional and personal experience as also location within the system, there are multiple strands that go into policymaking.

Decision-makers in Beijing strive to be consistent, make optional choices, in narrowly constrained, neatly defined situations and rank and maximize values by choosing the most efficient alternative. It is argued that there exists within the FPDM process in China a 'pluralized elite' who lay significant importance on a professional bureaucratic process as also a formalized policy consultation system. Think tanks and research institutes specializing in foreign policy, IR and strategic affairs are increasingly becoming influential voices within the 'policy network' in China.

Major policy outcomes in Beijing are the result of 'aggregation and mediation' at the highest levels in Zhongnanhai involving the participation of the FALSG, CPC Politburo and the Standing Committee. The Party Secretariat is the apex 'clearing house' for decisions discussed, considered and taken. The policymaking process in China, over the last few decades, is more systematic, regularized and institutionalized than before with major policy issues being carefully considered by a variety of institutions before a decision is taken. Increasingly, 'policy choices' and the 'decision' are influenced by the coming together/interplay of crises, opportunities, actors/participants and solutions.

For decision-makers in China the paralysis of the Chinese state and arbitrary decision-making during the Cultural Revolution act as a powerful factor motivating the creation of plural institutions within the government and also to ensure that there are no such episodes affecting the polity in the future. Following the Liberation in 1949, decision-making on strategic and security concerns while guided by 'major intellectual and political concerns' was determined according to the ideological perspective of Mao Zedong. In the reform period three powerful factors—(a) weakened personal authority of the leadership, (b) growing bureaucratic interests and the (c) changing domestic and international situation—have brought about a complete transformation in the decision-making processes.

It is important to assess the influence analysts have on policy formulation in China. A constant process of identifying different institutions, assessing their views, strengths, resources, and depth of linkages with important government bureaucracies will in many ways have a bearing on China's policy towards India. Chinese policymakers and the leadership approach security and strategic policy decision-making on a case-by-case basis, depending on the gravity of the issue. The calculation of costs and benefits plays a significant role in arriving at a decision.

The decision-making process of China provides a methodology to identify the degree of problems as also the relative influence of various actors. Finally, China's decision-making mechanisms are yet to take/regard India seriously and consequently, policymaking regarding India is of a 'low priority'. India is an irritant to be treated in a condescending manner. This could in the mid-term impinge bilateral relations with rational perspectives being overwhelmed by strong rhetoric from several quarters.

In this chapter, an attempt is made to examine strategic decision-making in China by detailing the growing significance of think tanks as policy deliberating and creating institutions. The roles and functions of Chinese intellectuals and think tanks is a sphere that is constantly expanding as reforms get more institutionalized and have a bearing on China's strategic policymaking. The horizontal synergies created are an indicator of the dynamics at play that reinforce the policymaking process in China—a significant feature of interest to policymakers in India. This chapter argues that as an influential part of the strategic decision-making process in China, policy think tanks supplement the ideas and opinions of key political leaders and more importantly provide policy alternatives to the leadership. Policy research institutes, think tanks and intellectuals in China fulfil the role of 'expressing' what the party–state articulates on various issues. While welcome, this expression of policy positions exists in a space created by the party–state to accommodate the new interests that have developed in a post-Mao political setting. In spite of four decades of reform, research institutes and policy think tanks are subject to the strict supervision of the party–state machinery.

The effect of China's economic reforms following the implementation of 'Open Door' policy has been when it comes to decision-making and how the CPC has reworked itself to display new facets. As Shaoguang Wang details, we notice several of these as discussed in the following list.

1. Closed Door Model
   In this model, decision-makers exclude the participation of the public in any manner. A primary consideration influencing the decision-makers is their belief that it is easier to frame a policy agenda and implement policies that result from it if they (the decision-makers) can prevent the issue from expanding to the mass public. This model reveals the defensive and insecure nature of decision-makers, who by excluding social organizations from the policymaking process, do so from the apprehension that the adopted decision might be rejected. In other words, it is an 'exclusionary' process that remains elite as the domain for making decisions is limited in size.

2. Mobilization Model
   The difference between the 'closed door model' and the 'mobilization model' lies in the detail that in the latter case, policymakers go out of their way to arouse the interest of the public and convince them (with and without coercion) to support an agenda. Several instances of the 'mobilization model' in China include the Land Reform, The Three-Anti and Five-Anti campaigns, the Great Leap Forward, the People's Communes, the Four Clear-ups all the way to the GPCR. The 'mobilization' model does not preclude the use of the state's vast propaganda machinery to influence a pre-determined outcome.
3. Inside Access Model
   This model refers not to an agenda prepared by policymakers but rather to the proposals made by an official 'brains trust' close to the very core of power. These proposals are made through internal channels for the appreciation of decision-makers and are not for public consumption. This model could be applied to elements of a 'micro' nature within the larger holistic domain of foreign policy, for example, China's approach to Climate Change Talks.
4. Reach-Out Model
   This model, even for one-party systems is a radical departure from the previous typologies. Rather than conceal proposals, policymakers publicize policy intentions to generate feedback through suggestions and also to scuttle any chances of the suggested policy measures from being implemented in a hurry.
5. Outside Access Model
   This model refers to a situation in which a citizen or a group of citizens submits suggestions on public affairs in the form of letters or reports to central decision-makers.
   It is not known how far Chinese citizens petition government authorities to bring about change in a particular aspect of foreign policy.101
6. Popular-Pressure Model
   The force to change the agenda comes from outside the government. Popular participation is the key catalyst here. Contemporary events generating heated public debate in China on foreign policy matters include the May 1999 bombing of the

Chinese Embassy in Belgrade by the United States and the 2001 EP-3E Aries 2 'Spy Plane Incident' involving a USAF aircraft flying inside Chinese airspace and being forced to land following a 'sky-collision' with a PLAAF aircraft whose pilot was killed. Both these incidents apart from being reported prominently by the state media have had the effect of convincing many policy-makers in China that the United States does not want China to 'rise' amongst the comity of nations.

Notes

1. See Alexander George, 'The Operational Code: A Neglected Approach to the Study of Political Leaders and Decision-Making', *International Studies Quarterly* 13, no. 2 (June 1969): 190–220; Judith Goldstein and Robert Keohane, eds., *Ideas and Foreign Policy: Beliefs, Institutions and Political Change* (Ithaca, NY: Cornell University Press, 1993).
2. Samuel T. Shelton, 'Jury Decision Making: Using Group Theory to Improve Deliberation', *Politics & Society* 34, no. 4 (December 2006): 706–725.
3. Jean Garrisson, 'Constructing the 'National Interest' in U.S.–China Policy Making: How Foreign Policy Decision Groups Define and Signal Policy Choices', *Foreign Policy Analysis* 3, no. 2 (April 2007): 106.
4. Alice Miller, 'The CPC Central Committee's Leading Small Groups', *China Leadership Monitor* 26 (Autumn 2008). Avaikable at http://www.hoover.org/publications/clm/issues/27770964.html (accessed on 30 August 2021).
5. A. Doak Barnett, *The Making of Foreign Policy in China: Structure and Process* (London: I.B. Tauris, 1985), 33.
6. The China Institutes for Contemporary International Research (CICIR) was reported to be well connected 'vertically' and 'horizontally' as it was bureaucratically subordinated to the FALSG and linked to the Ministry of State Security and its reports are read by the Politburo.
7. Lu Ning, *The Dynamics of Foreign Policy Decision-making in China* (Boulder, CO: Westview Press, 1997), 130–135.
8. See Lai Hongyi, 'External Policymaking under Hu Jintao—Multiple Players and Emerging Leadership in China', *Issues and Studies* 41, no. 3 (2005): 209–244.
9. James Conachy, 'Chinese Think-tank Warns of Growing Unrest Over Social Inequality', *World Socialist Website*. Available at http://www.wsws.org/articles/2001/jun2001/chin-j15.shtml (accessed on 15 June 2001).
10. The China Institute for International Strategic Studies (CIISS) is the premier intelligence analysis think-tank of the PLA and is directly subordinate to the General Staff Department Second Department (Intelligence). The Chairman of the CIISS is also the Deputy Chief of Staff of the PLA. See Bates Gill

and James Mulvenon, 'Chinese Military-Related Think Tanks and Research Institutions', *The China Quarterly* 171, (September 2002): 617–624.

11. The China Defence Science and Technology Information Centre (CDSTIC) is an overt intelligence collection and military technical affairs think tank and is subordinate to the General Armaments Department (GAD) of the PLA. The Chinese Academy of Engineering Physics (CAEP) and the Institute for Applied Physics and Computational Mathematics (IAPCM) hosts numerous specialists working on arms control and non-proliferation. Other GAD think tanks include the Northwest Institute for Nuclear Technology (NINT), Institute of Fluid Physics (IFP), Institute of Structural Mechanics (ISM) and the Institute of Laser and Plasma Physics (ILPP) as cited in Gill and Mulvenon, 'Chinese Military-Related Think Tanks and Research Institutions', 622.
12. The Foundation for International Strategic Studies (FISS) serves as a kind of liaison organization between foreigners and the Chinese military. It has close ties with the PLA General Staff Department (GSD).
13. See Michael Swaine, 'The Role of the Chinese Military in National Security Policy', 'Revised edition, (Santa Monica, CA: RAND Corporation, 1998) 80.
14. David Shambaugh, 'China's International Relations Think Tanks: Evolving Structure and Process', *The China Quarterly* 171 (September 2002): 576.
15. Examples include the following: (a) during the Korean War in the early 1950s, Lei Yingfu, an analyst with the PLA General Staff in the Operations Room, rightly predicted an American invasion despite 90 per cent of the peninsula being under the control of Pyongyang; (b) during the peak of the Sino-Soviet crisis over the Zhenbao/Damansky islands on the Wusuli/Ussuri river in the late 1960s, many Chinese analysts assumed that the Soviet Union will concentrate forces on its eastern borders, while some others thought that it will retain focus on its western borders to maintain strategic leverage over Europe in its Cold War with the United States. Following a report from Wang Shu, a staff reporter for *Xinhua*, who wrote that the Soviet Union's interests were with Europe and that China needed to develop relations with West Germany as it would be mutually beneficial, China and West Germany established relations in 1972 as cited in Shaoguang Wang, 'Changing Models of China's Policy Agenda Setting', *Modern China* 34, no. 1 (January 2008): 64–65.
16. See Murray Scott Tanner, 'Changing Windows on a Changing China: The Evolving "Think Tank" System and the Case of the Public Security Sector', *The China Quarterly*, 171 (2002): 559–574.
17. Also see Li Jijun, *Traditional Military Thinking and the Defensive Strategy of China* (Carlisle Barracks, PA: Strategic Studies Institute, 1997), 4; for a definition of what 'sovereignty' means to China. Available at http://www.fas.org/nuke/guide/china/doctrine/china-li.pdf (accessed on 30 August 2021).
18. See Huang Shuofeng, *On Comprehensive National Power* (Beijing: Chinese Academy of Social Science Press, 1992). According to the Federation of

American Scientists (FAS) in a chapter on 'Geopolitical Power Calculations' accessible on their website:

> Chinese assessments of Comprehensive National Power (CNP) are done both qualitatively, in general discussions of country strengths and weaknesses, as well as quantitatively, using formulas to calculate numerical values of CNP. China's forecasts of CNP reject using gross national product (GNP) indexes or the measurement methods of national power used in the United States. Instead, Chinese analysts have developed their own extensive index systems and equations for assessing CNP. Their analytical methods are neither traditional Marxist–Leninist dogma nor inspired by Western social sciences, but something unique to China. Available at www.fas.org/nuke/guide/china/doctrine/pills2/part08.htm (accessed on 30 August 2021).

19. Intellectuals are very high in China's social hierarchy, as reflected in paintings and poetry of every dynasty.
20. Milton D. Yeh, 'Ideological Flux and Intellectuals in Mainland China Since 1978', *Issues and Studies* 26, no. 9 (September 1990): 31 as cited in Ming Shen Chai and Shaun Breslin, no. 47.
21. Ibid., 30–33, as cited in Ming Shen Chai and Shaun Breslin, no. 47.
22. Deng Xiaoping, 'Respect Knowledge, Respect Trained Personnel', in *Selected Works of Deng Xiaoping (1975–1982)* (Beijing: Foreign Languages Press, 1984), 54. The 'Four Modernizations' were originally spelt out by Zhou Enlai in 1975 at the Fourth National People's Congress and later implemented by Deng Xiaoping. They stand for modernizing agriculture, industry, science and technology and defence.
23. David Shambaugh and Wang Jisi, 'Research on International Studies in The People's Republic of China', *PS: Political Science & Politics 17*, no. 4 (Fall 1984): 758–764.
24. See, for example, Daniel N. Nelson, 'Charisma, Control, and Coercion: The Dilemma of Communist Leadership', *Comparative Politics* 17, no. 1 (October 1984), 6. Also see, David Shambaugh, ed., *Deng Xiaoping: Portrait of a Chinese Statesman* (Oxford: Clarendon Press, 1995).
25. See Nikolas Rose and Peter Miller, 'Political Power Beyond the State: Problematics of Government', *British Journal of Sociology* 43, no. 2 (1992): 173–205.
26. Timothy Cheek, 'From Priests to Professionals: Intellectuals and the State under the CPC', in *Popular Protest and Political Culture in Modern China*, ed. Jeffrey N. Wasserstrom and Elizabeth J. Perry (2nd ed.; Boulder, CO: Westview Press, 1994), 185.
27. The term 'establishment intellectuals' used in this study is similar to the concept of 'politically engaged intellectuals' suggested by Merle Goldman. Specifically, establishment intellectuals are those with proper university degrees and willing to serve the political regime, though 'some members of this group may on occasion criticize the regime (in a friendly way)'. See Merle

Goldman, Timothy Cheek and Carol Lee Hamrin eds., *China's Intellectuals and the State: In Search of a New Relationship* (London: Harvard University Press, 1987).
28. Hung-yok Ip, *Intellectuals in Revolutionary China, 1921-1949 – Leaders, Heroes and Sophisticates* (Abingdon: Routledge, 2005), 3–4.
29. See Peter Moody, *Opposition and Dissent in Contemporary China* (Stanford, CA: Hoover Institute, 1977) as cited in Chai and Breslin, no. 47. A third category comprises the 'anti-establishment intellectuals' who are mostly living in exile and were at one time 'establishment intellectuals'. Prominent 'anti-establishment' intellectuals include Liu Binyan, Fang Lizhi and Yan Jiaqi. Perhaps the most radical Chinese 'anti-establishment' intellectual is Wei Jingsheng who as editor-in-chief of the short-lived journal *Exploration* had demanded 'freedom, democracy and radical change in socialist China as the Cultural revolution, bureaucratic malpractice and dictatorial rule had exposed the myth of socialist ideals'. As cited in Ka-ho Mok, *Intellectuals and the State in Post-Mao China* (London: Macmillan, 1998), 22.
30. Doak A. Barnett, *The Making of Foreign Policy in China: Structure and Process* (Boulder, CO: Westview Press, 1985), 143.
31. See Merle Goldman, *China's Intellectuals: Advise and Dissent* (Cambridge, MA: Harvard University Press, 1981).
32. See Michel Bonnic and Yves Chevrier, 'The Intellectual and the State: Social Dynamics of Intellectual Autonomy During the Post-Mao Era', *The China Quarterly* 127 (September 1991) as cited in Chai and Breslin, no. 47.
33. Shiping Hua, *Scientism and Humanism—Two Cultures in Post-Mao China (1978-1989)* (Albany, NY: State University of New York, 1995), 26.
34. See Zhidong Hao, *Chinese Intellectuals at a Crossroads: The Changing Politics of the Chinese Knowledge Workers* (Albany, NY: State University of New York Press, 2003) as cited in He Li, 'Emergence of the Chinese Middle Class and Its Implications', *Asian Affairs – An American Review* 33, no. 2 (Summer 2006): 67–84.
35. Ding Xueliang, *The Decline of Communism in China's Legitimacy Crisis, 1977-1989* (New York, NY: Cambridge University Press, 1994) as cited in Merle Goldman, 'Politically—Engaged Intellectuals in the Deng-Jiang Era: A Changing Relationship with the party-State', *The China Quarterly* 145 (March 1996): 35–52.
36. Merle Goldman, 'The Emergence of Politically Independent Intellectuals' in *The Paradox of China's Post-Mao Reforms*, ed. Merle Goldman and Roderick MacFarquhar (Cambridge, MA: Harvard University Press, 1999), 283.
37. See Shiping Hua, Ibid., 136, 7.
38. See Tang Tsou, 'The Tiananmen Tragedy: The State-Society Relationship, Choices, Mechanisms in Historical Perspective', in *Contemporary Chinese Politics in Historical Perspective*, ed. Brantly Womack (Cambridge: Cambridge University Press, 1991), 284–291; and Edward X. Gu, 'Cultural Intellectuals and the Politics of the Cultural Public Space in Communist China

(1979-1989): A Case Study of Three Intellectual Groups', *The Journal of Asian Studies* 58, no. 2 (May, 1999): 389–431.
39. See Yan Jiaqi, *Towards a Democratic China* (Honolulu: University of Hawaii Press, 1992).
40. See Pan Wei, 'Toward a Consultative Rule of Law Regime in China', in *Debating Political Reform in China – Rule of Law vs. Democratization*, ed. Suisheng Zhao (New York: M.E. Sharpe, 2006), 3–40.
41. The May Fourth movement of 1919 emerged after the Versailles Treaty awarded Shandong province to Japan despite China having been part of the Allied Triple Entente. This movement rallied together intellectuals, students and lay people against imperialism and fostered a powerful sense of nationalism into the domestic politics of China.
42. Hung-yok Ip, '*Intellectuals in Revolutionary China, 1921-1949*', 32.
43. The 'Two Whatevers' stand for 'uphold whatever policy decisions Chairman Mao made, and unswervingly follow whatever instructions Chairman Mao gave' that appeared in the *People's Daily, Liberation Army Daily* and the party journal *Hongqi* (Red Flag) shortly after Mao's demise.
44. See Ruan Ming, *Hu Yaobang on the Turning Point of History* (Hong Kong: Global Publishing, 1991), 27–31.
45. Lucian W. Pye, *The Dynamics of Chinese Politics* (Cambridge, MA: Oelgeschlager, Gunn & Hain, 1981), 13.
46. Goldman, Cheek and Hamrin, *China's Intellectuals and the State*, 19.
47. Ministry of Foreign Affairs, PRC, 'Independent Foreign Policy of Peace',. Available at http://www.fmprc.gov.cn/eng/wjdt/wjzc/t24881.htm (accessed on 30 August 2021).

China's 'Independent Foreign Policy of Peace' was first adopted at the 12th National Congress of the CPC in 1982. See Hu Yaobang, 'Report to the Twelfth CPC National Congress – Create a New Situation in All Fields of Socialist Modernisation', as cited in Harold C. Hinton, *The People's Republic of China 1979-1984: A Documentary Survey* (Wilmington, DE: Scholarly Resources Inc., 1986), 210–212.
48. See Ministry of Foreign Affairs, PRC, 'China's Position Paper on the New Security Concept', 6 August 2002. Available at http://www.fmprc.gov.cn/eng/wjb/zzjg/gjs/gjzzyhy/2612/2614/t15319.htm (accessed on 30 August 2021).
49. See Li Qinggong and Wei Wei, Chinese Army Paper on New Security Concept, *Jiefangjun Bao* (Liberation Army Daily), December 24, 1997, 5\ FBIS-CHI-98-015, Jan 15, 1998.
50. Hongying Wang, 'Multilateralism in Chinese Foreign Policy: The Limits of Socialization', *Asian Survey* 40, no. 3 (2000): 478. Also see, Injoo Sohn, 'Learning to Cooperate: China's Multilateral Approach to Asian Financial Cooperation', *The China Quarterly* 194 (June 2008): 318.
51. Karl Deutsch, *The Nerves of Government: Models of Political Communication and Control* (New York, NY: The Free Press of Glencoe, 1963), 4.

52. See Gu Xin, 'From Intellectuals to Technocrats: The Formation and Development of Chinese Reformist Think-Tanks in the 1980s', *Stockholm Journal of East Asian Studies* 8 (1997): 89–135.
53. Margaret Sleeboom-Faulkner, 'Regulating Intellectual Life in China: The Case of the Chinese Academy of Social Sciences', *The China Quarterly* 189 (March 2007): 83–99.
54. The concept of '*Zhonghua Minzu*' was often used in the 1990s to express 'racial political correctness'. (Sleeboom, 2004, p.31) *Zhonghua Minzu* was a term used by scholars often to point out the importance of '*Zhonghua*' as an organic unity between different clans and ethnic groups. A literal translation of *Zhonghua Minzu* refers interchangeably to the 'Chinese race' and 'Chinese nation'.
55. The writings of Chinese scholars Hao Shiyuan, Ma Dazhang and Zhao Yuntain in the 1990s is pointed out by Margaret Sleeboom as representing this 'statist' genre of academic literature. See Margaret Sleeboom, 95, 127.
56. Ming-Chen Shai and Shaun Breslin, 47, 20–22.
57. Hanwen Chen, 'Structural Changes and Foreign Policy Transformation: Structural – Institutional Contexts of Chinese Foreign Policy Evolution since 1979' (Unpublished PhD diss., University of Maryland, 1995), 187.
58. See Daniel C. Lynch, *After the Propaganda State – Media, Politics, and 'Thought Work' in Reformed China* (Stanford: Stanford University Press, 1999).
59. Kang Xiaoguang and Han Heng, 'Graduated Controls: The State-Society Relationship in Contemporary China', *Modern China* 34, no. 1 (January 2008): 38.
60. Nina P. Halpern, 'Information Flows and Policy Coordination in the Chinese Bureaucracy', in *Bureaucracy, Politics and Decision Making in Post-Mao China*, ed. Kenneth G. Lieberthal and David M. Lampton (Berkeley and Los Angeles, CA: University of California Press, 1992), 131.
61. According to Ming-Chen Shai and Shaun Breslin in their paper on Chinese think tanks,

> The CIS was established in 1982 in Beijing to provide policy suggestions on international affairs and domestic political and economic development under its Director, Huan Xiang. Huan was an international relations specialist and had strong personal ties with the top leaders, including Deng Xiaoping and Zhao Ziyang. The DRC was established in 1980 as the main research unit under Zhao Ziyang. Ma Hong, an economic specialist and personal advisor of Zhao, was the honorary head of the DRC. However, both the CCIS and DRC have lost influence in terms of policy suggestions because of leadership change and the political climate following Tiananmen'. (p. 17)

62. Chen Ziming and his friend Wang Juntao were sentenced to long prison terms after the 'Tiananmen Incident' and have till date are officially termed as 'the black hands behind the black hands' by the Chinese government regarding their role in the events leading up to the crackdown in 1989.

63. See Wang Chaohua, ed., *One China, Many Paths* (London: Verso, 2003), 9–45.
64. Yongjin Zhang, 'Review: International Relations Theory in China Today: The State of the Field', *The China Journal* 47 (January 2002), 101. A remarkable endeavour on the part of IR specialists in China has been the setting up of a web portal www.irchina.org that discusses, explains and features articles on International Relations from a Chinese perspective.
65. See Margaret Sleeboom-Faulkner, Ibid., 83–99.
66. Chih-Yu Shih, *China's Just World – The Morality of Chinese Foreign Policy*. (Boulder, CO: Lynne Reiner, 1993), 18.
67. Efforts in this direction as also to explain to a wider audience the importance of IR in China have among other works, included, Zhi Zhongyun, ed., *Guoji Zhengzhi Lilun Tansuo Lai Zhongguo* (Explorations of Theories of International Politics in China; Shanghai: Shanghai Renmin Chubanshe, 1998), 332; Wang Yizhou, *Xifang Guoji Zhengxixue: Lishi Yu Lilun* (The Discipline of International Politics in the West: History and Theory) (Shanghai: Shanghai Renmin Chubanshe, 1998), 771); and Lu Yi, Gu Guanfu, Yu Chenglian and Fu Yaozu, ed., *Xin Shiqi Zhongguo Guoji Guanxi Lilun Yanjiu* (Research on International Relations Theories in China's New Era; Beijing: Shishi Chubanshe, 1999), 422.

See Yongjin Zhang, 'Review: International Relations Theory in China Today: The State of the Field', 101–108.
68. Sujian Guo and Shiping Hua, eds., *New Dimensions of Chinese Foreign Policy* (Lanham, MD: Lexington Books, 2007), 2.
69. See Bonnie S. Glaser and Phillip C. Saunders, 'Chinese Civilian Foreign Policy Research Institutes: Evolving Roles and Increasing Influence', *The China Quarterly* 171 (2002): 597–616.
70. Chen Binhua, 'Cross-Straits ties research center established in Beijing', *Xinhua* (Beijing), September 6, 2000.
71. The CACDA is accessible at http://www.cacda.org.cn/english/activity/INDEX.ASP (accessed on 24 May 2008).
72. The 'Hundred Flowers' campaign was aimed solely at local bureaucracies for non-communist-affiliated officials to speak out about the policies and the existing problems within the central government in a manner previously considered illegal. During a Communist Politburo Conference in 1956, Zhou Enlai emphasized the need for intellectuals to speak out about the policies of the government, in theory allowing for better governance. An ideological crackdown later followed and re-imposed Maoist orthodoxy in public expression, effectively crushing the campaign. See Narnarayan Das, 'A Fresh Look at China's Hundred Flowers Period', *China Report* 12, no. 5–6 (1976): 45–53.
73. The 'Anti-Rightist Campaign' was a reaction against the Hundred Flowers Campaign which had promoted pluralism of expression and criticism of the government. It is still not clear whether the Hundred Flowers Campaign was a deliberate tactic to smoke out 'rightists', or whether Mao simply decided

that it had gone too far in its criticism of the CPC. See Denis C. Twitchett, John K. Fairbank and Albert Feuerwerker, *The Cambridge History of China*, Vol. 10–15, (New York, NY: Cambridge University Press, 1978).

74. The 'Socialist Education/Four Clean Ups Campaign' was launched by Mao Zedong in 1963 to 'cleanse politics, economy, ideology and organisation' and is widely believed to have set the stage for the Cultural Revolution. See Joseph Esherick, Paul G. Pickowicz and Andrew G. Walder, eds., *The Chinese Cultural Revolution as History*, (Stanford, CA: Stanford University Press, 2006).

75. The Great Proletarian Cultural Revolution (GPCR) was a political struggle for power within the CPC which drew into its vortex large sections of society, intelligentsia and the military. See, Roderick MacFarquhar, *Origins of the Cultural Revolution – Vol. 1* (New York, NY: Columbia University Press, 1974); and Roderick MacFarquhar and Michel Schoenhals, *Mao's Last Revolution* (Cambridge, MA and London: The Belknap Press of Harvard University Press, 2006).

76. Joseph Fewsmith, *China Since Tiananmen – The Politics of Transition* (New York, NY: Cambridge University Press, 2001), 105.

77. Participants from the Chinese side included the Chinese Institute of International Studies (CIIS), the Renmin University of China, the CICIR, the School for International Studies at Beijing University and the Shanghai Institute for International Studies (SIIS). European participants included, the European Policy Centre, The Hague; the United Nations University, the Netherlands Institute of International Relations, Clingendael; The Centre for Liberal Strategies, Bulgaria; Notre Europe, Paris; The Universidad Autonoma de Madrid; and the Copenhagen Business School. See Stanley Crossick et al., 'EU–China Think Tank Roundtable', *EPC Issue Paper 21*, no. 6–7 (December 2004), The Hague (Clingendael). Available at: http://www.epc.eu/TEWN/pdf/606913435_EPC%20Issue%20Paper%2021%20EU-China%20Roundtable.pdf
See Mumin Chen, 'Going Global: The Chinese Elite's Views of Security Strategy in the 1990s', *Asian Perspective* 29, no. 2 (2005): 150.

78. See Margaret Sleeboom, 96, 126.

79. The concept of 'harmony' has a rich connotation in Chinese 'seeking common ground while shelving differences'; 'the unity of Heaven and the Human' etc. See Zhao Qizheng, 'Diversity of Civilizations and A Harmonious World', *Foreign Affairs Journal* Special Issue (December 2007): 209–214.

80. See Timothy Cheek, 'Xu Jilin and the Thought Work of China's Public Intellectuals', *The China Quarterly*, 186 (June 2006): 401–420. 'Public Intellectuals' in China are those 'who have academic backgrounds and professional knowledge, address and participate in public affairs, and maintain a critical spirit and moral ideals' (p. 401).

81. An editorial in the *China Daily* (Beijing) of 2 February 2004 titled *Policy-making needs revamping* had this to say on policymaking in China–'...problem

in China's current policy lies in its wilfulness'. The article later states that '...shortcomings in policymaking have caused enormous damage to the country' and that '...the lack of solid institutional foundations, including policymaking consulting, hearings, assessments and a system of responsibility is the major reason for the flaws'. Available at http://www.chinadaily. com.cn/en/doc/2004-02/02/content_302175.htm (accessed on 30 August 2021).
82. Edward X. Gu, '"Non-Establishment" Intellectuals, Public Space, and the Creation of Non-Governmental Organizations in China: The Chen Ziming-Wang Juntao Saga', *The China Journal* 39 (January 1998): 39.
83. See Xudong Zhang, ed., *Whither China? Intellectual Politics in Contemporary China* (Durham: Duke University Press, 2001).
84. See Susanne Weigelin-Schwiedrzik, 'In Search of a Master Narrative for 20th Century Chinese History', *The China Quarterly*, 188 (December 2006): 1070–1091.
85. See Li, 'Emergence of the Chinese Middle Class and Its Implications', 67–84.
86. Tadashi Yamamoto & Susan Hubbard, 'Conference Report' in Tadashi Yamamoto (ed.) *Emerging Civil Society in the Asia Pacific Community*, Singapore, Institute of Southeast Asian Studies and Japan Centre for International Exchange, 1995 as cited in Diane Stone, 'Think Tanks and Policy Advice in Countries in Transition', paper prepared for the Asian Development Bank Institute Symposium: 'How to Strengthen Policy-Oriented Research and Training in Vietnam' 31st August 2005. Available at www.adbi.org/discussion-paper/2005/09/09/1356.think.tanks/ (accessed on 30 August 2021).
87. He Qinglian, 'China's Changing of the Guard: A Volcanic Stability', *Journal of Democracy* 14, no. 1 (January 2003): 69.
88. See, for example, Stephen Gill, *American Hegemony and the Trilateral Commission*. (Cambridge: Cambridge University Press, 1995), 51–55; Joseph Fewsmith, *Dilemmas of Reform in China: Political Conflict and Economic Debate* (New York, NY: M.E. Sharpe, 1994), 34–49.
89. During the Cultural Revolution, scholars and intellectuals were called the 'stinking ninth'—comprising the last rung in society.
90. Margaret Sleeboom-Faulkner, 'Regulating Intellectual Life in China: The Case of the Chinese Academy of Social Sciences', *The China Quarterly* 189 (March 2007): 83.
91. See Merle Goldman, 'Literary Dissent in Communist China', *Harvard East Asian Series* No. 29 (Cambridge, MA: Harvard University Press, 1967), 8.
92. Jonathan D. Pollack, 'Chinese Military Power: What vexes the United States and Why?' *Orbis* 51, no. 4 (Fall 2007), 636.
93. Xiaoguang and Heng, 'Graduated Controls—The State–Society Relationship in Contemporary China', 38.
94. Xiaoguang and Heng, 'Graduated Controls', 39.
95. See Margaret Sleeboom-Faulkner, 127.

96. See Xuanli Liao, 86, 53–99.
97. Most of the independent think tanks work on the Chinese economy. Some of them are the Unirule Institute of Economics and Unirule Consulting Firm, founded in 1993 and funded on a project-by-project basis by provisional grants from domestic and foreign foundations. The Institute of China and the World (ICW) based in Beijing focuses on elections at the village and county level and is funded by foreign foundations. The China Development Institute (CDI) and the Shanghai Institute of American Studies are some of the (relatively) independent think tanks that have earned a name for themselves in China.
98. Bruce J. Dickson, 'Cooptation and Corporatism in China – The Logic of Party Adaptation,' in *China's Deep Reform—Domestic Politics in Transition*, eds. Guoli Liu and Lowell Dittmer (Lanham: Rowman & Littlefield, 2006), 122.
99. Daniel C. Lynch, 'Envisioning China's Political Future: Elite Responses to Democracy as a Global Consultative Norm', *International Studies Quarterly* 51, no. 3 (September 2007): 703.
100. Fewsmith, *Dilemmas of Reform in China*, 15

CHAPTER 2

FPDM and India–China Relations
Identifying Decision-making Themes

Introduction

The modern state is a complex institutional construct that enforces laws and rules of a government within a territorially defined extremity. Each state has adopted for itself a system of governance that is represented by political actors who legitimize their roles through various means. The functioning of a state is a process that goes through constant change and experimentation. A state cannot survive in isolation and has to interact with other states thereby bringing into the picture a set of norms and processes. In order to constantly engage with other states, the fulfilment of norms and processes is performed through the medium of institutions like the bureaucracy. Each state has specialized actors/bureaucracies that serve various functions. Among the most important actors/bureaucracies of a state are the ones to do with its foreign policy. The mechanism/s by which a state performs its foreign policy and ensures for itself security among the comity of nations is a complex series of micro- and macro-specific processes. These processes leading to the adoption of an overall/holistic policy by a state is called FPDM.

FPDM is an increasingly specialized field of academic enquiry that explores processes governing the 'decision' through a range of different approaches. Among the nation states of the world, China is no exception when it comes to the 'decision-making context'. Questions such as—'Which individuals, groups and institutions play key roles in decision-making in China?'; 'What are the mechanisms that exist to coordinate foreign policy decisions?'; 'Where do information and counsel come from?' and 'What is the influence of experts and through which channels do they voice their opinions?'—keep scholars, specialists and policymakers constantly on the lookout for fresh insights, clues and approaches to interpret the decision-making process in Beijing.

To understand the decision-making processes of a state, the analysis of established structures of 'causal interpretation and expectations' provides insights into institutional and individual linkages that lead up to a decision. The value chain leading to a decision is a complex process that identifies categories, typologies and behaviour, establishes historical precedents and decision rules, collates information and encourages alternative courses of action.

Where are Sino-Indian relations in this? There are two hypotheses motivating this chapter. First, the process of FPDM in China is varied and reflective of influences spawned over the last four decades since the reform process was initiated; and second, these variations in decision-making have exercised their influence over the dynamic nature of Sino-Indian relations, especially since May 1998. This year and month are chosen as a template for what India–China bilateral is. The five nuclear tests conducted by India in Pokharan, stunned the world and China alike. These nuclear tests had several linkages with political and bureaucratic interests coalescing with science and technology providing a valid claim for India to be acknowledged as a nuclear power.

Section I
Decision-making and Foreign Policy—China

'Chinese foreign policy today is complex, variegated, flexible and refractory, defying any neat characterization or confident prognostication'.[1]

Decision-makers comprehend a complex world of uncertainty. Each decision-maker has a particular image of the world, shaped by his/her interpretation of a whole range of factors—history, events, cultural stereotypes, etc. The political capabilities of a state are in many ways constricted by the nature of its political culture.[2] Decision-making and the ability to reach decisions thus vary from country to country. As regards decision-making/policymaking in China, there are several competing models such as 'fragmented authoritarianism', 'new authoritarianism' and 'bureaucratic institutionalism'.[3] In states where political culture is defined and regulated by a dominant 'Party', agenda-setting as regards policy assumes immense importance.

In the past four decades, theoretical approaches to the study of foreign policy have generated a wealth of literature on the specific aspect of decision-making. A few questions—Who decides? What is the process that leads to the decision? How is the process of decision arrived at? What are the approaches constructing a framework of decision-making? have led to a generic debate on FPDM.

A 'decision' is political by nature and initiates a process of 'cause' and 'effect'. For Fei-ling Wang, the making of foreign policy in China is 'deeply politicized'.[4] For Deborah Stone, rational analysis is a political struggle, with analysis being a 'strategically crafted argument' creating 'ambiguities and paradoxes'.[5]

Foreign policy decisions in China were, and are always made, at the central level. Decision-making for the Chinese leadership involves considering different policies and their related variables as also the process of minimizing doubt. It is a matter of scholarly debate whether a consensus is arrived at before a decision is taken in China. National role conception plays a very important role in foreign policy behaviour. In most analyses of China's FPDM, the emphasis on national interest, cultural tradition and ideology as 'imperatives' predominate.[6] For prominent Chinese foreign policy analyst Chih-Yu Shih, several variables go into the creation of a 'national role conception' for China.[7] These are: a description of the national mission in the world; analyses of current inter-state relationships; the specific notion of world justice; and stability over time.

The variables and determinants that go into the making of a nation's foreign policy find expression in its policy statements as enunciated from time to time by its leadership. These statements abide by an established set of principles that guide 'national behaviour' on the 'international stage'. China is no different in these aspects and articulates its leadership articulates policy statements within a framework that encompasses national identity, interests, expectations, values and goals. The generic temperament of FPDM is such that it is a sphere of competitive approaches guided by the maximizing of national self-interest.

Why Do Policies Change and How?

To most analysts, the field of FPDM became an important aspect of overall foreign policy since the early 1960s primarily through the work of Richard Snyder, H.W. Bruck and Burton Sapin. For Richard Snyder, operating environments account for specific actions and continuities, that inform choices made with values and norms to be ascribed or not.[8]

There are two significant features or 'decision lines' that come to bear when a change in policy is contemplated and later (after winning acceptance) is implemented. The first feature is the 'expansion of the sphere' wherein 'policy entrepreneurs' are willing and able to initiate efforts to change long-standing policies that have run their course. John Kingdon argues that there is a 'variability' to this sphere with 'policy entrepreneurs' always actively promoting their new ideas and waiting for 'windows of opportunity' when different streams of problems, politics and policies do converge.[9] An 'expansion of the sphere' encourages the coming together of effective policy coalitions. These coalitions include bureaucrats, politicians, interest groups, journalists, researchers and other actors at the policymaking levels.

The second feature exercising a significant bearing on 'policy change' is the 'scope of conflict'. Policy outcomes can be changed by altering the scope of conflict over the issue in question. According to Elmer E. Schattschneider, 'the outcome of every conflict is determined by the extent to which the audience becomes involved in it'.[10] In contemporary times the 'scope of conflict' over an issue could be expanded when the proponents involved engage the media. Media attention expands the sphere influencing even policy outcomes. Baumgartner and Jones describe a policy process of 'punctuated equilibrium' wherein policy remains fairly static until an issue is redefined and made more salient.[11] Decision-makers represent the country's interests and serve as the mechanics of a nation's adaptation. Once the decision-makers realize that a 'course correction' is required, they will introduce a process of 'adaptive restructuring' to ameliorate the vulnerability and pressures arising out of the shift in policy course. This leads to the next question of 'who decides'.

Who Decides?

Although it is still difficult to discern precise decision-making mechanisms in Beijing, it may be cautiously said that there has been reasonable continuity in the composition of 'actors' involved in the process of decision-making. The central leadership as represented institutionally by the CPC Politburo Standing Committee is considered to be at the apex of decision-making on strategic affairs. The role of the MFA is to provide the requisite information for policy formulation and implement 'strategic decisions' taken by the central leadership.[12] For Samuel S. Kim, a strictly analytical approach would necessitate the conceptualization of China's FPDM process as a 'pyramid-shaped structure with the most visible and flexible domains at the top and the most invisible and invariant ones at the base'.[13] The four levels to the pyramid are:

1. Policies, where policy content and behaviour inform and define issue/s.
2. Principles, defining general and moral orientations involved.
3. Basic strategies and Lines, identify threats and alliances to policies adopted.
4. Worldview and National Identity, being the conceptual foundation of foreign policy.

At the apex are 'policies' that are most variable and are followed by principles that provide the most vocal element to an adopted policy line. The third level adheres to the 'basic line' (e.g., China's foreign policy of peace and development) and is re-affirmed and revised at the Party Congress every five years. The fourth level comprises the *Weltanschauung* and national identity and as such are the foundational constructs of China's FPDM.

Within the decision-making process a function of 'differential access' operates prior to the final decision. The 'differential access' operates at several levels and reflects the vertical and horizontal processes of many sub-systems within a larger system. First, in a decision-making context, from among the participants/actors, some groups have more resources than others and are better able to mobilize. Second, some groups are located strategically in the social and economic structure of society and their interests cannot be ignored. Third, some groups inspire higher social esteem and consequently have greater access to decision-makers. Fourth, decision-makers themselves might be either ideologically inclined towards a particular group or identify themselves as representing the interests of that group.

Why Is Foreign Policy Decision-making Important?

A limited comprehension of others' FPDM processes makes for a tenuous foundation for foreign policy choice and interpretation.[14] In order to understand decision processes there is the need to identify historically established categories, decision codes/rules and behaviour. FPDM is not a physical event, but rather a mental one. Decision-making (including on foreign policy) is not observed directly; rather it is inferred from speeches by official personages or the publication of official documents by any one of the 'actors' involved in the decision-making process. For this reason, 'there is an unavoidable element of uncertainty in any assertion that a decision has been made'[15] and the field of enquiry, of immense value.

FPDM in China is a privilege to those on top of the power pyramid. During the Maoist period, the entire process was tightly controlled by a few top leaders, with Mao at the helm, and this 'monopolistic control' was a process hidden from those within administrative structures and beyond the realm of discussion by common people. In recent years however, there has been a 'professionalizing' of the system and diversification of interests, priorities and issues, necessitating the creation of 'pools of expertise' channelized primarily through the bureaucracy.

Briefly, the significance of decision-making arises when a process is well underway. The socialization of nation-states on the international stage requires that they understand, interpret, assess, qualify and categorize each other on the basis of knowledge that they have generated through experience and interaction. The constant nature of demands on the international arena for a nation state makes it that much more imperative for it to have a domestic process of feedback and debate. These provide for arriving at a 'decision' after several hypotheses have been tested and validated and make for a rational approach.

Review of Literature

The whole process of FPDM is a vast field of academic enquiry with a disparate set of inputs. It is imperative at this stage to undertake a review of literature that captures the scope, issues and potential of the subject of enquiry of this chapter.

A key factor influencing the final decision taken by a leader/leadership is the immediate circle of 'advisors' surrounding the 'power core'. Regarding the 'advisor/s', two questions that arise are: What are the resources at the disposal of an 'advisor'? What are the power bases of 'advisors'? A foundational work on political power and the role of the 'political/policy advisor' is Harold Lasswell and Abraham Kaplan's *Power & Society: A Framework for Political Inquiry* (New Haven, CT: Yale University Press, 1950). To Lasswell and Kaplan, advisory power is akin to 'enlightenment' (i.e., the use of knowledge) to influence change. With requisite expertise and access to exclusive information, advisors are in a unique position to affect change. Advisors thus perform the role of 'policy entrepreneurs' with their specific, technocratic expertise.

Alexander George's classic work *Presidential Decision making in Foreign Policy: The Effective Use of Information and Advice* (Boulder,

CO: Westview Press, 1980) examines the interface of different presidential management methods and the organization of a President's foreign policymaking system, describing in detail the pitfalls and benefits of 'collegial', 'competitive', and 'formalistic' approaches. George concedes the impact of three different advisory roles that of 'devil's advocate', 'formal options', and 'multiple channels of advocacy', to widen the presidential scope of inquiry and side-step bureaucratic biases. From an American perspective, George's work provides fascinating insights into decision-making in an established democratic political culture.

Attempting to explain the relationship between 'change' and FPDM, James Rosenau's *The Study of Political Adaptation* (New York: Nichols Publishing Company, 1981) introduces the concept of 'adaptive behaviour' in FPDM. The 'adaptive behaviour' model assumes that state's like organizations have to adapt constantly to their changing environment while protecting their basic interests. To Rosenau, the linkage between objective changes and subjective responses is provided by the state's basic need to survive and prosper in the extremely competitive international system. A precursor to Rosenau's 'adaptive behaviour' model is Donald Nuechterlein's identification of four features that determine a country's 'persistence' in the international system—'physical safety', 'material well-being'; 'political-diplomatic order'; and 'basic social values'.[16]

K.J. Holsti had argued that domestic structures do act as a major determinant, though not the only determinant in the restructuring of a nation's foreign policy.[17] Moving from the 'general' to the 'specific', Joseph Fewsmith's study of think tanks and the Central Party School (CPS) in Beijing highlights 'ideology' and 'ideological justification' (e.g. the 'Three Represents') remaining crucial to political decisions and the decision-making process in China.[18]

Doak Barnett's *The Making of Foreign Policy in China – Structure and Process* (London: I.B. Tauris, 1985) analyses the structure and process of foreign policymaking focusing on the institutions and individuals involved. Barnett examines the policymaking process by including the party and governmental structure, the nature of foreign policy issues, relationships among institutions, the role of the policymakers, etc.

In the 1980s, David Lampton, Kenneth Lieberthal and Michel Oksenberg brought forward the 'fragmented authoritarianism' model to study China's policymaking process. The 'fragmented authoritarianism' model posits that 'as authority below the very peak of the Chinese political system becomes fragmented and disjointed, a bogged down policy process appears that is characterized by extensive bargaining'.[19] While the model offers only a static description of how the core apparatus worked, it accurately highlights the problems of coordination inherent in China's policymaking process.[20] Since the emphasis on decision-making revolves around arriving at a consensus, the involvement of more actors with equal status in decision-making has the effect of increasing the time and effort needed for policy coordination and compromise.

Kjell Goldmann in his *Change and Stability in Foreign Policy* (Princeton, NJ: Princeton University Press, 1988) hypothesizes that in any nation's FPDM process there exist some factors from within the government that are given to resisting change in policy. He terms them as 'policy stabilizers' whose typology is the following: 'blocking change in policy unless removed'; 'reducing the scope of policy change' and 'delay policy change'.

Alastair Iain Johnston in his widely cited *Cultural Realism: Strategic Culture and Grand Strategy in Chinese History* (Princeton, NJ: Princeton University Press, 1995) argues three significant points. First, from a historical point of view, China's strategic culture has been offensive despite its weak material capability. Second, as seen from its grand strategy, a realpolitik 'Parabellum' strategic culture—not a Confucian strategic culture—guides FPDM in China. Third, Chinese decision-makers have internalized this strategic culture, such that China's strategic behaviour exhibits a preference for offensive uses of force, mediated by a keen sensitivity to relative capabilities.[21]

Writings on FPDM include an ever-growing range of subjects. As Charles Todd Kent's *Politically Rational Foreign Policy Decision-Making*, Texas A&M University, 2005, reveals, the influence of 'interest groups'[22], 'knowledge-based experts'[23], 'business interests'[24], 'inter-state war and domestic considerations'[25], 'territorial disputes'[26], 'crisis bargaining',[27] 'two-level games'[28] and the ever-growing salience of public opinion in influencing FPDM, primarily in democratic systems, are part of the growing literature in this field.

A fresh approach to decision-making has been provided by Xuanli Liao in her book on the role of think tanks and decision-making.[29] Liao's model on decision-making in China is predicated on the shift from 'centralized elitism' under Mao Zedong to 'pluralistic elitism' under Jiang Zemin. While the 'top elite' still holds power over decision-making, this process has become more 'pluralistic' by involving regular policy inputs from different sources, such as government departments and foreign policy think tanks. Liao identifies two important 'features' in analyzing the role of think tanks and decision-making in China today. The first 'feature' refers to the 'levels of decision-making in China's political hierarchy' and the second feature refers to the 'levels of political sensitivity'. Liao argues that the former is more important than the latter. Decisions taken at the highest levels of government are more than likely to have benefited from a range of inputs from foreign policy think tanks.

The growing literature on China's FPDM from a non-western perspective is that of Huiyun Feng in *Chinese Strategic Culture and Foreign Policy Decision-Making* (Abingdon: Routledge, 2007). Huiyun Feng terms the 'constructivist cultural realist' argument by Alastair Iain Johnston a 'failure' for its 'deterministic insistence on the exclusive impact of a Parabellum strategic culture of offensive realism in Chinese grand strategy', which results in the erroneous assumption that Chinese strategic culture and leadership is 'offensive in nature'. Theoretically drawing heavily from the cognitive branch of social psychology and from game theory in political science, she argues that Chinese decision-makers have followed the norms of a 'defensive strategic culture'.

As can be inferred from the above, foreign policy decision-making (FPDM) as a dynamic field of government activity has generated several models and approaches with which to identify, study and delineate the decision-making characteristics of different political systems. Prior to this study selecting a particular approach or model, it is imperative to elucidate a few prevalent models of FPDM.

'Rational Actor' Model

IR is an arena where different actors make their contestations. These contestations are fed by practical considerations, history, legality, greed and little altruism. The 'rational actor model' is most popular in determining the trajectory of FPDM. To quote James Morrow, 'actors do what they believe is in their best interests'.[30] The typology of 'rational actor model' is clarified by three elemental assumptions—first, 'unitary actors or states make foreign policy decisions'; second, 'these unitary actors calculate the cost and benefits of different courses of action and choose the alternative that maximizes their utilities'; third, 'the international environment is the primary determining factor in foreign policy decisions'.[31]

By adopting a rationalistic approach an actor becomes aware of a 'problem', posits a goal, carefully weighs alternative means, and chooses among them according to his/her estimates of their respective merit, with reference to the state of affairs he/she prefers.[32] Since states are assumed to be 'unitary rational actors' it is also assumed that the decision-making processes within the leadership groups proceed as if there was a single dominant leader who controls the outcome. As in politics, 'actors' tend to behave rationally, meaning to maximize their interests, where the 'outcomes depend upon the prevailing institutions, shaping how much power the political actors may exercise, especially enhancing their bargaining power'.[33]

The 'rational actor model' suits the temperament of 'neo-realism' best. The five central suppositions of 'neo-realism' are: one, the international system is anarchic; two, states are unitary actors; three, states are rational; four, states desire to maximize their security; and five, states seek to gain power when it does not threaten their security. A significant limitation of the 'neo-realist' framework is that it ignores the context and realities surrounding a given domestic political environment. Several other assumptions that follow the earlier suppositions are: first since states are the primary actors for neo-realists, the primary drivers of FPDM are 'foreign policy elites;' second, since 'states act on the basis of the rational calculation of self-interests'[34] arriving at a definition of the situation/crises forms the basis for foreign policy elites to act; and third, since the world is 'anarchical' the quest for security is endless and motivated by relationships and alliances forged through power.

FPDM is the result of 'linked actions' and 'reactions' influenced significantly by 'domestic' and 'international' levels. A set of primary provisions influencing FPDM are that of regarding the' foreign policy arena' as a system linking together with other 'influences' to shape an integrated whole. Other important conditions involve the finality of FPDM stemming from the interface of the 'international system', 'domestic politics' and 'individual actors'.[35] The 'Rational Actor' model pre-supposes that decision-makers know what their wants, goals, means and actions are. It is to be assumed that the desire to maximize net benefits from foreign policy choices guides leaders and decision-makers. Put simply 'a policymaker will never choose an action that is expected to produce less value or utility, than some alternative policy'.[36]

Bureaucratic/Organizational Decision-making

The 'bureaucratic model' alternately known as the 'organizational model' categorizes decisions as 'outputs' flowing from large governmental ministries/departments/bureaus/agencies who generate opinions through 'standard operating procedures' (SOPs). This model posits that institutional interests are important in determining policymaker's preferences. A less generous way of looking at the 'bureaucratic model' is to assume that governmental decision-making by different organizations and agencies is a conflictual process as each 'bureaucratic' arm tries to succeed in presenting its views on national security policymaking.

In a complex centralized system of government for effective preparation of policy choices, there is the requirement of coordination between different centres of responsibility through 'standard patterns of decision-making'. The government on its part will rely on the advice or policy options suggested by the organization known for its experience, expertise and capability in the relevant field.

The bureaucratic/organizational' model does not discount the role of 'bargaining' between the 'actors' within a centralized framework.

Rather, there is 'active' participation and competition between different 'actors' to get across their point to the decision-making authority. Ultimately, elements of 'compromise', 'persuasion', and an acceptable 'cost-benefit analysis' prevail. In other words, most 'actors' see foreign policy issues from their parochial considerations and fall short in trying to evolve a policy consensus. Decisions are made through a highly politicized process involving bargaining, coalition-building, compromise as well as organizational/institutional power struggles. With domestic political interests also a factor, it is the skill and power of the winning combination that decides the outcome.[37]

Increasing institutionalization of the FPDM process in the reform period has witnessed the emergence of bureaucracies as powerful voices in the policy process. It is interpreted that all shades of opinions participate in the policymaking process and thereby promote their interests.

Linkage Politics Model

FPDM and foreign policy analysis in China is also reflective of the 'linkage politics model'. The 'linkage politics model' posits that since foreign policy is made by the very same leadership groups who exercise an influential role in domestic politics, those factors that are significant in domestic policymaking are most likely to be instrumental in foreign policymaking.[38] Those factors include: national political and economic attributes; policymaking procedures; the motivation, role and organization of policymakers, history and cultural traditions, national and government capacity, etc.

The 'Linkage Politics model' influences the processes involved in FPDM in two ways. First, the model may become critical in reshaping the policymaker's perception of the international environment as also in the execution of specific policies on issues. Second, the model may play a role in altering the conditions of foreign policy formulation and execution and transform the manner in which national resources are allocated and consumed.[39]

K.J. Holsti had typified the different variables impacting on the process of FPDM reveals the inherent dynamics of the process leading to decision-making.

Broadly, they were Independent variables, Intervening variables and Dependent variables. Independent variables comprise external, domestic, historical and cultural factors with colonial experiences – if any. Intervening variables comprise the perceptions and calculations of policymakers, the policymaking process, personalities and attitudes of elite towards the world beyond. Dependent variables focus on re-orientation, disengagement policies—if any, restructuring actions, and actions motivated by external aggression. To study the foreign policy choices of a country, it helps to understand the internal political dynamics, domestic political and institutional arrangements.

Pluralist Model

The 'Pluralist model' of FPDM is a recent approach with which to deconstruct the methodologies involved in arriving at a decision in China. This model rests on five primary beliefs.

The first belief of the 'pluralist model' is that 'interest groups compete with each other to gain access to the process of policymaking'. The second belief is that 'power is dispersed within a society through different interest groups'. Some of these groups have greater access to FPDM and hence a greater probability of influencing outcomes [e.g., the PLA's and the Taiwan Affairs Leading Small Group (TALSG's) respective views on Taiwan]. The third belief believes that a process of 'bargaining' and 'compromising' among the different interest groups precedes the eventual policy outcome. The fourth belief is that in spite of the concentration of power with the leadership in influencing FPDM, the post-Mao foreign policy process has opened up enough space for government departments, local governments and think tanks to have a say'. The fifth belief predicates the 'pluralist model' as being heavily influenced by two other models: 'arbiter model' and 'arena model'. The 'arbiter model' visualizes the government as standing above the group battle, setting ground rules for the conflicts, ensuring a balance between different groups and only inviting groups into the policy arena when required. The 'arena model' sees policy as a matter of mutual recognition, negotiation and bargain between the state and interest groups.[40]

A glaring shortcoming of the 'pluralist model' is that lays too much importance on 'interest groups' and ignores the existing institutional structure. The FPDM process comes to bear when a state decides to respond to a set of stimuli, in either a pre-determined manner or in a manner influenced heavily by the circumstances surrounding a crisis. Influenced by the approaches detailed in the earlier sections, this chapter adopts the methodological framework of a 'multi-causal approach'[41] that consciously avoids futile attempts to elucidate the complex phenomenon of FPDM by a single 'causal variable'. A 'multi-causal approach' highlights several salient features that illuminate the external behaviour of a state—China in this case. Under this approach, these salient features also hint at the existence of broader relationships amongst themselves. The 'multi-causal approach' adopted for this chapter are:

- Historical legacy, Ideological principles, Military doctrines, Security and Economic interests, Domestic political process, Actors and Interest groups with the fulcrum being FPDM.
- 'Historical Legacy'[42] where events of the past having a bearing on the decision-making process as the past experience gets transmitted to present times and are reflected in the attitude, behaviour, perceptions and decisions taken by policymakers and leaders.
- 'Ideological Principles'[43] assume that the actors subscribe to a set of beliefs that frame overall approaches in the conduct of foreign policy. From 'Marxist-Leninist-Maoist' ideological framework in the past, China today espouses a 'post-Dengist' ideology of 'peace and development'.
- 'Military Doctrines'[44] assume the importance of the 'use of force' to defend 'core national interests' and the role of the PLA in the decision-making process.
- 'Security and Economic Interests'[45] assume the existence of 'objectives' that are listed before any significant decision is taken. These 'objectives' could also morph into 'goals' or 'outcomes' that have a dynamic of their own once a decision is taken.
- The 'Domestic Political Process'[46] is a feature that cannot be ignored while computing FPDM. Political processes bring to bear on the decision-makers a set of assumptions, values, interests and options.

- 'Actors and Interest Groups'[47] assume that in every system, leading up to the 'decision' are individuals and groups with their own agendas and interests involved. Bureaucratic clusters are also powerful groups that may influence a decision owing to their sectoral interests.

Section II
Praxis

Flowing from the earlier section detailing concepts and approaches applicable to China's FPDM, the chapter in its second section examines Sino-Indian relations as a case study where theoretical approaches detailed earlier are reflected in their various nuances. To lend relevance, the author has focused on two decades since the Indian nuclear tests of 1998 in examining the contours and substance of Sino-Indian relations and attempted to highlight the commonalities, divergences, institutions, actors and other aspects of a constantly evolving dynamic relationship.

Introduction

A bilateral relationship needing deeper scrutiny from scholars and commentators is undoubtedly the growing 'engagement' and 'divergences' between India and China. For close to five decades India and China predicated their relations on the Panchsheel principles.[48] Representing more than a third of humanity, the two countries apart from impressive economic growth—more in China's case—symbolize different political cultures. In India's case, a federal, democratic experiment in its seventh decade in contrast to a Chinese version of socialism with its innate characteristics marks a primer to bilateral complexities. As Asia's largest countries, India and China, for many, symbolize the shifting contours of geopolitics and geo-economics of the Asia-Pacific region—a role that will assume more importance in the coming years. As neighbours with a disputed boundary, the two countries have bitter memories of the 1962 war[49] and maintained a frosty relationship until the late 1980s.

The behaviour type dominating Sino-Indian relations oscillates between 'estrangement' and 'rapprochement'. As powerful forces, these behaviour types exercise significant influence over the decision-making mechanisms of both the countries towards each other. For long, the Sino-Indian relationship was determined by the rather exclusive nature of critical enquiries related to the events leading to, and the aftermath of the brief border war of 1962.[50] Being on the defeated side, the outcome of this conflict, to date inhibits and influences the decision-making process towards China in New Delhi. From a Chinese perspective, the decision-making process towards New Delhi is representative of a mix of 'cautious engagement' tinged with 'historical grievances' regarding the boundary dispute.

To retain focus on the primary objectives of the chapter, and as mentioned before, the author will examine the Sino-Indian relationship since the Indian nuclear tests of 1998. This has been done so as to capture new vectors emerging in the bilateral relationship that have provided an ameliorative dynamic to what was a 'static relationship'. The decade since India's nuclear tests in May 1998 witnessed the emergence of 'closer' relations between India and China. The decade after has witnessed the emergence of China as a global economic determinant with strategic undertones. India, in contrast, wishes to be acknowledged as a global power, with a growing economy and norm abiding behaviour. The 'political' and 'economic' content of the growing relationship reflects a maturity not witnessed before, while their bilateral perspectives towards each other influence the strategic landscape. There are three determining features of Sino-Indian relations—first, a 'political connective' that is reflected in the regularity and importance of high-level visits on both sides; second, an 'economic incentive' that has witnessed trade emerge as a significant 'driver' influencing relations between the two sides; and third, a 'strategic imperative' that guides, and informs each other of their perceptions and apprehensions regarding each other. Apart from these powerful 'commonalities' there are outstanding issues of 'divergences' as well—the unresolved boundary dispute and Tibet that remain potent challenges to a constantly deepening relationship with inconsistencies galore as also the trade surplus China has with India revealing economic disparities.

The Nuclear Tests of 1998: Impact on Sino-Indian Relations

India's nuclear tests of May 1998 transformed its foreign and security policy objectives, the effects of which are more pertinent two decades later. The National Democratic Alliance (NDA) coalition led by the Bharatiya Janata Party (BJP) that took office in March 1998 was perhaps the first Indian political party that prior to assuming office had promised in its election manifesto[51] to deal more assertively with what it claimed was India's deteriorating security environment.

The first pointed statement made by an Indian cabinet minister against China was by then defence minister, George Fernandes, who during the course of a lecture described China as India's 'potential threat number one'.[52] Reflecting the oscillating temperament of the bilateral relationship, the MFA in China responded by stating that the Indian defence minister's statement was 'ridiculous and not worth refuting'. The MFA statement added that Fernandes' remarks had 'seriously destroyed the good atmosphere of improved relations between the two countries' and that '[T]he Chinese side has to express extreme regret and indignation over this'.[53]

The week after Fernandes' remarks, India conducted three underground nuclear tests on May 11 which drew a rather subdued statement from Beijing to the effect that the tests were 'detrimental to peace and stability in the South Asian region'.[54] On May 13, India conducted two more nuclear tests and these coincided with the publication of a letter by the *New York Times*, written by the Indian Prime Minister A.B. Vajpayee to US President Bill Clinton justifying the nuclear tests by naming China as the proximate cause for India going nuclear.[55] The contents of Vajpayee's letter had the effect of mobilizing opinion in China against the Indian nuclear tests. China's decision-makers arrived at a twin strategy of internationally highlighting the dangers posed to the non-proliferation regime by the nuclear tests and bilaterally by asking India to take 'practical action' to 'untie the knot' and not 'jeopardize the future of Sino-Indian relations'.[56] From China's perspective, India was regional 'hegemon' in South Asia actively modernizing its armed forces as also entering into defence cooperation agreements with countries such as the United States and Japan that some Chinese analysts point out is representative of a 'new containment' strategy against China.[57]

Displaying remarkable flexibility and sobriety, India took the initiative with the then Principal Secretary to the Indian Prime Minister and later National Security Adviser, Brajesh Mishra articulating the Indian position on China, stating that the Indian government did not regard China as its 'enemy' and would like to resolve all 'substantive problems' through dialogue.[58] India's initiatives aimed at 'untying the knot' continued with the President K.R. Narayanan taking personal interest in restoring bilateral ties to normalcy.[59]

Two instances of these were—President K.R. Narayanan meeting Ambassador Zhou Gang and former Chinese ambassador Cheng Ruisheng in January 1999 and undertaking a state visit to China in May-June 2000 to commemorate the 50th anniversary of the establishment of bilateral relations. China on its part quietly resumed the Joint working group (JWG) mechanism (suspended since the nuclear tests).

The moderate tone to Chinese statements was in evidence during the Kargil conflict[60] between Pakistan and India in the summer of 1999 when Premier Li Peng and Foreign Minister Tang Jiaxuan issued statements calling for both countries 'to maintain peace and stability in South Asia' and to resolve the 'Kashmir issue politically...through negotiations and consultations'.[61] The Chinese position on Kashmir went down well with Indian policymakers who were anticipating China's backing of Pakistan's position on the issue. In maintaining a neutral stance, the Chinese leadership was articulating a continuation of President Jiang Zemin's position on the Kashmir issue.[62] The seriousness on the part of the Indian government to bring back bilateral relations to normality was demonstrated by then External Affairs Minister Jaswant Singh's visit to Beijing and Shanghai from 29 March to 2 April 2002. The purpose of Jaswant Singh's visit was to impress upon the Chinese leadership the importance of maintaining continued dialogue between the two countries and also to prepare the grounds for a visit by Vajpayee.

After the five-year term of the NDA government came to a close, the general elections of 2004 produced another coalition government in India. The Indian National Congress (INC) led United Progressive Alliance (UPA) formed a coalition government in May 2004 and released the Common Minimum Program (CMP) that would serve as a template for governance for the period 2004-09. In the section on 'Foreign Policy' the CMP stated,

> '[T]he UPA government will give the highest priority to building closer political, economic and other ties with its neighbors in South Asia...Trade and investment with China will be expanded further and talks on the border issue pursued seriously'.[63]

Reflected in this statement are the sentiments expressed by all the coalition partners of the UPA including those parties who supported the government from outside. Inheriting a foreign policy charted by the previous NDA, the UPA government did not make any significant policy reversals and emphasized a 'spirit of continuity' in maintaining and enhancing relations with China. In large measure the 'spirit of continuity' in India's foreign policy towards China is the logical consequence of coalition governments becoming the norm in New Delhi since the commencement of India's economic reforms. Since the nuclear tests of 1998, the BJP-led NDA and the INC-led UPA have provided 'coalitional stability' in completing their terms.[1]

This phase has also witnessed a maturing of Indian foreign policy with 'economics' and 'active multilateralism' becoming the preferred policy outcome from New Delhi in its interactions with neighbouring countries and beyond. Prima facie it could be argued that first, since the turn of the century, Indian foreign policy has exhibited a strong 'positive value' in economic diplomacy, and second, closer engagement with China is evidence of the success of India's 'Look East' policy[65] adopted in 1992. To quote India's former foreign secretary Shyam Saran:

> More than an external economic policy or a political slogan, the 'Look East' policy was a strategic shift in India's vision of the world and her place in the evolving global economy. It was also a manifestation of our belief that developments in East Asia are of direct consequence to India's security and development.[66]

The Political Connective: High-level Visits

The first argument laid out by the author in this chapter is the emergence of a political connective as highlighted by regular high level visits by the leadership of both the countries in the period since 1998. During the NDA government's tenure, the Chinese Premier Zhu Rongji undertook a very successful visit to India from 13-18 June 2002. His visit was considered a landmark as it encouraged the growth of bilateral trade that today has emerged as the most dynamic vector of Sino-Indian relations.

Former Prime Minister A.B. Vajpayee's visit to China from 22-27 June 2003 was noteworthy for several reasons. First, the visit was advertized as the culmination of several years' effort since the nuclear tests of May 1998 to bring about a sense of direction and ballast to the bilateral relationship between the two countries. Second, the visit aimed at expediting the process of settling the boundary dispute between the two countries by creating new mechanisms with the political brief to finalize an eventual settlement. Third, increasing trade between the two countries was sought to be heralded as a new vector that would benefit both the sides. Fourth, the Indian side was hoping to secure recognition of Sikkim's accession to India. [67] Fifth, linked to Sikkim was the question of opening new transit points for trade on the Himalayas that would be of immense benefit to settled populations on both the sides of the border.[68]

The Vajpayee visit culminated in the signing of a total of ten agreements and a 'Declaration on Principles for Relations and Comprehensive Cooperation between India and China'.[69] The 'Joint Declaration' of 2003 created 'Special Representatives' with the express political brief of arriving at a 'mutually agreeable settlement to the boundary dispute'. The importance of such a mechanism as the 'Special Representative' is to create institutional leverages within the bilateral framework that would address core security issues that dominate the bilateral ties between the two countries. The most welcome aspect of Vajpayee's visit from a Chinese perspective was the declaration on Tibet. To quote from the Declaration: 'The Indian side recognizes that the Tibetan Autonomous Region is part of the territory of the People's

Republic of China and reiterates that it does not allow Tibetans to engage in anti-China political activities'.[70]

From an Indian perspective, the recognition of Nathu La as a designated pass for trade, entry and exit was interpreted as a restrained gesture from China in acknowledging India's sovereignty over Sikkim. The lack of an official statement from China acknowledging Sikkim as being a part of India coupled with media reports of repeated Chinese incursions in that region[71] as also Tawang in Arunachal Pradesh have generated some heat in New Delhi providing an illustration of the obstacles prevalent in a growing relationship.

During the UPA government tenure, the first high level visit was of Chinese Premier Wen Jiabao from April 9-12, 2005. Twelve bilateral documents[72] were signed during the visit and of these the most important was the 'Agreement on Political Parameters and Guiding Principles for the Settlement of the India–China Boundary Question'. The eleven articles comprising this agreement detail the cornerstones of an eventual political solution to the lingering boundary dispute. The spirit of the 'Political Parameters' is revealed in the phraseology of the articles where both the sides solemnly declare that 'differences on the boundary question' will not be 'allowed to affect the overall development of relations'. The two sides further agreed to 'resolve the boundary question through peaceful and friendly consultations'. For Chinese foreign minister Li Zhaoxing, the agreement on 'Political Parameters' was the '...first official document on the border issue in more than twenty years... (laying) a foundation for peaceful negotiations'.[73]

A decade after Jiang Zemin's visit in 1996, the Chinese president, Hu Jintao became the second president from China to visit India from November 20 to 23, 2006. The highlight of the visit was the Joint Statement issued that commits both the countries to follow a 'ten-pronged strategy' to further improve bilateral relations.[74] Maintaining the 'high level' political connectivity between the two countries, the Indian Prime Minister Dr Manmohan Singh visited China from January 13-15, 2008.

In an address delivered at the Chinese Academy of Social Sciences, Dr Manmohan Singh had stated that:

India's domestic and foreign policy priorities are closely linked. The primary task of our foreign policy is to create an external environment that is conducive for our rapid development. Our policy seeks to widen our development choices and give us strategic autonomy in the world. The independence of our foreign policy enables us to pursue mutually beneficial cooperation with all major countries of the world.[75]

Dr Manmohan Singh's visit to China was significant for several reasons—first, it reflected the determination of both the countries to deepen relations despite the existence of 'differences' over the boundary dispute; second, the visit highlighted the growing recognition of trade as an entirely new dimension between the two countries and third, the visit brought out the importance for both the countries to enunciate their common perspectives on a whole range of issues as reflected in the 'Vision Statement' released by Dr Manmohan Singh and Wen Jiabao during the visit. The 'Vision Statement' marks a departure from the earlier bilateral joint statements and aims to project a shared commitment and approach by both the sides to issues of global import.

The political connective content in the 'Vision Statement' is reflected in its call to 'promote the building of a harmonious world of durable peace and common prosperity'.[76] The civilizational ties that bind the two countries together finds an echo in 'the two sides recognizing that' they 'bear a significant historical responsibility to ensure comprehensive, balanced and sustainable economic and social development'[77] of each other. The political nuances emerging from the 'Vision Statement' underline the importance of both the countries concentrating their abilities in harnessing their economic potential to achieve comprehensive growth and social stability.

The similarities of the developmental experience are too many to be missed. For India, the reform process since 1991 has ushered in major changes across the socio-political spectrum. The days of one-party majority in the Indian parliament were a thing of the past with coalition alliances the mainstay. The General Elections of 2019 brought the BJP to power with a majority in parliament. Regional political parties have grown in stature and electoral alliances are forged on the basis of societal permutations and combinations that were unthinkable a decade ago.[78] In China, while the Communist Party holds hegemony on power, the groundswell of change is felt in the manner in which loose associations of those marginalized from the reform process are increasingly making themselves heard. The Communist Party has also changed with a technocratic-legalist elite displaying signs of 'consensus building' replacing the 'paramount leader' of yesteryears.[79] Xi Jinping however appears to be a throwback in time, tailor-made for this century! In China's case however, the Party has made the success of the reforms its ticket to legitimacy along with political institutionalization and systemic leadership transition. In India, the debate over the extent of reforms is indeed a lively one, with all shades of opinion finding some level of acceptance and vocal adherents.[80]

The Economic Incentive: Bilateral Trade as the New Vector

The second argument laid out by the author is that economic incentive as a new powerful vector has transformed bilateral relations between China and India.

The India–China engagement has 'economics' as the new buzzword motivating closer and deeper Sino-Indian relations. The 'Vision Statement' of Dr Singh and the Chinese premier, Wen Jiabao, calls for both sides to 'support and encourage the processes of regional integration that provide mutually beneficial opportunities for growth, as an important feature of the merging international system'.[81] Regional cooperation mechanisms such as the East Asia Summit (EAS)[82], the Asia-Europe Meeting (ASEM)[83], the South Asian Association for Regional Cooperation (SAARC)[84]—in which China is an observer; the Bay of Bengal Initiative for Multi-Sectoral Technical and Economic Cooperation (BIMSTEC)[85] and the Shanghai Cooperation Organisation (SCO)[86]—in which India is an observer—have been identified as structures for future cooperation and coordination by both the sides. It indeed will be welcome if India and China could drive momentum into the SAARC—a mechanism held hostage so far due to the insecurities of India's neighbours regarding India's centrality and dominance in the region. A flip side to this—India must be prepared to acknowledge the growing centrality of China in its trade with other member countries of the SAARC.

As a powerful 'driver' Sino-Indian trade dynamics have surpassed all expectations. At the end of November 2007 the bilateral trade between the two countries was to the tune of USD 38.6 billion dollars making China India's second largest trading partner. It is expected that in the coming months China will become India's largest trading partner, supplanting the United States. For China, the world's fourth largest trading power, India was its tenth largest trading partner in 2007. Remarkably, a decade ago, Sino-Indian trade was negligible. In 2005 a Joint Study Group[87] to identify economic complementarities and opportunities between the two countries had predicted a bilateral trade figure of USD 20 billion by 2008. The Manmohan Singh visit saw the both the sides setting a target of USD 60 billion in bilateral trade by 2010.

The 'global content' of the 'Vision Statement' acknowledges the combined status of India and China as being the largest developing nations in the world. The two countries while embracing the process of globalization and its challenges have sought the 'establishment of an open, fair, equitable, transparent and rule-based multilateral trading system'[88] and for an early conclusion of the Doha Development Round. The reality remains different beyond the gloss of India's superlative performance in software and business process outsourcing (BPO) sectors[89] and China's emerging as the 'factory floor' of the world. Even after four decades of reforms in China and three decades in India a majority of the population supports itself by agriculture and related activities. Although agriculture forms a diminishing percentage in the GDP of both the countries, the demographics involved in creating sustainable non-farm sectors is mind-numbing and requires decades of economic restructuring. In India, the question of agriculture being opened to 'market forces' is a controversial one affecting the lives of millions and that could well affect the political outcome of electoral competition in many states and even at the centre when in the summer of 2024, the current BJP/NDA government completes its term.

The 'Vision Statement' also highlighted the need for both countries to coordinate their strategies in supporting developing countries within the World Trade Organization (WTO). With large populations to support, the introduction of market forces too quickly could lead to the unravelling of the relative gains accrued from years of 'fine-tuning' the economy to face the challenges of globalization.

The Security Imperative: Common Aspirations

The third argument the author makes is that the two countries are, sometimes, motivated to arrive at a security imperative that is guided by common aspirations.

The common aspirations of India and China are best revealed in their 'positive value' approach towards multilateralism.[90] Active participation in multilateral forums is from a pragmatic realization of several factors. First, a conducive international environment is a necessity for the successful and stable implementation of domestic economic reforms in both the countries; second, multilateral economic and security arrangements in the region are inevitable and non-participation is a liability; third, multilateral institutions go further in promoting 'stability' and a 'multi-polar' order that benefits members most and, fourth, 'a pragmatic foreign policy that is ideologically agnostic is more goal fulfilling and national interests driven'.[91]

The security concerns the two sides share is revealed by their common approach to non-traditional security issues. With the quest for energy increasingly determining the future trajectory of growth for both the countries, the 'Vision Statement' calls for the 'international community to establish an international energy order that is fair, equitable, secure, stable and to the benefit of the international community'. The opportunity presented by the International Thermonuclear Experimental Reactor (ITER) in which China and India are participating nations is identified as 'meeting the global energy challenge in an environmentally sustainable manner'. On climate change, the two countries 'welcome the outcome of the United Nations Framework Convention on Climate Change (UNFCCC)' and 'agree to work closely during the negotiation process laid out in the Bali Road Map for long term cooperative action under the Convention' and in adherence to the principles and provisions of the Kyoto Protocol. The two sides emphasized the need for moving forward the processes of 'multilateral arms control, disarmament and non-proliferation', and their shared aspiration to 'peaceful uses of outer space'. The two sides also 'condemned terrorism in all its forms' and pledged to work together bilaterally and in consonance with the international community to 'strengthen the global framework against terrorism'.[92] The shared sentiments on non-traditional security issues should be seen as an emerging methodology in building structures for future cooperation.

Analysing Bilateral 'Notes of Dissonance'— The Boundary Dispute and Tibet

As in most bilateral relationships, Sino-Indian ties are not without their 'negative value features'. These are most visible as regards the unresolved boundary dispute and the recurrent influence of Tibet in an overall bilateral perspective. In total, while bilateral relations are beginning to reflect a maturity never seen before, the centrality of arriving at a settlement to the lingering boundary dispute cannot be wished away. The March 2008 riots in Lhasa and other parts of Tibet could in the near to middle term be a factor exercising strains in bilateral relations.

The Boundary Dispute

India and China share a disputed boundary stretching more than 3000 km. The boundary dispute between the two sides remains unresolved despite the creation of special mechanisms[93] and evolving political parameters[94] to arrive at an eventual settlement.[95] While Hu Jintao's 2006 visit demonstrated a commitment at the political level to maintain and improve upon existing ties between both the countries what however dominated the visit were the 'utterances' of Sun Yuxi, then Chinese ambassador in India. Prior to Hu's visit, Sun Yuxi had created a furore by claiming the whole of Arunachal Pradesh as belonging to China. From an Indian perspective, Sun Yuxi had crossed the 'red line' by making a contention during the course of an interview with a television channel that 'the whole of Arunachal Pradesh is Chinese territory and Tawang is only one place in it',[96] Sun Yuxi succeeded in bringing the touchy boundary issue to the centre stage of India–China bilateral relations. His statements and the emotions it unleashed eclipsed the slew of agreements signed during Hu's visit. Not only did Sun Yuxi's statements throw a shadow on the discourse that preceded and followed Chinese President Hu Jintao's otherwise successful visit to India in November 2006, it also had the effect of diluting his predecessor Hua Junduo's widely applauded statement made in 2003.[97]

Sun Yuxi's statement brought to the fore Indian concerns over China's aggressive polemics of making territorial claims. Sun's repeated 'assertions' were contrary to the 'comfortable bonhomie' created in the last couple of years by the rhetoric over 'growing congruence of interests' and 'mutual complementarity' as also debates on the 'simultaneous rise of India and China'—the Chindia factor. These remarks had the effect of alienating public opinion in India, that since economic reforms of 1991, had been favourable about enhancing relations with China.

Sun's remarks were met by a robust response by India's External Affairs Minister, Pranab Mukherjee's statement, that 'Arunachal Pradesh is an integral part of India'.[98] From the Indian perspective, Sun's statement, was interpreted as going beyond the text of the agreement between India and China on the 'Political Parameters and Guiding Principles for the Settlement of the India-China Boundary Question',[99] that was signed during the visit of Chinese premier Wen Jiabao to New Delhi in April 2005. To cite, Article I of the Agreement specifically states that 'the differences on the boundary question should not be allowed to affect the overall development of bilateral relations. The two sides will resolve the boundary question through peaceful and friendly consultations'.[100] Article V further states that 'the two sides will take into account, inter alia, historical evidence, national sentiments, practical difficulties and reasonable concerns and sensitivities of both sides, and the actual state of border areas (emphasis added)'. Article VII crucially states that 'in reaching a boundary settlement, the two sides shall safeguard due interests of their settled populations in the border areas'.[101]

It has not gone unnoticed in India that since Xi Jinping's assuming the leadership of the Party, State and the Central Military Commission

(CMC), China has become more vocal in its claim over Tawang district in the Indian state of Arunachal Pradesh.[102] It is precisely this kind of 'aggressive posturing' that needs to be kept under check as the emotive element in Sino-Indian relations is never far from the surface. The eventual settlement of the boundary dispute is therefore the litmus test facing the growing bilateral engagement of the two countries, despite multiple strains. From the Indian perspective, a primary question that arises is—are Sun Yuxi's remarks characteristic of a negotiating posture or are they reflective of China's methodology when it comes to handling territorial disputes?

Tibet

In March 2008, the riots in Tibet came at a time most embarrassing for the Chinese government. First, the 11th National People's Congress (China's parliament) was in session when large-scale violence was reported from Tibet. The Chinese political leadership, not conditioned to citizens protesting or articulating their interests was initially taken aback by the protests. Second, the demonstrations against Chinese rule in Tibet, questioned the claims propagated by the CPC that 'Tibet is an oasis of prosperity and stability under the leadership of the CPC'. Third, and perhaps most significantly, the violence against Chinese rule in Tibet came at a time when China was gearing up to host the Olympic Games in Beijing, in August of that year. The Olympics are not without a political agenda for the leadership in China. They were visualized by the CPC as the signature event highlighting in one stroke, China's 'economic prosperity', 'peaceful rise and development', 'harmony of people' and 'global outlook'. Fourth, for the current leadership of Xi Jinping, any 'mass' developments in Tibet that happened during Hu Jintao's are of paramount concern as the 'discontent' could spread to other minority regions especially Xinjiang, where reside the restive Uighurs; and fifth, it is not a comforting thought for Chinese policymakers that the XIV Dalai Lama and his followers exiled from China are living as refugees articulating their grievances against China through the 'Tibetan government in exile' based in Dharamshala, India.

As in the past when faced with 'internal disturbances', the leadership in China typically applied itself to describing the supposed perpetrators of the violence in the vilest terms.[102] The terms used to describe the Dalai Lama for instance hark back to the lexicon of the Cultural Revolution. The emotive content of the 'Tibet issue' for China is linked to its sovereignty and territorial integrity over which it brooks no compromises. For China, any 'instability' in Tibet challenges the unity of the country and has to be dealt with 'severely'. To cite John Rowland, '[T]ibet for Chinese leaders and Mao included was a 'palm whose five fingers were Ladakh, Nepal, Bhutan, Sikkim and NEFA' (the North Eastern Frontier Agency now known as Arunachal Pradesh). [103]

Despite India's repeated statements acknowledging the TAR being part of China,[104] there is considerable disquiet among official and academic circles in China about the 'ambiguity' that New Delhi is projecting. It flusters Indian policymakers that their efforts over the years in 'curtailing' the anti-China rhetoric from Tibetan exiles based in India has not been acknowledged by Beijing. At the level of the Special Representatives discussing an eventual settlement to the boundary dispute between the two countries, it is to be expected that China will raise the pitch over the presence of 'exiled Tibetans in India led by the Dalai Lama' and the 'Tibetan government in exile'. China can even be expected to ask India to stop providing 'sanctuary' to the Dalai Lama for his 'splittist' activities. Should such a development take place, India faces the delicate choice of not alienating the Tibetan exiles and at the same time not to be seen as appeasing Beijing. For all practical purposes, the Tibetan refugee community in India is well entrenched and could be considered politically an 'interest group' and a 'strong voice of moral suasion' primarily due to the charismatic influence of the Dalai Lama.

While no restrictions or obstacles are expected on the trade and economic relations between the two countries, the recent violence in Tibet has increased the level of 'political distrust' of India on the Chinese side. The visit of Nancy Pelosi, Speaker of the US Congress, heading a bipartisan delegation to express support to the Dalai Lama in the immediate aftermath of the violence in Tibet was highlighted by the Chinese media to advocate 'conspiracy theories' linking the role of the United States and India (in a lesser manner) in tacitly encouraging the 'splittists' and the 'Dalai clique'.[105]

FPDM and Sino-Indian Relations—Inferences

High level visits by the political leadership from both the countries, the emergence of trade as a significant determinant and a shared aspiration of a global strategic order are but one important part of the dynamic nature of Sino-Indian relations. Impressive strides in bilateral relations have been made by both the countries in the last decade and multiple levels of interaction exist to address the entire gamut of relations between India and China. To address 'trust deficit' between the two countries, it is imperative to maintain existing arrangements of interaction at the highest levels and institutionalize a framework for cooperation that settles outstanding bilateral disputes by separating its emotive content and create new opportunities for deepening ties. Adopting the 'multi-causal' approach in trying to capture the essence of FPDM and their relation to Sino-Indian relations, the following characteristics emerge.

For the sake of clarity, the inferences made have been grouped in two categories: 'FPDM in Beijing' and 'Perceptions influencing the decision-making process of Sino-Indian relations'

FPDM in Beijing

1. Flowing from the adoption of a 'multi-causal' approach as the methodological framework to situate this chapter, there emerge several 'determinants' that have a significant bearing on the decision-making process in Beijing. These determinants are: 'domestic', 'international systemic' and 'domestic- international linkage'. The 'domestic' determinant lays stress on domestic factors—political, cultural, historical, leadership traits and ideology—that influence China's FPDM. The 'international systemic' determinant is a value system that believes in China's international position, power, prestige, influence, etc. deciding China's FPDM. The 'domestic- international linkage' determinant is a blend of those factors that merge from the domestic to international and influence FPDM.
2. The concept of 'peaceful development' in China's foreign policy is a continuation of Deng Xiaoping's concept *tao guang yang hui*

('keep a low profile and never take the lead'). Jiang Zemin had subscribed to the concept of *duo ji shi jie* ('multipolar world')[107] while his successor Hu Jintao in his foreign policy forays has laid stress on China's role as a peace loving, people based (*yi ren wei ben*) tolerant and responsible power.[108] China's soft power[109] is to enhance China's in regional and world affairs and aid its economic development. Xi Jinping's phraseology is *zhongguo meng* (China dream). Not mentioning the world and responsible aspects of global governance are missing!

3. The decade from 1979 to 1988 was marked by a Chinese approach to territorial sovereignty that could be characterized as a 'cautious attempt to concurrently de-escalate conflict along each of the China's main borders and maintain China's pre-existing stance on the location of those borders'.[110] The decade from 1988 to 1998 witnessed China actively pursuing mechanisms to resolve outstanding boundary disputes that met with success as regards the Central Asian states, Vietnam and Russia. A tactical approach highlighting the salience of border relations, while not compromising on strategic goals and territorial claims became the policy line.

4. The realm of FPDM for China reflects a 'non-ideological temperament' and could even be termed as 'ideologically agnostic'. It is the interests and objectives of a particular adopted policy line that resonate and influence decision-makers. The phase since 'Tiananmen Incident' of 1989, reveals a political stridency matched with an economic aspiration to become world's largest economy.

5. With the hierarchy of the CPC dominated by 'technocrats' and 'legalists' the role of the 'revolutionary elite' is over. Reflecting the professional and personal experience as also location within the system, there are multiple strands that go into policymaking.

6. There exists within the FPDM in China a 'pluralized elite' who lay significant importance on a professional bureaucratic process as also a formalized policy consultation system. Think tanks and research institutes specializing on foreign policy, IR and strategic affairs are increasingly becoming influential voices within the 'policy network' in China. Major policy outcomes in Beijing are the result of 'aggregation and mediation' at the highest levels in

Zhongnanhai involving the participation of the FALSG, CPC Politburo and the Standing Committee.
7. Following the Liberation in 1949, decision-making on strategic and security concerns while guided by 'major intellectual and political concerns' was determined according to the ideological perspective of Mao Zedong. In the reform period three powerful factors (a) weakened personal authority of the leadership, (b) growing bureaucratic interests and the (c) changing domestic and international situation—have brought about a complete transformation in the decision-making processes.

Perceptions Influencing the Decision-making Process of Sino-Indian Relations

1. The official statements issued by both the countries during such high level visits captures the element of 'realism' that guides bilateral relations. As developing countries, India and China above all yearn for 'peaceful environment' to focus on developing their domestic economies. 'Realism' also guides the establishment of mechanisms to find an eventual settlement to the outstanding boundary dispute.
2. The role of interest groups and powerful bureaucracies in the decision-making process towards India cannot be ignored. A hypothesis laid out by Vernon Aspaturian more than four decades ago was that 'certain groups in Beijing tend to benefit from tension producing policies (sic.) mainly because they receive additional resources and may prompt a hostile action externally in order to further parochial bureaucratic interests'.[111]
3. The 1998 nuclear tests have accrued for India 'relative gains' and that the post-Pokharan scenario has unfolded with India seeking strategic parity with China. The culmination of the Indo-US nuclear deal only reinforces this notion.[112] From an Indian perspective, Pakistan is no longer a factor in its relations with China, irrespective of the China–Pakistan Economic Corridor (CPEC) and its progress, so far.
4. To the Chinese, the irresolution of the boundary dispute has two legacies—the 'historical' and the 'contemporary'. The 'historical'

relates to the unfairness of treaties[113] drawn up by colonial powers and the 'contemporary' relates to India's position on the boundary dispute being 'Nehruvian' and that as long as the Congress is in power there is no hope for resolution.
5. From a geopolitical perspective, 'China historically has sought to keep regional powers weak, divided or deferential and to exclude competitors in order to minimize threats (from its neighbouring countries)'.[114]
6. An important distinction to be drawn by analysts of Sino-Indian relations is to assess the resources and 'relative strengths of different research institutions and their relationship to different agencies within the Chinese government'. This facilitates the creation of an overall construct that details the variables and determinants influencing China's India policy.[115]
7. The Indian political system does not find many enthusiasts in China. Most Chinese experts on India are perplexed by the 'dynamic processes' and 'personality centric politics' governing India's coalition governments. It could be construed that Chinese pressure to settle the boundary dispute will increase if Chinese analysts were to conclude that there is a fragile coalition at the centre.
8. It is significant to note that across the political spectrum in India, improving relations with China is important, minus the increase in belligerence from Beijing in Tibet. This consensus does not however mean that there needs to be a quick solution to the lingering boundary dispute. The same however cannot be said of China, as relations with India are but one of the many issues Chinese foreign policy decision-makers must address.

Notes

1. Samuel S. Kim, 'China and the World in Theory and Practice', in *China and the World: Chinese Foreign Relations in the Post-Cold War Era*, ed. Samuel S. Kim (Boulder, CO: Westview Press, 1994), 3.
2. See Paul R. Viotti and Mark V. Kauppi, *International Relations and World Politics – Security, Economy, Identity* 3rd ed. (New Jersey: Pearson Education, 2007).
3. The 'bureaucratic institutionalism' model is another name for the 'structural institutional context model' that revolves around the fundamental predicates of (a) systemic constraints influencing the shaping of policy outputs,

(b) within a FPDM context institutional relationships are impersonal, and (c) the configuration of institutional relationships is automatic and not intentional.

4. Fei-ling Wang, 'Beijing's Incentive Structure: The Pursuit of Preservation, Prosperity and Power', in *China Rising: Power and Motivation in Chinese Foreign Policy*, eds. Yong Deng and Fei-ling Wang (Lanham, MD: Rowman and Littlefield, 2005), 22.
5. Deborah Stone, 'Policy Paradox: The Art of Political Decision Making', in *Classics of Public Policy*, eds. Jay M. Shafritz, Karen S. Layne, and Christopher P. Borick (New York: Pearson/Longman, 2005), 65.
6. Davis B. Bobrow, Steve Chan and John A. Kringen, *Understanding Foreign Policy Decisions: The Chinese Case* (New York: Macmillan – The Free Press, 1979), 2.
7. Chih-Yu Shih, *China's Just World – The Morality of Chinese Foreign Policy* (Boulder, CO: Lynne Reiner, 1993), 1.
8. Richard C. Snyder, H.W. Bruck and Burton Sapin, eds., *Foreign Policy Decision-Making: An Approach to the Study of International Politics* (New York: Free Press of Glencoe, 1962), 5.
9. See John W. Kingdon, *Agenda's Alternatives and Public Policies*, 2nd ed. (New York: Harper Collins, 1995).
10. E. E. Schattschneider, *The Semi-Sovereign People* (New York: Holt, Rinehart & Winston, 1960) as cited in Andrew C. Mertha and William R. Lowry, 'Unbuilt Dams – Seminal Events and Policy Change in China, Australia, and the United States', *Comparative Politics* 39, no. 1 (October 2006): 1.
11. Frank R. Baumgartner and Bryan D. Jones, *Agenda's and Instability in American Politics* (Chicago, IL: University of Chicago Press, 1993) as cited in Andrew C. Mertha and William R. Lowry, 'Unbuilt Dams – Seminal Events and Policy Change in China, Australia, and the United States', Comparative Politics 39, no. 1 (October 2006): 2.
12. See David M. Lampton, *The Making of Chinese Foreign and Security Policy in the Era of Reform, 1978-2000* (Stanford: Stanford University Press, 2001).
13. Samuel S. Kim, *China and the World: New Directions in Chinese Foreign Relations*, 2nd ed. (Boulder, CO: Westview Press, 1989), 16.
14. Davis B. Bobrow et al., *Understanding Foreign Policy Decisions*, 2.
15. Nicolaus Tideman, *Collective Decisions and Voting – The Potential for Public Choice* (Aldershot: Ashgate, 2006), 3.
16. See Donald E. Nuechterlein, 'The Concept of National Interest: A Time for New Approaches', *Orbis* 23 (Spring 1979): 76.
17. Kal J. Holsti et al., *Why Nation's Realign: Foreign Policy Restructuring in the Postwar World* (London: George Allen & Unwin Ltd., 1982). Holsti lists 17 national conceptions—'bastion of revolution-liberator'; 'regional leader'; 'regional protector'; 'active independent'; 'liberator supporter'; 'anti-imperialist agent'; 'defender of the faith'; 'mediator- integrator'; 'regional sub-system collaborator'; 'developer'; 'bridge'; 'faithful ally'; 'independent'; 'example'; 'internal developer'; 'isolationist' and 'protectee'.

18. See Joseph Fewsmith, 'Where do correct ideas come from? – The Party School, key think tanks and the intellectuals', in *China's Leadership in the 21st Century: The Rise of the Fourth Generation*, eds. David M. Finkelstein and Maryanne Kivlehan (Armonk, NY: M. E. Sharpe, 2003).
19. See David M. Lampton, *Policy Implementation in Post-Mao China* (Berkeley and Los Angeles: University of California Press, 1987); Kenneth G. Lieberthal and David M. Lampton, *Bureaucracy, Politics and Decision Making in Post-Mao China* (Berkeley, CA: University of California Press, 1992)
20. See Michel Oksenberg, 'China's Political System: Challenges of the Twenty-First Century', *China Journal* 45 (January 2001): 21–35; Kenneth G. Lieberthal and Michel Oksenberg, *Policy Making in China: Leaders, Structures and Processes* (Princeton, NJ: Princeton University Press, 1988).
21. Alastair Iain Johnston, *Cultural Realism: Strategic Culture and Grand Strategy in Chinese History* (Princeton, NJ: Princeton University Press, 1995), 117.
22. See Robert Keohane and Helen Milner, eds., *Internationalization and Domestic Politics* (New York: Cambridge University Press, 1996), 25–47.
23. Peter M. Haas, 'Introduction: Epistemic Communities and International Policy Coordination', *International Organization* 46 (Winter 1992): 1.
24. See Helen. V. Milner, *Interests, Institutions, and Information: Domestic Politics and International Relations* (Princeton, NJ: Princeton University Press, 1997).
25. Bruce Bueno de Mesquita and David Lalman, *War and Reason: Domestic and International Imperatives* (New Haven, CT: Yale University Press, 1992).
26. Paul Huth, *Standing Your Ground* (Ann Arbor: University of Michigan Press, 1996).
27. Helen. V. Milner, *Interests, Institutions, and Information*, 24.
28. Robert D. Putnam, 'Diplomacy and Domestic Politics: The Logic of Two-Level Games', *International Organization* 42 (Summer 1988): 427–460.
29. Xuanli Liao, *Chinese Foreign Policy Think Tanks and China's Policy Towards Japan* (Hong Kong: The Chinese University Press, 2006).
30. See James D. Morrow, 'A Rational Choice Approach to International Conflict', in *Decision Making on War and Peace: The Cognitive Rational Debate*, eds. Nehemia Geva and Alex Minz (Boulder, CO: Lynne Reiner, 1997).
31. Charles Todd Kent, 'Politically Rational Foreign Policy Decision-Making' (Unpublished PhD diss., A&M University, 2005): 2–3.
32. Amitai Etzioni, 'Mixed Scanning: A "Third" Approach to Decision Making', in *International Relations and World Politics – Security, Economy, Identity* 3rd ed., eds. Paul R. Viotti and Mark V. Kauppi (New Jersey: Pearson Education, 2007), 41–50.
33. Jan-Erik Lane, *Comparative Politics – The Principal-Agent Perspective* (Abingdon: Routledge, 2008), 23.
34. David Patrick Houghton, 'Reinvigorating the Study of Foreign Policy Decision Making: Toward a Constructivist Approach', *Foreign Policy Analysis* 3, no. 1 (January 2007): 25.
35. See Charles Todd Kent, Ibid., 6–14.

36. Bueno de Mesquita, as cited in Greg Cashman and Leonard C. Robinson, *An Introduction to the Causes of War – Patterns of Inter-State Conflict from World War I to Iraq* (Lanham, MD: Rowman & Littlefield, 2007), 6.
37. Graham Allison, *Essence of Decision: Explaining the Cuban Missile Crisis* (Boston: Little Brown, 1971), 8.
38. Readings on 'Linkage Politics Model' include, James N. Rosenau, *Linkage Politics: Essays on the Convergence of National and International Systems* (New York: The Free Press, 1969); Richard Snyder, H. W. Bruck and Burton Sapin, 'The Decision Making Approach to the Study of International Politics', in *International Politics and Foreign Policy*, ed. James N. Rosenau (New York: The Free Press, 1969), 199–206.
39. Hanwen Chen, 'Domestic Reform, Structural Changes and Foreign Policy Transformation: Structural – Institutional Contexts of Chinese Foreign Policy Evolution since 1979' (Unpublished PhD diss., Graduate School, University of Maryland, 1995), 22–23.
40. See Xuanli Liao, *Chinese Foreign Policy Think Tanks and China's Policy Towards Japan*, 8–9.
41. The author acknowledges Ho Joon Kim, 'Why China Goes to War – Risk-Taking Factors and Patterns of Crisis Behavior: Three Comparative Case Studies' Graduate School of Arts and Sciences, George Washington University, 1990 for clarifying methodological approaches to this study and introducing the 'multi-causal approach'.
42. See Mark Mancall, 'The Persistence of Tradition in Chinese Foreign Policy', *The Annals of the American Academy of Political and Social Science* 349 (September 1963): 14–26; C. P. Fitzgerald, *The Chinese View of Their Place in the World* (London: Oxford University Press, 1964); John King Fairbank, 'A Preliminary Framework', in *The Chinese World Order*, ed. J.K. Fairbank (Cambridge, MA: Harvard University Press, 1968), 1–19 and 'Chinese Foreign Policy in Historical Perspective', *Foreign Affairs* 47, no. 3 (April 1969): 449–463.
43. Communist ideology is frequently classified by political scientists into three ideal types: Seliger's 'fundamental' and 'operative' ideology, Moore's 'ideology of ends' and 'ideology of means', and Schurmann's 'pure' and 'practical' ideology. While at a fundamental level it refers to the body of theories considered as 'universal truth', such as the end goal of communism, class and class struggle, democratic centralism and the historical mission of the proletariat, at an operative level it designates sets of political ideas and values put forward by political elites to guide or justify their concrete policies and actions. It is not always easy, however, to draw a clear distinction between fundamental and operative ideology, as there is frequently a degree of overlapping between the two. See Martin Seliger, *Ideology and Politics* (New York: The Free Press, 1976); Barrington Moore, *Soviet Politics- The Dilemma of Power, the Role of Ideas in Social Change* (Cambridge, MA: Harvard University Press, 1950), 402–403; Franz Schurmann, *Ideology and Organisation in Communist China* (Berkeley,

CA: University of California Press, 1966), 18; Stuart Schram, *Ideology and Policy in China since the Third Plenum, 1978-1984* (London, Research Notes and Studies, No.6, SOAS/University of London, 1984); Lucien Pye, 'On Chinese Pragmatism', *The China Quarterly* 106 (June 1986): 230; Malcolm B. Hamilton, 'The Elements of the Concept of Ideology', *Political Studies* 35, no.1 (March 1987): 18; and Donald S. Zagoria, 'Ideology and Chinese Foreign Policy', in *Ideology and Foreign Policy*, ed. George Schwab (New York: Cycro Press, 1978), 103–116.

44. See for instance, Lin Biao, 'Long Live the Victory of People's War', *Peking Review* 8, no. 36 (3 September 1965).

45. An illustration of security and economic interests was Hu Yaobang's pronouncing China's new foreign policy in 1982 that has evolved several times over and currently reads as follows:

'China unswervingly pursues an independent foreign policy of peace. The fundamental goals of this policy are to preserve China's independence, sovereignty and territorial integrity, create a favourable international environment for China's reform and opening up and modernization construction, maintain world peace and propel common development'.

China's 'Independent Foreign Policy of Peace' was first adopted at the 12th National Congress of the CPC in 1982. See Hu Yaobang, 'Report to the Twelfth CPC National Congress – Create a New Situation in All Fields of Socialist Modernisation', as cited in Harold C. Hinton, *The People's Republic of China 1979-1984: A Documentary Survey* (Wilmington, DE: Scholarly Resources Inc., 1986), 210–212.

46. Lucien W. Pye, *The Dynamics of Chinese Politics* (Cambridge, MA: Oelgeschlager, Gunn & Hain, 1981), 13; Parris H. Chang, *Power and Policy in China* (University Park: The Pennsylvania State University Press, 1975) and Ming-Cheng M. Lo and Eileen M. Otis, 'Guangxi Civility: Processes, Potentials, and Contingencies', *Politics & Society* 31, no.1 (March 2003): 131–162.

47. Parris Chang, 'The Emergence of Reform Forces and Politics', in *China's Reform Politics*, ed. San-Woo Rhee (Seoul: Sogang University Press, 1986), 36–39.

Lowell Dittmer and Yu-Shan Wu. 'Chinese Politics'. *World Politics* 47 (1995): 467–494; Andrew Nathan, 'A Factionalism Model for Chinese Politics', *The China Quarterly* 53 (January-March 1973): 34–66 and Tang Tsou, 'Prolegomenon to the Study of Informal Groups in Chinese Communist Party Politics', *The China Quarterly* 65 (January 1976): 98–114.

48. The Five Principles of Peaceful Coexistence also called the 'Panchsheel', were first elaborated at the Bandung Conference of Asian and African nations in April 1955. In brief the 'five principles' stand for mutual respect for sovereignty and territorial integrity; mutual non-aggression; non-interference in each other's internal affairs; equality and mutual benefit; and peaceful coexistence. They were part of the ten principles adopted by the Bandung

Conference, which in sequence are: (a) Respect basic human rights and the aims and principles of the UN charter; (b) respect sovereignty and territorial integrity of every nation; (c) recognize that all races are equal and all nations, big or small, are equal; (d) non-intervention or interference in other nation's internal affairs; (e) respect every nation's right of individual or collective defence in accordance with the UN Charter; (f) to not make use of collective defence arrangements to serve any great power's special interest and to not impose pressure upon each other; (g) to not offend any nation's territorial integrity or political independence by aggressive behaviour or aggressive threat or resort to force; (h) to solve all international disputes through peaceful means such as negotiation, mediation, arbitration or judicial solution and any other peaceful means chosen by the concerned parties in accordance with the UN Charter; (i) promote mutual interests and cooperation and (j) respect justice and international obligation.

49. In October and November 1962, China and India fought a war, in which Indian troops were convincingly defeated, over the disputed boundary called the McMahon line. The Sino-Indian border is more than 3300 km long and divided into three sectors: the western sector from the Karakoram Pass to Demchok on the Indus; the middle sector from Demchok to the Nepalese boundary and covering on the Indian side the states of Uttaranchal and Himachal Pradesh; and the eastern sector from Bhutan to Myanmar.

50. See Alfred P. Rubin, 'The Sino-Indian Border Disputes', *The International and Comparative Law Quarterly* 9 (January 1960): 103–104; George N. Patterson, *Peking versus Delhi* (New York: Praeger, 1964); Arthur A. Stahnke, 'The Place of International Law in Chinese Strategy and Tactics: The Case of the Sino-Indian Boundary Dispute', The *Journal of Asian Studies* 30, no. 1 (November 1970): 95–119; Alastair Lamb, *The China-India Border: The Origins of the Disputed Boundaries* (London: Oxford University Press, 1964) and *The McMahon Line: A Study in the Relations between India, China and Tibet, 1904-1914* (London: Routledge & Kegan Paul, 1964). Scholarly Indian views on the dispute include, Parshotam Mehra, *The North-eastern Frontier: A Documentary Study of the Internecine Rivalry between India, Tibet, and China* (Delhi: Oxford University Press, 1979); *Negotiating with the Chinese, 1846-1987: Problems and Perspectives* (New Delhi: Reliance Publishing House, 1989); *An 'Agreed' Frontier: Ladakh and India's Northernmost Borders, 1846-1947* (Delhi: Oxford University Press, 1992); *Essays in Frontier History: India, China, and the Disputed Border* (Delhi, Oxford: Oxford University Press, 2007); and John P. Dalvi, *Himalayan Blunder* (Delhi: Pocket Books, 1969).

51. See BJP Election Manifesto 1998, Ch. 8 'Our Nation's Security' http://library.bjp.org

52. '"China is enemy no. 1": George', Indian Express (New Delhi), May 4, 1998.

53. See Foreign Ministry News Briefings, Beijing Review, May 25 – 31, 1998, p. 7. For the Chinese policy makers, George Fernandes remains a favourite target of opprobrium linked as he is to pro-Tibet activists based in India.

54. Xinhua, 13 May 1998, in Foreign Broadcast Information Service, Daily Report, China (FBIS-CHI, No.98-133). http://www.wnc.gov.
55. 'India's letter to Clinton on the Nuclear testing', New York Times, May 13, 1998. A12.
56. (a) Following the publication of Vajpayee's letter to Clinton by the New York Times, for some Chinese commentators it was clear that the 'anti-China justification of India's nuclear tests was of greater concern to Beijing than the tests themselves'. See, Ye Zhengjia, 'Wushi nianlai de Zhong Yin guanxi: jingyan he jiaoxun' ('Experience and lessons in 50 years of Sino-Indian relations') Guoji wenti yanjiu (Beijing) (International Studies), no. 4 (1999): 17–23. Also, Wang Hongwei, 'Tancheng duihua shi yi zeng xin' ('Frank dialogue, dispelling doubts, increasing trust') Nanya yanjiu (Beijing) (South Asia Research) 1 (1999): 14–17.

(b) To India's discomfiture, China played an active role in joining the members of the Security Council to pass Resolution 1172 condemning India and Pakistan's nuclear tests.
57. Yu Bin, 'Containment by Stealth: Chinese Views of and Policies toward America's Alliances with Japan and Korea after the Cold War', Institutional Paper, Asia Pacific Research Center (Stanford), September 1999.
58. John Cherian, 'Wrong Signals', *Frontline* 15, no. 23 (November 7–20, 1998).
59. The author argues that former President K. R. Narayanan had genuine personal interest in restoring relations with China that had suffered since the nuclear tests of May 1998. Since the war with China in 1962, and the consequent downgrading of diplomatic relations, India did not have an ambassador in China until 1976, when K.R. Narayanan was appointed to that position by the Indian government.
60. The summer of 1999 witnessed the second confrontation since the conclusion of the World War II of two 'nuclear capable' states—India and Pakistan. The two countries fought, what is now called 'half a war' in the mountains of Kargil and Batalik in Kashmir. India considered this 'half a war' a betrayal of trust since then Prime Minister Vajpayee had visited Pakistan to initiate a process of rapprochement and met with the civilian government led by Nawaz Sharif. The political outcome of this conflict for Pakistan was a military coup that brought Gen. Pervez Musharraf to power.
61. Xinhua, 11 June 1999, FBIS-CHI 1999-0611
62. During his visit to South Asia in 1996, Jiang Zemin stunned Pakistan by stating that China 'no longer recognizes [Kashmir] as an international issue, notwithstanding the UN resolutions'. See George Perkovich, *India's Nuclear Bomb – The Impact on Global Proliferation* (Berkeley: University of California Press, 1999), 387.
63. Text of the CMP released by the UPA, The Hindu (New Delhi) 28 May 2004. Available at http://www.hinduonnet.com/2004/05/28/stories/2004052807371200.htm

64. Coalitional continuity since 1998 has been a feature of democracy in India, with the Congress-led UPA and BJP-led NDA in power alternately.
65. It was the Narasimha Rao government (1991–1996) that launched India's 'Look East' policy influenced no doubt by several factors—the collapse of the Soviet Union, the end of the Cold War and beginnings of a 'unipolar order', the economic success of Association of Southeast Asian Nations (ASEAN) and the need for 'strategic autonomy' in foreign policy. For detailed analyses on India's 'Look East' policy see, Frederic Grare and Amitabh Mattoo, eds., *Beyond the Rhetoric – The Economics of India's Look East Policy*, Vol. 2 (New Delhi: Manohar, 2003); and N. S. Sisodia and G. V. C. Naidu, eds., *Changing Security Dynamic in Eastern Asia: Focus on Japan* (New Delhi: Bibliophile South Asia/Promilla & Co., 2006).
66. 'Present Dimensions of the Indian Foreign Policy' – Address by Foreign Secretary, Mr Shyam Saran at Shanghai Institute of International Studies, Shanghai on November 11, 2006. Accessible at http://meaindia.nic.in/speech/2006/01/11ss01.htm
67. Following a referendum held on 14 April 1974, Sikkim voted to join the Union of India and became its 22nd state. China did not recognize this referendum and until 2003 used to maintain on its MFA website a page on 'China–Sikkim' relations.
68. The opening up of Nathu La pass on the Sikkim–China border for trade and transit is widely accepted as an opportunity to enhance trade in the Himalayan region as also become a 'spiritual gateway' for Tibetan Buddhists who comprise the majority of the population in that region. The Vajpayee visit saw the two countries agreeing to designate Changgu in Sikkim, India, and Renqinggang of the Tibet Autonomous Region (TAR), China, as venues for border trade. The two sides also agreed on using Nathu La as the pass for entry and exit for persons, means of transport and commodities engaged in border trade. Apart from Nathu La, India conducts border trade with China from two other high altitude passes—Lipulekh Pass in Uttaranchal and Shipki La in Himachal Pradesh.
69. The 'Declaration on Principles for Relations and Comprehensive Cooperation between India and China' is accessible at http://meaindia.nic.in/declarestatement/2003/06/23jd01.htm
70. Ibid.
71. For the recurring tensions on the boundary dispute, see, 'Chinese Army Personnel Transgress into Sikkim' The Indian Express (New Delhi) June 18, 2008; 'We'll sort out China incursions issue' Hindustan Times (New Delhi) June 20, 2008; 'Incursions, a matter of perception' The Hindu (Chennai) February 24, 2008; Pranab Dhal Samanta, 'Tip of Sikkim is latest India-China flashpoint' The Indian Express (New Delhi) May 18, 2008; and 'Dispute over Tawang Blocking India-China Border Talks' The Indian Express (New Delhi) August 12, 2008.

72. The 12 documents signed during Wen Jiabao's visit were:
   1. Agreement on Political Parameters and Guiding Principles for the Settlement of the India–China Boundary Question.
   2. Report of India–China Joint Study Group on Comprehensive Trade and Economic Cooperation.
   3. Protocol on Modalities for the Implementation of (Confidence-building measures) CBMs in the Military Field Along the Line of Actual Control (LAC) in the India–China Border Areas.
   4. Agreement on Mutual Administrative Assistance and Cooperation in Customs Matters.
   5. MOU on the Launch of the India–China Financial Dialogue.
   6. MOU on Civil Aviation.
   7. Protocol of Phytosanitary Requirement for Exporting Grapes from India to China.
   8. Protocol of Phytosanitary Requirement for Exporting Bitter Gourds from India to China.
   9. MOU on Provision of Hydrological Information of the Sutlej /Langqen Zangbo River in Flood Season by China to India.
   10. Protocol on India–China Film Cooperation Commission.
   11. MOU on Cooperation between the Indian Council of World Affairs (ICWA) and the Chinese People's Institute of Foreign Affairs.
   12. Memorandum on the Construction of an Indian-style Buddhist Temple on the Western side of the White Horse Temple in Luoyang, China.

   The Full Text of the Agreement is available on the Ministry of External Affairs (MEA), India, website http://www.mea.gov.in
73. 'Wen's visit has met desired targets: China' 13 April 2005, Rediff.com. Accessible at: http://www.rediff.com/news/2005/apr/13wen.htm
74. Briefly, the '10-pronged strategy' to improve bilateral relations is as follows:
   1. Ensuring comprehensive development of bilateral relations
   2. Strengthening institutional linkages and dialogue mechanisms
   3. Consolidating commercial and economic exchanges
   4. Expanding all-round mutually beneficial cooperation
   5. Instilling mutual trust and confidence through defence cooperation
   6. Seeking early settlement of outstanding issues
   7. Promoting trans-border connectivity and cooperation
   8. Boosting cooperation in science and technology
   9. Revitalizing cultural ties and nurturing people-to-people exchanges
   10. Expanding cooperation on regional and international stage
75. Speech by Dr Manmohan Singh, Prime Minister of India, titled 'India and China in the 21st Century' at the Chinese Academy of Social Sciences, Beijing, 15 January 2008. Accessible at http://meaindia.nic.in/speech/2008/01/15ss01.htm

76. See text 'A Shared Vision for the 21st Century of the Republic of India and the People's Republic of China' Press Information Bureau, National Informatics Centre, Government of India. Also accessible at: http://www.meaindia.nic. in/pressrelease/2008/01/14/pr03.htm.
77. Ibid.
78. The economic reform process in India is not without its political impact with a wider cross-section of society participating in politics and emerging to the forefront as stakeholders in governance. With single-party majority rule a thing of the past, political alliances are increasingly ideologically neutral and adopting postures where 'all politics is local'. See Zoya Hasan, *Quest for Power: Oppositional movements and Post-Congress Politics in Uttar Pradesh* (New Delhi: Oxford University Press, 1998) and Susanne Hoeber Rudolph and Lloyd I. Rudolph, *Explaining Indian Democracy: A Fifty Year Perspective, 1956-2006 The Realm of Ideas – Enquiry and Theory*, Vol. 1 (New Delhi: Oxford University Press, 2008).
79. Lowell Dittmer and Guoli Liu, eds., *China's Deep Reform – Domestic Politics in Transition* (Lanham: Rowman & Littlefield, 2006), 14.
80. See Amartya Sen, *The Argumentative Indian – Writings on Indian History, Culture and Identity* (New York: Farrar, Strauss & Giroux, 2005) and Arjun Sengupta, Archana Negi and Moushumi Basu, *Reflections on the Right to Development* (New Delhi: Sage Publication, 2005).
81. Ibid.
82. The EAS came into being in December 2005 at its first summit in Kuala Lumpur. It comprises 16 countries including India and was initiated by ASEAN and China. Significantly, the United States is not a member of this multilateral forum.
83. The ASEM has been a regular feature since its first summit in Bangkok in 1996. Beginning with 15 EU member states and 10 East-Asian countries, the process now includes the new members of the EU as well as ASEAN plus India, Pakistan and Mongolia since the 6th ASEM Summit (Helsinki) in 2006.
84. The SAARC was created in 1985 and is the only organization for regional cooperation in South Asia. Its eight members include Afghanistan, Bangladesh, Bhutan, India, Maldives, Nepal, Pakistan and Sri Lanka with Australia, China, European Union, Iran, Japan, Mauritius, Myanmar, South Korea and the United States as observers. The SAARC is expected to include Myanmar as a member at its next summit.
85. Earlier called the BISTEC (Bangladesh, India, Sri Lanka and Thailand Economic Cooperation) with Myanmar as observer and formed in June 1997, the organization changed its name to BIMSTEC at its first summit in Bangkok in 2004 and currently also includes Myanmar as full member as well as Nepal and Bhutan.
86. The SCO was primarily created by China with the active support of Russia in June 2001 as an inter-governmental forum involving the Central Asian republics.

87. See Report of the India–China Joint Study Group on Comprehensive Trade and Economic Cooperation. Available at www.hinduonnet.com/thehindu/nic/0041/report.pdf
88. Text – 'A Shared Vision for the 21st Century of the Republic of India and the People's Republic of China'.
89. India's software and services exports in 2007-08 were to the tune of USD 40.8 billion with a domestic market estimated at USD 23.2 billion comprising 5.5 per cent of the GDP.
90. Hongying Wang, 'Multilateralism in Chinese Foreign Policy: The Limits of Socialization', *Asian Survey* 40, no. 3 (2000) 478.
91. Suisheng Zhao, ed., Chinese Foreign Policy – Pragmatism and Strategic Behaviour (Armonk, NY: M.E. Sharpe, 2004), 4.
92. Text – 'A Shared Vision for the 21st Century of the Republic of India and the People's Republic of China'.
93. The mechanism of Special Representatives from either side to exclusively address the boundary dispute was created in 2003. The Special Representatives have held 12 rounds of talks so far without any hint of a final settlement.
94. The Political Parameters and Guiding Principles for the Settlement of the India–China Boundary Question was signed during Chinese premier Wen Jiabao's visit to India in April 2005.
95. The complicated nature of the dispute involves India accusing China of 'illegally occupying' 43,180 sq km of Jammu and Kashmir (in the Aksai Chin region) including 5,180 sq km 'illegally ceded' to Beijing by Islamabad under the Sino-Pakistan boundary agreement in 1963. China on its part accuses India of 'possessing' some 90,000 sq km of 'Chinese territory', mostly in the north-eastern state of Arunachal Pradesh.
96. The exact remarks made by Sun Yuxi during an interview with CNN/IBN television network were: 'In our position, the whole of the state of Arunachal Pradesh is Chinese territory. And Tawang is only one of the places in it. We are claiming all of that. That is our position'. Available at http://www.rediff.com/news/ 2006/nov/14china.htm
97. In a statement prior to Prime Minister Vajpayee's visit to China in June 2003, Hua Junduo, then Chinese Ambassador to India, outlined three peak periods in India–China relations. 'The first period' Hua Junduo wrote, 'can be traced to two millenniums back when Buddhism bound China and India together' in the earliest stage of the historic exchange between the two great ancient civilizations. The second period features mutual sympathy and support in the respective struggles for national independence and liberation in modern times. As the third period, Ambassador Hua Junduo mentioned the 'good-neighbourly relationship' in the 1950s between the two independent Asian nations newly emerging in the international arena and by the Five Principles of Peaceful Co-existence they jointly initiated after the World War II. See, Raviprasad Narayanan, 'India's Foreign Policy Towards China: The NDA Experience – Dominant Issues in Sino-Indian Relations', *Harvard Asia Quarterly* 7, no. 4 (Autumn 2003).

98. 'Arunachal is an integral part of India: Pranab' 14 November 2006, Accessible at: http://www.zeenews.com/articles.asp?aid=335503&sid=NAT
99. See text of the Agreement between the Government of the Republic of India and the Government of the People's Republic of China (PRC) on the Political Parameters and Guiding Principles for the Settlement of the India-China Boundary Question, MEA, India.
100. Ibid.
101. Ibid.
102. Zhang Qingli, Party Secretary for the TAR, has described the Dalai Lama as a 'wolf wrapped in monk's robes, a devil with a human face and a beast's heart'. This coming from the Party Secretary of Tibet is indicative of the attitude in Beijing after the violence in March.
103. John Rowland, *A History of Sino-Indian Relations: Hostile Coexistence* (Princeton, NJ: D. Van Nostrand Company Inc., 1967), xv.
104. See text of the; Declaration on Principles for Relations and Comprehensive Cooperation between the Republic of India and the People's Republic of China' issued by both the sides during former Indian prime minister A. B. Vajpayee's visit to China in June 2003. Accessible at http://www.meaindia.nic.in/declarestatement/2003/06/23jd01.htm
105. See He Zhenhua, 'Those falsely accusing others only discredit themselves' Opinion on People's Daily Online, 8 April 2008. Accessible at: http://english.people.com.cn/90001/90780/91342/6388602.html; 'Why some U.S. media going to such extreme?' (sic.) Opinion on People's Daily Online, 2 April 2008. Accessible at: http://english.people.com.cn/90001/90780/6385665.html and 'TYC: From violence to terrorism' Opinion on People's Daily Online, 18 April 2008.
106. <Missing Note please provide>
107. The concept of 'multipolarization' (duojihua) was adopted by the CPC at the 14th Party Congress in 1992. Chinese analysts in their theoretical construction of a multipolar world constantly refer to yi chao duo qiang ('one big power and four powers'). The United States is the 'big power' with the European Union, Russia, China and Japan being the 'powers'.
108. Sujian Guo and Shiping Hua, eds., *New Dimensions of Chinese Foreign Policy* (Lanham, MD: Lexington Books, 2007), 1–2.
109. Soft power is a state's ability to 'shape the preferences of others' and the ability to induce international compliance without resorting to coercive means. The comprehensively positive image a country/nation presents to others is the determinant of soft power. See Joseph S. Nye, *Soft Power—the Means to Success in World Politics* (New York: Public Affairs, 2004).
110. Allen Carlson, *Unifying China, Integrating with the World – Securing Chinese Sovereignty in the Reform Era* (Stanford: Stanford University Press, 2005), 50–51.
111. Vernon Aspaturian, 'Internal Politics and Foreign Policy in the Soviet System', in *Approaches to Comparative and International Politics*, ed. R. Barry Farrell

(Evanston: Northwestern University Press, 1966), 8, as cited in Byong-Moo Hwang, 'Chinese Motives in Foreign Crises: Domestic and Foreign Policy Interactions' (Unpublished PhD diss., University of California, Riverside, 1978).

112. See Lei Guang, 'From National Identity to National Security: China's Changing Responses Toward India in 1962 and 1998', *The Pacific Review* 17, no. 3 (2004): 399–422.

113. See Dong Wang, *China's Unequal Treaties – Narrating National History* (Lanham, MD: Lexington, 2005).

114. William S. Turley, 'Vietnam/Indochina: Hanoi's Challenge to Southeast Asian Regional Order', in *Asian Pacific Security: Emerging Challenges and Responses*, ed. Young Whan Kihl and Laurence E. Grinter (Boulder, CO: Lynne Rienner Publishers, 1986), 178–79 as cited in Sanqiang Jian, 'Foreign Policy Restructuring as Adaptive Behavior: China's "Independent Foreign Policy of Peace" 1982-1989' (Unpublished PhD diss., Kent State University, 1992), 50.

115. Jing-dong Yuan, 'Foe or Friend? The Chinese Assessment of a Rising India After Pokharan – II' Ch. 8 in *South Asia's Nuclear Security Dilemma – India, Pakistan, and China*, ed. Lowell Dittmer (New York: M.E. Sharpe, 2005), 168.

Part II

Praxis

CHAPTER 3

The India–China Bilateral and the Significance of Environmental Diplomacy

Introduction

China–India relations have for long been hostage to insular prisms of enquiry that are overwhelmingly based on 'zero-sum approaches'—made apparent in the earlier chapters. Salient aspects such as economic interaction and competition are ascendant variables providing much-needed variation to analyse their bilateral relationship. An investigation into their bilateral cooperation is warranted as, by many accounts, India and China are competitors, rather than partners. This chapter is to enquire and explicate the following questions—what are the levels of cooperation between China and India on environmental issues? What are the methodologies driving initiatives between the two countries? How is the China–India environment cooperation—if any—to be located in a wider discourse?

> States have, in accordance with the Charter of the United Nations and the principles of international law, the sovereign right to exploit

their own resources pursuant to their own environment policies, and the responsibility to ensure that activities within their jurisdiction of control do not cause damage to the environment of other states or of areas beyond the limits of national jurisdiction.[1]

(Principle 21 of Stockholm Declaration, 1972)

'It is clear that any agreement on climate change should respect the need for development and growth in developing countries. Equitable burden sharing should underlie any effective global climate change regime'.[2]

As developing countries, China and India face the challenges of climate change and sustainable development intrinsic to their overall economic development and global influence. The issues arising out of climate change for China and India are inextricably woven with issues of livelihood and development. Put simply, the status of the environment around us is not only a policy issue but also one around which economic development plans have to be reoriented. The stark warning issued below by the Intergovernmental Panel on Climate Change is a portent of alarming developments that could take place if the issue of climate change were to be ignored by states.

'Unmitigated climate change would, in the long term, be likely to exceed the capacity of natural, managed and human systems to adapt'.[3]

The importance of climate change as a global issue became salient in the 1980s, and institutional constructs around the issue have been evolving over the past four decades since the United Nations Conference on the Human Environment (UNHCE) held in Stockholm in 1972. In the next two decades, climate change and the environment made the difficult transition from the margins of international relations to its very centre owing to its policy-centric nature and being an issue influenced by international political cross-currents. The acceleration of 'policy interest' guided by scientific and technical expertise in climate change witnessed the creation of the Advisory Group on Greenhouse Gases (AGGG) in July 1986 in Villach (Austria). Workshops in Villach and Bellagio (Italy) in 1987 came to the conclusion that 'the issue of climatic change merited the attention of policymakers' and that 'a coordinated international response seems inevitable....'[4] The importance of the meetings in Villach and Bellagio is that climate change as an issue began absorbing the attention of policymakers and not just involving the scientific community. The Villach/Bellagio workshops informed the deliberative process of the Toronto Conference on the Changing Atmosphere in 1988 and the subsequent decision by the United Nations General Assembly (UNGA) to initiate climate negotiations following the World Commission on Environment and Development Report of 1987—the Brundtland Commission Report.

The 'security impact' of climate change has undoubtedly cast its influence in the years since. Climate change, particularly global warming, made a transition to becoming what Barry Buzan terms as an issue characteristic of 'macrosecuritization'—the highlighting of which it is believed would lead to quick action.[5] The importance of sustaining the environment around us and the impact of human activity plausibly responsible for inducing climate change has been a powerful hypothesis for close to two decades with the 1992 UNFCCC Earth Summit at Rio defining Climate Change as the following:

'"Climate change" means a change of climate which is attributed directly or indirectly to human activity that alters the composition of the global atmosphere and which is in addition to natural climate variability observed over comparable time periods'.[6]

Several common loci motivate China and India to cooperate on climate change, chiefly the following: the rapidity with which their economies have been growing; their respective socio-economic needs and the 'ideal of common but differentiated responsibility (providing) legal and philosophical basis for the existing legal obligations ... designed to achieve the objectives of the Kyoto Protocol'.[7] Since 1978, China has had a four-fold increase in its GDP per capita and it has been forecast that by 2025, China will become the world's largest economy. Between 1990 and 2004, 17.5 per cent of global CO_2 emissions were from China and its continued economic growth indicates that it has become the world's largest emitter of greenhouse gases (GHGs) since 2007.[8] Being developing countries with relatively low per-capita emissions, China (4.9 tons in 2007)[9] and India (1.5 tons in 2007)[10] have development priorities that cannot be ignored. Both countries are focusing on reducing greenhouse emissions by adopting energy-efficient technologies as also renewables.[11]

This chapter, inclusive of the introduction, theoretical approach and hypotheses is divided into eight sections that give an insight into the complexities of environmental diplomacy and cooperation with specific emphasis on climate change negotiations and Sino-Indian cooperation, environmental diplomacy and cooperation, negotiating climate change, China's environmental bureaucracies and emerging trends of hydro-politics and hydro-cooperation between the two countries. The concluding section makes policy recommendations.

Theoretical Approach and Hypotheses

Environmental threats are asymmetrical and unlike conventional threats are non-reciprocal. As an existential threat, the prospect of climate change assumes stark overtones since its impact (and influence) go beyond the territorial limits of nation-states. With every year witnessing a march towards a global compact on climate change, we are participants in a process where the 'transformative' power of the 'global ecology' triumphs over other contentious issues. The construction of a 'new social episteme'—comprising 'the spatial, metaphysical and doctrinal'—is renovating global governance as never before.[12] Climate change as an issue is 'sovereignty' neutral and establishes a conundrum for states that legitimize themselves and the political system they have created around this core precept. Policies directed towards addressing climate change are to be seen as a reaction to environmental problems at an overarching level. Below this level are units that make up the national and sub-national levels and are driven by interests. The interests-based politics of the environment primarily focuses on the domestic determinants that influence negotiations in international forums.[13]

The importance of the two-level game can also be applied to negotiations on contentious issues—climate change being one—and the direction in which current negotiations are headed. 'International outcomes' it is argued by Robert Putnam are 'significantly improved by understanding internal bargaining' when faced with the prospect of making minimally acceptable compromises.[14] Putnam's two-level game resonates more with India owing to its democratic ethos and established role of interest groups debating and participating in policy processes. National governments adopt policy postures that maximize their own capabilities to accommodate domestic pressures while looking to minimize the adverse fallout from international developments or processes of negotiations that have their own set of dynamics. Any international concord gaining wide acceptance still has to be ratified domestically and internal political considerations could derail a government's tacit acceptance of an international agreement. A fractious issue like climate change has its own domestic reciprocal influences and it is the decision-makers' job to reconcile the divergent views of the 'domestic' and the 'international' and achieve a modicum of congruence.

There are three hypotheses motivating this chapter:

1. The inevitability of climate change is creating the world's largest developing countries, China and India to coordinate diplomatic positions at international forums.
2. The diplomatic cooperation on climate change by China and India is motivated by domestic constituencies propelling economic development.
3. The influence of climate change in diplomatic priorities for China and India is transforming internal debates on development and influencing policymaking dynamics

India–China Cooperation: Overview

At the outset, the history of China and India's cooperation on environmental issues began close to four decades ago at the UNCHE Stockholm Conference in 1972. China's environmental diplomacy at the UNCHE Stockholm Conference was a landmark event that symbolized an end to its hiatus from post-war international multilateral fora and its assumption of an important role in UN activities for the first time. Until 1971, China's place in the international system was represented by the Republic of China (ROC; Taiwan). Not known to bypass an opportunity on the international stage Chinese Premier

Zhou Enlai, treated the conference as a means of re-engaging ties with the rest of the world and quickly positioned itself as the leader of the developing world.[15] The Chinese delegation to the UNHCE was an indication that China was serious about addressing environmental concerns and willing to shoulder its environmental responsibilities.[16]

At the same conference, countries of Asia, Latin America and Africa did not see the importance of environmental issues as their focus on poverty was more pressing.[17] Delegates from Brazil, China and India argued that poverty is a greater polluter and development was the solution. Indira Gandhi had famously asked, 'How can we speak to those who live in villages or slums about keeping the oceans, the rivers and the air clean?'[18] Brazil and China accused the Developed North of employing environmental arguments to keep developing countries poor[19]—an argument that echoes even today, though the semantics are different. It is assumed that China and India may have cooperated with each other in this conference owing to their respective national positions articulating the cause of the global south, and not by design. Any 'intentional' cooperation on their part could be ruled out as the two countries were still to re-establish diplomatic relations at the highest levels following the 1962 war. It was only in 1976 that ambassadorial-level relations were re-established between China and India.

For long the two countries have had the same position in climate change negotiations in symmetry with the Global South. It was Indira Gandhi who rightly pointed out, that development—India's crucial electoral plank and China's regime survival formula—is the top priority for both countries. The Global South has its roots in the Non-Aligned Movement (NAM) consisting of states that adopted a neutral stance during the Cold War, and the G77 which derived from the New International Economic Order that sought to end the South's economic dependency on the North.[20] The G77 which represents the number of original member states has now grown to more than 130 countries, and China as only an associate member has been acting as a loyal club member in supporting the position of the South. Yet the G77 is not a monolithic group. Within it, the Organization of the Petroleum Exporting Countries (OPEC) decelerate the environmental negotiation process while the Alliance of Small Island States (AOSIS) becomes ever more vulnerable to climate change and will be most likely to enjoy benefits from any firm commitment.[21]

Documented cooperation between China and India did not happen until the 1987 Montreal Protocol on ozone depletion. Both countries collaborated in bargaining for USD 80 million during the first three years after their accession to the Montreal Protocol to Protect the Stratospheric Ozone Layer.[22] China and India normalized their relationship, helped by Rajiv Gandhi's 1988 visit to Beijing. This visit seems to have provided a foundation for cooperation in generating a developing world coalition but it does not explain existing cooperation at the 1987 Montreal Conference.

After Rajiv Gandhi's visit, both countries adopted a cooperative attitude in international environmental conferences. At the 1992 Rio Earth Summit, India and China, reflecting the views of most developing countries, argued that the North should transfer technology as a requirement for the South's support for the agreement on global warming.[23] The theology behind this line was that of 'equity' that could only be achieved if there were to be a clear and time-bound programme to stabilize and reduce GHG's from developed countries.[24] The most notable case of India–China cooperation came at the Kyoto Protocol of 1997. The two countries with other developing countries held the principle of 'common but differentiated Responsibilities', and successfully convinced the developed countries to set up Clean Development Mechanism (CDM) and provided financial and technical assistance to the South.[25]

Both China and India want technology transfer and funding from UNFCCC in addition to the CDM projects. As of April 20, 2012, a total of 4023 CDM projects had been approved by the Department of Climate Change of National Development and Reform Commission (NDRC) of China.[26] India is able to take advantage of CDM because of stable governance and higher allocations to clean technology. The 4,000th project registered with the UNFCCC was a wind power project in the state of Maharashtra which expects to reduce GHG emissions by 21,807 ton a year; the equivalent of removing emissions from 4,275 cars each year.[27]

Ganapati and Liu had pointed out the strength and weaknesses of the respective institutions of Chinese and Indian designated national agencies (DNAs).[28] The institutional setup of the Chinese DNA is directly under the powerful NDRC. The authority of the NDRC extends beyond economic development and includes environmental issues, as evidenced in bureaucratic design with the head of the National Coordination Committee on Climate Change (NCCC) also serving as the chairperson of the NDRC. This institutional setup allows development policies to go hand-in-hand with environmental policies, especially with CDMs; and thus makes for a more efficient system. In India, the National CDM Authority (NCDMA), under the Ministry of Environment, Forest and Climate Change (MoEF) is in charge of all India CDM projects. The NCDMA is headed by the Secretary of the MoEF. While the MoEF may not be at the same high level as China's NDRC in the bureaucracy ladder, India's CDM policies can be debated through a democratic process involving a vibrant civil society, unlike China.

While the two countries have shown efforts to increase the number of CDM projects, CDM has evolved into a financial instrument that requires the participation of financial institutions, but China's carbon market is still in the infancy stage that makes its financial institutions especially banks less interested in this potentially lucrative investment at the moment.[29] India may be facing the same challenge as well.

At the COP8 in New Delhi in late 2002, China joined India in reiterating its opposition to GHGs emission cuts for developing countries proposed by the EU. Both countries reiterated that increased emissions would be needed to lift their citizens out of poverty.[30] Prior to the 2007 Bali climate summit, China had taken the position that developing countries should not have to meet compulsory targets set by rich nations.[31] It is after the proposed 'Bali Roadmap' that India and China have had regular meetings on environmental matters which led to an 'Agreement on Cooperation in Addressing Climate Change' signed by the NDRC on behalf of China and the Indian MoEF in November 2009.[32] The NDRC deals with the overall coordination and response to climate change in China.[33] The two countries have maintained close contacts since Bali (2007) and throughout the Copenhagen

Conference in which they joined Brazil, the United States, and South Africa in making the Copenhagen Accord non-binding.[34]

The Copenhagen Conference was perhaps the clearest illustration of India and China working jointly. To quote Shyam Saran,

> 'Copenhagen also marked a turning point in India's relations with China, though it remains to be seen how enduring this proves to be... It was India and China which were able to ensure that the red lines for developing countries did not get erased'.[35]

There was however, friction within the G77 comprised as it was by various internal groupings [the Coalition for Rainforest Nations, the AOSIS and the OPEC group among others] with the AOSIS largely supporting the position of the European countries to cut emission drastically—a position opposed by other developing countries. The AOSIS, threatened by rising sea levels, had taken a more aggressive position in hoping to secure a deal. In 2005, the Coalition for Rainforest Nations headed by Brazil had raised the proposal to voluntarily reduce carbon emissions by conserving forests, in exchange for capital, technology compensation or entering the carbon trade market. This proposal from Brazil was entirely jettisoned by politics and individual hubris with Amazon forests facing the brunt of commercial greed. In brief, political faultlines and 'group bargaining' over climate change have proven themselves to be resilient.[36] Post-Copenhagen, China and India cooperated with each other by sending letters agreeing to be listed in the chapeau of the Copenhagen Accord, but with the reiteration that negotiations on climate change must take place under the aegis of the UNFCCC and that the Accord does not open up a parallel track. The timing of the letters sent suggested that India and China may have coordinated their moves. The Chinese letter of 9 March 2010 contained one sentence—'the [UNFCCC] Secretariat can proceed to include China in the list of Parties included in the chapeau of the Copenhagen Accord'.[37] The Indian letter sent a day before stated that it 'may be listed in the chapeau of the Copenhagen Accord', with its understanding of the Accord 'indicated in an appropriate footnote'—where India stated that the Accord could not become a new track for negotiations bypassing the UNFCCC.

The dual challenges of climate change and sustainable development are beginning to influence the development trajectory of China and India. As neighbours with the primary agenda of creating the internal infrastructure for continued economic growth the challenge facing the two countries is to strike a balance between domestic expectations and global conformity to environmental norms. The two countries face similar challenges with large populations, modernization and urbanization.[38] Their different political and administrative systems notwithstanding, the two countries are currently at that phase where choices they make are going to influence global developmental trends.

Environment Diplomacy and Cooperation

'Cooperation' in any aspect requires the consent and willingness of the actors involved. Environmental cooperation is no different and in an international setting provides an interface at different levels. The first level involves two actors displaying the requisite temperament to sort common problems. At the second level, we have two distinct political cultures and institutional sub-systems striving to create a common methodology to address the common problems. The third level provides the necessary interface between science and policy where narrow self-interests are to be restrained and make way for a scientific prediction that dovetails with the issue of common grievance.[39] To quote Zhang Yan, a former Chinese ambassador to India,

> 'Climate change, one of the most important issues of 2009, has also become a facet of China-India cooperation. Both countries share similar concerns and positions in addressing climate change and closely consulted and coordinated with each other.'[40]

The Agreement signed between China and India to cooperate on Climate Change in October 2009 chiefly highlights the following:

1. Adopting a common position on an eventual deal
2. Cooperating in creating mechanisms to reduce GHGs
3. Cooperating in areas such as energy efficiency, renewable and transfer of technology

The agreement is for a period of five years and a Joint Working Group will also be set up to exchange views on climate change talks, adoption of domestic policies and to monitor the implementation of joint cooperative projects.[41] Crucially, the five-year period will inform analysts and others whether the two countries have managed to generate levels of coordination, communication and implementation of the nuances emerging from the high-level summitry around climate change. If the 'cooperation' between the two countries is bound to generate an accommodation of their views (however diluted) in an eventual agreement on climate change it would undoubtedly be a positive development. The agreement on cooperation between China and India is one of the several joint initiatives undertaken by both sides to negotiate their way through climate change as a process of international negotiation. An earlier agreement signed by both sides in 1993 for a period of five years was not renewed, owing perhaps to the developments in bilateral relations following Pokhran II in May 1998. Apart from bilateral cooperation, the two countries have actively participated in multilateral forums and issued regular statements on environmental cooperation displaying an approach that values bilateral and multilateral approaches to climate change negotiations (see Table 3.1).

The most common explanation for India's and China's cooperation is that of self-interest. Economic development is the key to any domestic political legitimacy, but along with high growth rates in recent years, come higher emission levels (see Table 3.1). As the world's largest manufacturer, a high portion of China's emissions is a 'substitute' for energy consumption in other countries and regions.[42] Every 1 per cent of GDP growth in India requires an increase of 0.82 per cent or more in energy use. [43] And between 1990 and 2005, India's petroleum consumption rose by 5.5 per cent per annum. Future emission is destined to rise as suggested by the Japanese and South Korean model, India's demand for fossil fuel, will grow at a much faster rate until personal incomes reach USD 20,000. There is still a long way for India and China to go and bring down their emissions.

As the two countries have intensified their domestic process of economic transformation, their relative success has attracted disparate coalitions who have invoked the phenomenon of 'global warming' to

Table 3.1 Bilateral and Multilateral Environmental Agreements/Statements Issued Emphasizing Cooperation on Climate Change between India and China

Agreement/Joint Statement	Date
Agreement on environmental cooperation between the government of the People's Republic of China and the government of the Republic of India	7 September 1993
Agreement on cooperation on addressing climate change between the Government of the People's Republic of China and the Government of the Republic of India	21 October 2009
Joint statement issued at the conclusion of the third BASIC ministerial meeting on climate change, Cape Town	25 April 2010
Joint statement issued at the conclusion of the fourth BASIC ministerial meeting on climate change, Rio De Janeiro	25-26 July 2010
Joint statement issued at the conclusion of the fifth BASIC ministerial meeting on climate change, Tianjin	11 October 2010
Joint communique at Tenth Russia-India-China Ministerial Meeting, Wuhan	15 November 2010
Joint statement issued at the conclusion of the sixth BASIC ministerial meeting on climate change, New Delhi	26-27 February 2011
Joint statement issued at the conclusion of the seventh BASIC ministerial meeting on climate change, Zimbali, Durban	29 May 2011
Joint statement issued at the conclusion of the eighth BASIC ministerial meeting on climate change, Inhotim, Minas Gerais	26-27 August 2011
Joint statement issued at the conclusion of the ninth BASIC ministerial meeting on climate change, Beijing	1 November 2011
Agreed minutes of the first China-India Strategic Economic Dialogue, Beijing	26 September 2011
Joint statement issued at the conclusion of the tenth BASIC ministerial meeting on climate change, New Delhi	13-14 February 2012
Joint statement on climate change between India and China during prime minister's visit to China	15 May 2015

Source: Compiled by the author.
Note: The author acknowledges Dr Liao You-te's help. The importance and intensity of consultations revolving around climate change are evident from the five meetings held in 2011 by the countries comprising the BASIC.

ensure compliance in adhering to nascent international norms that seek to address environmental concerns. By initiating cooperation on climate change, China and India have displayed an atypical characteristic to their otherwise tense relationship fraught with the constant recalling of events that led to a rupture six decades ago. Cooperation between the two countries could go a long way in mitigating climate change, reduce environmental stress and damage to the ecology regionally and globally.[44] The flip side however is that international environmental cooperation is a long-term process with satisfaction to its participants, not a guaranteed outcome. To quote Matthew Paterson,

'There remains an analytical gap in the understanding of processes of international cooperation with regard to the issue of global warming'.[45]

An outcome of China–India cooperation on climate change is the initiation of 'linkages'. The linkages emergent are politically neutral and policy-oriented with their value sets. Three value sets clearly noticeable are as follows:

1. Functional linkages—when an action (natural) leads to a variety of consequences applicable to both sides, for instance, the melting of glaciers or the formation of a high-altitude lake following a cloudburst or landslide with the potential to cause destruction on both sides.
2. Actor linkages—when one or the same set of actors is involved in different issues and positions adopted. For instance, the 'group bargaining' approach ascribed to the G77 or the AOSIS at climate change conventions.
3. Value linkages—when the perception gains ground that different events are part of the same issue with the same invoking of values. For instance, the developed countries' position on capping CO_2 emissions motivates China and India to coalesce their arguments with strong overtones of national interests cloaked within overall values and their merits.

India's approach to international concerns over climate change and the need for a global compact revolve around three fundamental positions:

no absolute emission cuts; no commitment to any accord that sidelines Kyoto Protocol and no signing of any agreement or treaty without domestic consensus. Adherence to the Kyoto Protocol, principles of the UNFCCC according to the mandate of the Bali roadmap are a basic issue of faith for China and India with the expectation that industrialized countries will not hollow out these precepts.[46] India also wants to play a key role in facilitating a solution to climate change by being a consensus builder. It is said that when former Prime Minister Manmohan Singh appointed Jairam Ramesh as the Minister of Environment and Forests, he instructed him, 'India has not caused the problem of global warming. But try to make sure that India is part of the solution'.[47]

The need for domestic consensus also agrees with policy debates in China and India that call for directing development towards a sustainable path. To quote Yu Hai,

> 'In dealing with international environment cooperation, we insist on a basic principle that international issue (sic.) is an extension of domestic issue'.[48]

Positive spillovers of the China–India cooperation are also encouraging regional initiatives on environmental cooperation with China, India and Nepal launching a trans-boundary project to conserve the 'highly diverse' and 'environmentally fragile area' spanning the mountainous and sacred Himalayan region of Mount Kailash.[49] With both countries investing substantially in renewable energy, there is a need for active bilateral cooperation on 'renewables' as this aspect is still in its primary stages.[50] There is the probability of negative spillovers too. Trans-boundary risks especially those involving rivers and glaciers could get aggravated in the absence of specific dialogue mechanisms addressing the fears of lower riparian countries of the Himalayan sub-region.

Climate change coupled with increased levels of pollution—terrestrial and atmospheric—in an alarming manner is beginning to influence weather patterns across the Indian sub-continent. The shrinking of glaciers in the Himalayas, distorted rainfall patterns, intense spells of summer and winter are without doubt in the future going to influence the economic trajectory and livelihoods of more than a billion people in India alone. Stretching this point, if it were to be noticed that climatic change is influencing agricultural output and also responsible for internal displacement owing to rising sea levels, nothing short of a catastrophe awaits policymakers and the affected.[51] Echoing these concerns was Jairam Ramesh, the former Minister of Environment and Forests in India during a parliamentary debate.

> The most vulnerable country in the world to climate change is India. We are dependent on monsoons…they are the lifeline of our country… We are depressed when the monsoons fail and happy when the monsoons are good… The uncertainty caused by climate change on the monsoons is of first and overriding priority of India.[52]

For China and India, environmental sustainability and economic development are inextricably linked. To quote former President of China, Hu Jintao,

> Climate change is an issue arising in the course of human development. It is associated with both natural factors and human activities. It is an environmental issue, but also, and more importantly, a development issue, as it is closely connected with the development stage, way of life, size of population and resource endowment of different countries and their places in the international division of labor. In the final analysis, we should and can only advance efforts to address climate change in the course of development and meet the challenge through common development.[53]

The above quote is a considered position adopted by China and articulated by its then President, is an illustration of how climate change and environment negotiations have matured in the past four decades since the Stockholm Conference of 1972. For long, anguish felt by the Global South was that they counted for little and their collective weight was not of strength but of 'marginalization, disenfranchization' imposed on it by the international system. To Adil Najam, the Global South has always received short shrift in negotiations where the powerful and developed countries have held an upper hand. Najam sees three phases in the Global South's negotiating posture on the Environment—the pre-Stockholm period marked by the politics of 'contestation'; the Stockholm to Rio period highlighted by 'reluctant participation' and the post-Rio period marked by 'engagement'.[54]

Negotiating Climate Change

An ironic aspect of government decision-making is that unless an issue assumes the dimensions of a crisis, measures to address it do not feature on its priority list.[55] Environmental policymaking also suffers from the same malady. For decades, countries such as India and China were deciding policy options on the basis of 'self-perceptions that encouraged marginalization and capacity-limitations'. The modicum of cooperation achieved by China and India in negotiating climate change did not commence until they began to feel two diametrically opposite forces—first, the historic position they were occupying in spreading equitable wealth domestically by the adoption of sound economic policies and second, the pressure of being isolated and criticized at international forums and worse, being labelled as 'spoilers' and 'deal breakers' acting as a galvanizer and not a deterrent.

Negotiations represent a salience to the issue at hand and bring to the table bilateral faith and expectations that solutions are at hand. As such negotiations do not need to conform to a template or model and are unique in their approach and methodology.[56] The participants in such an exercise are aware that environmental issues are varied and each category has different solutions and they need not agree with the next category of issues at hand. In the case of neighbours, the same issue is invariably seen through different prisms. They bring to the 'negotiating sphere' not only their interests and official 'lines' but also other variables such as attitudes, political culture, bureaucratic temperament, institutional rigidity and emotions. Negotiations are to be seen as an 'instrument that manages trans-boundary environmental risks'[57] and evolves a position on issues of common import. The importance of regular negotiations between actors is that they lead to a socialization of each other that could lead to a routine procedural process and increased consensual knowledge. To quote Gunnar Sjostedt,

> The problems of coping with environmental issues in international decision-making ultimately depend on how those issues are framed

and conceived by the policy makers in the negotiating arena. This arena includes not only those negotiating the issues at the table, but also the authorities and other actors 'back home', to whom the negotiators are accountable.[58]

The MoEF has been representing India at international forums on climate change and its allied debates. India's negotiating behaviour broadly emphasizes the following three salient points:

1. Adherence to the principle of 'common but differentiated responsibilities'.
2. Reliance on multilateral approaches that reflect the voice of the majority over that of the powerful minority.
3. Right to domestic development being a non-negotiable aspect.[59]

India's principled stand on climate change does find appreciation amongst a few scholars in China and Huang and Huang summarize India's position as follows. For Huang Yunsong and Huang Min, India will only take on reduction under the principle of common but differentiated responsibility, and reduction must be made under the principles of equity and justice. The position on 'common but differentiated responsibilities' advocates the rationale of climate change as a 'common' issue facing humanity and it not being restricted in scale or scope. The aspect of 'responsibility' being 'differentiated' clearly makes the case for developed countries to acknowledge their share in contributing to climate change over a historical time-frame and take the lead in providing the developing world with the necessary wherewithal to mitigate the fallout from climate change.

They further opine that India will not accept any legally binding reduction agreement, and advanced countries must fulfil the obligation under the climate change agreements.[60] This creates space for India and China to cooperate in emission reduction issues as developing countries but with the caveat that India has always pointed out its emissions as being half of China's—and that is quite a substantial difference.[61]

Within the negotiating frameworks of the UNFCCC there are significant categories by which states can be grouped. According to a study,[62] there are broadly four types of states involved in the contentious debates over climate change. 'Lead states' are those who take the initiatives to set the agenda, prepare backgrounders and detailed technical bulletins, persuade others of the seriousness of the issue and volunteer mitigation by providing funding and expertise. 'Supporting states' are the ones that go along with the agenda set by 'lead states'. The third category comprises 'swing states' who are vociferous in demanding concessions to go along with the agenda and the fourth category comprises 'veto states' who are labeled so as they block initiatives and dilute proposals. These categorizations assume importance every time a summit or meeting on climate change does not live up to the expectations of groupings like the EU.[63]

Hence, China and India to the so-called agenda-setting states are the centrifugal force driving the last category. The 'veto coalition' or dyad made up of the two countries is undoubtedly an irritant to those groupings having solutions to mitigate climate change.

China's climate change diplomacy is a key component of its foreign policy primarily owing to its global significance and the opportunities it presents for China to display its ever-increasing responsibilities.[64] An ideological veneer to climate change was also inherent within the concept of 'harmonious society' that talks of attaining 'harmony between Man and Nature'.[65] The significance of climate change to China's leadership is evidenced by the First National Climate Change Assessment it undertook in 2006. The document titled China's National Climate Change and released by the NDRC in 2007 was the outcome of the assessment made the previous year.[66] The importance of the issue was underlined by the setting up of a National Climate Change Leading Group under the leadership of the Premier, Wen Jiabao. The National Climate Change Leading Group is responsible for participating in international negotiations, protect domestic interests and coordinate bureaucratic interests.[67]

China's basic lines guiding its negotiations on climate change are as follows:

1. Climate change is human-induced.
2. Developed countries are largely responsible for current elevated CO_2 levels.

3. Common but differentiated responsibilities are a fundamental tenet of climate change negotiating process.
4. China's per-capita emissions are less in comparison with advanced countries.
5. The need for curbing emissions requires technical and financial wherewithal.
6. China seeks to create a positive image while addressing climate change issues.
7. China's responsibilities on climate change are owing to its developing country status.

China attaches importance to issuing official white papers on contentious issues and climate change and the environment are not exempted from this kind of approach.[68] The White Paper issued in November 2011 is a case in point: To quote

> 'China has been playing a constructive role in international negotiations on climate change, actively pushing forward the negotiation process, thereby making a significant contribution to addressing global climate change'.[69]

The release of the White Paper coincided with the Conference of Parties 17 to be held in Durban and is to be seen as an instance of China's environmental diplomacy at work. Most significant is China's pitch on the 'responsibilities' involved in negotiating climate change and its role as being a 'constructive' one. Other behavioural aspects of China's ongoing efforts in negotiating for itself a deal at the climate change talks include:

1. A constant emphasis on its active role in international negotiations under the UN framework.
2. International consultation and consensus to be the basis of any eventual agreement.
3. Calling for more exchanges and coordination between developed and developing countries on climate change.

As an associate member of the G77, China lays emphasis on evolving a developing countries' united front in climate change negotiations.

The consistent position of the G77 and China and India has been that the developed world tends to ignore its historical responsibility in generating unacceptable levels of CO_2 emissions and the disparity in per-capita emissions needs to be acknowledged.[70] The nuanced manner in which China puts forward its negotiating position brings together domestic considerations and the symbiosis between economic development, poverty alleviation and social stability—issues that are also dear to the legitimacy of the Chinese Communist Party (CCP)! The importance of climate change for China owes much to resource management and energy use with China's energy policies and climate change policies having strong linkages. The pro-active approach adopted by Beijing does not restrict itself to the confines of bureaucracies and encourages other forms of participation in the debate on climate change. In November 2011, China established the National Strategic Research and International Cooperation Center for Climate Change, a think-tank especially to discuss, debate and formulate positions on climate change. This think-tank is affiliated with the NDRC.[71]

China's internal debates on climate change also bring out interesting aspects. Chinese scholars have different views regarding China's climate change policies. Zhang Haibin views that China is likely to accept reduction commitments if the cost is low, but the commitments will be divided into four phrases: voluntary, conditional, voluntary and conditional, and legally binding reductions.[72] However, the process can be speeded up if China reaches a much-desired goal of becoming a middle-income country. Wang Limao holds similar views arguing that China's per capita emission is only half the world's average and before China becomes a middle-income country, it can consider holding the intensity of carbon dioxide emission constant.[73] Qin Dahe recognizes the increasing pressure on China to reduce emission, but it is economically infeasible for China to do so at this moment because 70 per cent of China's energy comes from coal and there exists no economic model of low emission leading to high growth.[74] Zhang Kunmin and Wen Zongguo also view that advanced countries should adhere to the Kyoto Protocol and other reduction agreements. At the same time, China should increase energy efficiency, develop renewable energy and control population as the means to assist the reduction of CO_2 emissions.[75] All authors have mentioned common but differentiated responsibility.

For China and India, negotiations on climate change are contentious, to say the least, since their respective policymaking segments and domestic polity view the 'environment' as being an indivisible part of 'sovereignty'. It could be argued that their institutional frameworks are predisposed to a 'monolithic understanding of sovereignty'.[76] Further, the discourse on climate change in both the countries has strong shades of 'a political and cultural framing' which to the developed countries is an approach that typifies a 'self-serving exercise' scripted by powerful domestic actors on the environment.[77]

The intensity of negotiations on climate change perhaps reached a peak at the COP 17 in Durban in November 2011. It appears that China and India face two prospects—to cooperate more intensively and ensure their basic interests are not hollowed out or to be gradually marginalized as their positions are considered 'rigid' even by sections within the G77. As pressure mounts, many in the 'Global South' are inclined to accept a legally binding agreement. At Durban, India's former Environment Minister Jayanthi Natarajan, emphasized India's unequivocal opposition to the Durban Road Map by stressing equity. In a significant speech, she said,

> India is asking for space for basic development for its people and poverty eradication. Is this an unreasonable demand? ...Equity has to be the centerpiece of the Climate discussion and our negotiations should be built on it.[78] ...We're talking of livelihoods and sustainability here. I'm not accusing anybody, but there are efforts to shift the (climate) problem to countries that have not contributed to it... If that is done, we're willing to reopen the entire Durban Package. We did not issue a threat. But are we being made into a scapegoat? Please don't hold us hostage.[79]

Echoing India's position on 'common but differentiated responsibility', Chinese representative Xie Zhenhua, vice chairman of the NDRC, reiterated China's position that '[T]he developed countries should confront their historical responsibilities and high-level percapita emissions, take the lead in large-scale emission reduction, and provide developing countries with financial and technical supports'.[80] Despite calls from Indian and Chinese officials, the Durban Platform was adopted which requires a legally binding agreement applying to all countries be completed by 2015. To quote from the UNFCCC – 17th COP:

> Decides that the Ad Hoc Working Group on the Durban Platform for Enhanced Action shall complete its work as early as possible but no later than 2015 in order to adopt this protocol, legal instrument or agreed outcome with legal force at the twenty-first session of the Conference of the Parties and for it to come into effect and be implemented from 2020.[81]

Ten days after the Durban Conference, India issued a statement stating that 'It (the Durban pact) does not imply that India has to take binding commitments to reduce its emissions in absolute terms in 2020'.[82] India's seventeen paragraph submission to the UNFCCC following the Durban Conference made on 28 February 2012 reiterated its core position to the need for "… efforts for increase in the level of ambition must be made, inter alia, in accordance with the principle of equity and the principle of Common But Differentiated Responsibilities of the Parties'.[83] The Chinese submission made on 8 March 2012 stated in clear terms the following:

> Developed country Parties should take the lead in reducing their emissions by undertaking ambitious mitigation commitments and fulfill their obligations of providing financial resources and transferring technology to developing country Parties in accordance with the principles and provisions of the Convention, in particular the principle of common but differentiated responsibilities. The key to increase the level of ambitions to reduce emissions lies with the developed country Parties' political will and the recognition of their historical responsibility.[84]

To conclude this section, with its work cut out, the legal phraseology adopted by the Ad Hoc Working Group will be a highly contested process. China and India on their part will be facing more international pressure since the G77 does not appear to be speaking in one voice and by 2015 there will be a legally binding agreement on emission reductions. Yet development is the top priority for India and China and a slowdown in economic growth may have an internal political impact in both countries—more in India.

China's Environmental Bureaucracy

The vast Chinese bureaucracy subsumes within it competing agencies differentiated by rank and function. It is assumed that there are 'conflicts' in policymaking owing to 'vertical' and 'horizontal' channels of communication and authority. The Chinese bureaucracy interprets 'environmentalism' atypically as not only an issue of salience with the potential to derail economic growth but also as an ideological challenge that subverts the socialist market economy it is creating for itself.

The National People's Congress (NPC) passes laws which the State Council implements by tasking ministries. The State Environmental Protection Agency (SEPA) is the national agency responsible for environmental regulation and is the administrative wing of the NPC. The SEPA focuses on policy-specific issues especially related to terrestrial (land and water) and atmospheric (air) pollution. The Commission for the Protection of Environmental and Natural Resources (CPENR) reports to the State Council and coordinates environmental protection efforts and outlines general policies. The Ministry of Environmental Protection (MEP) has full ministerial status but does not control SEPA or the ENPRC. The NDRC is the main institution within China's bureaucratic firmament to coordinate Climate Change and Energy policy since 1998. The NDRC leads a 15-member ministerial National Climate Change Coordination Committee and does the agenda-setting on Climate Change. The NDRC and the Ministry of Foreign Affairs (MOFA) have a coordination mechanism through the NCCC also known alternately as the NC4. Reports brought out by the NDRC include the National Assessment Report on Climate Change (2006); National Climate Change Programme (2007); and China's Policies and Actions for Addressing Climate Change (2008). The MOFA has the brief of ensuring that China's political and economic interests are met during international negotiations. Climate Change for the MOFA is also an issue that has to display China's sensitivities and initiatives by catering to the common aspirations of developing countries to which it belongs.

The National Energy Commission, Ministry of Water Resources and the State Forestry Administration are other actors involved in participating, coordinating and implementing measures stemming from policy commitments made by the leadership to alleviate the impact of climate change domestically. The State Forestry Administration has 16 allied institutes to assist its work. At the grassroots, Environmental Protection Bureaus (EPBs) are the responsible agencies enforcing and implementing laws and regulations flowing from the top. The charter of the EPBs flows from local congresses adopting local regulations that do not differ from the legislation above. The EPBs manage cities, townships and counties and are substantially aided by monitoring stations and research institutes.[85] As local actors are influenced by the regulations of the central government on environmental protection, EPBs are for the most part the bottom end of the policy chain. Yet they display streaks of autonomy in decision-making especially in regions where minorities comprise the predominant resident population. In Yunnan for instance, forested areas where minorities are resident is considered to be a 'collective' and common property rights influence policy formulation.[86]

Perhaps the landmark documented national initiative on the Environment as a policy issue and one that attracted government attention was the First National Conference on Environmental Protection convened by Premier Zhou Enlai in August 1973. The conference adopted a 32 character 'guiding principles' that emphasized overall planning, recycling, public participation, environmental protection, and overall benefit to society. The creation of a Leading Group on Environmental Protection in 1974 was an indicator of the seriousness attached to the issue of environment by the Chinese leadership. The Leading Group's functions involved the creating of an administrative structure to monitor the environment, generate laws and regulations to protect the environment and coordinating environmental planning.[87] The relative strength of China's environmental bureaucracies today and their administrative and coordination skills flow from this initiative from the early 1970s. Despite this experience of administratively handling the environment, China lacked international exposure and it was only in 1988 that China involved itself in international negotiations on climate change. In 1992, China ratified the UNFCCC and in 2002 ratified the Kyoto Protocol.

There are other actors/groups[88] involved in the discourse on the environment and climate change in China and some of these are:

1. Civil servants representing not only the bureaucracies but also the legal, scientific and academic communities, who while seemingly representing a differentiated power constituency, are in their entirety, a powerful group.
2. Environment experts embedded within the Chinese policymaking circles and who have had training and experience of working with international environmental agencies especially the United Nations and international financial institutions are a group with their interests.
3. The emergence of non-governmental organizations (NGOs) focusing on environmental issues is an aspect that needs more attention. The environmental NGOs in China inhibit a space where they are respected for their genuine concerns regarding the state of China's overall environment and the recommendations they put forward are acceptable to the government. However, the government does not want these NGOs to become trenchant critics of the political system and tolerates them as long as they keep their focus on pointing out grave environmental lapses.

In sum, China's approach to climate change is a mix of multilateral and bilateral agreements. The Asia-Pacific Partnership on Clean Development and Climate (APP)—of which India is a member—is an instance of a multilateral initiative.[89] The APP has established eight government and business taskforces on cleaner fossil energy, renewable energy and distributed generation, power generation and transmission, steel, aluminium, cement, coal mining and buildings and appliances. This non-binding compact consistent with the principles of UNFCCC will 'complement, but not replace, the Kyoto Protocol'. The countries comprising the APP later negotiated and signed the

Charter of the APP on 12 January 2006. The partnership seeks to 'advance clean development and climate objectives, recognizing that development and poverty eradication are urgent and overriding goals internationally'. Complementing the multilateral are bilateral initiatives such as the EU–China Partnership on climate change[90] and the Australia–China partnership on climate change.[91] By adopting a methodology that enables it to be at the forefront of the G77[92] and at the same time initiate bilateral and multilateral environment agreements, China reveals a sophisticated strategy of negotiation that increases its benefits and decreases costs.

The next section examines the bilateral challenge facing China and India as regards trans boundary waters and its potential to expand into a regional issue requiring enhanced levels of cooperation and coordination at many levels.

Hydro-politics or Hydro-cooperation: A Game Changer for China and India

The salience of transboundary river waters between China and India and its relation to the 'domestic'—especially its linkages to environment and development—and the 'external'—with inescapable strategic consequences—is an issue needing some elaboration.

A potential threat facing the downstream region comprising India and Bangladesh is China's quest to create a cascade of dams on the upstream Yarlung Tsangpo/Brahmaputra that is feared would lead to the downstream nations of India and Bangladesh facing water shortages and its consequent economic impact in the years to come. Maps from reliable sources available in open domains reveal a large number of hydropower projects on the Yarlung Tsangpo (Brahmaputra river) introducing hydro security into China–India relations.

Flowing down from its watershed in Tibet, the Brahmaputra and its main branches from the Indian Himalaya's—the Lohit, Dibang, Dihang, Subansiri and Jia Bharali—are civilizational lifelines to India's northeast.[93] With copious water flows, these rivers sustain millions of people and their livelihoods. It has been estimated that around 12 per cent of the water flows in the Brahmaputra basin are from glacier flows, and if this figure were to increase, it would be evidenced that Himalayan glaciers are indeed melting at a faster rate, owing perhaps to human-induced causes. The classified nature of available data on Himalayan rivers only serves to accentuate existing fears—real and imagined.

The outcome of China's plans to divert water from the highlands poses many questions including the vital one of 'downstream effects of changing water flow regimes' which are a big unknown.[94] Arguably, China's evolving 'water policy' has strong domestic connotations and hence as a category, 'water security' is an issue exhibiting overlaps of 'domestic-external linkages'[95] and by default elements of the 'two-level game' since its impact goes beyond the territorial extremities of a single state. At another level, the manner in which China is emerging as a central axis in potential water-related disputes in Asia (the Mekong and the Brahmaputra rivers being cases in point) is an expansive issue—beyond the scope of this paper—that calls for more attention from nations that form the riparian constituents to rivers originating from the highlands of Tibet.

The internal acceleration of utilizing hydro-resources in China has led to the emergence of a discourse in India that straddles a wide spectrum. It has been argued that 'domestic considerations' influencing China's long-term plans to divert river waters from Tibet into its 'water stressed' northern regions might involve a conflict between the two countries. To Mohan Malik, the 'ecological impact on the Indian subcontinent' with China exercising control of the upper reaches of rivers in Tibet, could lead to a conflictual situation.[96]

If China were to be successful in carrying out its plans to divert water from the Brahmaputra/Yarlung Tsangpo to its central and northern provinces, it undoubtedly will lead to deep fissures in bilateral relations between the two countries. Also, it will complicate India's own plans to utilize the relatively untapped potential of the Brahmaputra and its tributaries to generate hydel power to its northeastern states. In totality, it is the strong imperatives from domestic constituencies in both the countries that are encouraging the rapid construction of large dams on the same river system that is giving the issue strategic undertones.

The argument put forward is that though the utilization of river waters by China for its domestic consumption has multifarious strategic connotations for India, the issue does hold the potential of encouraging cooperation between the two sides. The aspect of 'Cooperation' in matters pertaining to 'water security' does have its adherents in China. For Zhang Jincui, 'water conservancy (sic.) projects are the bridge linking China and India' and 'water should be the beginning of bilateral cooperation, not conflict'.[97] Adding a unique perspective, Zhang Jincui introduces a game theory aspect to 'water security' between China and India, and opines that the two countries are caught between a 'prisoner's dilemma' and a 'coordination game' owing to two factors—extant bilateral difficulties and differences, and lack of information nodes regarding water security between the two countries.

Continuing along this line is Wang Bin who is of the opinion that with more than three decades of international environmental diplomacy expertise, China and India need to encourage a 'flow of dialogue, share experiences in environmental protection and sustainable development and look for innovative solutions' since the sustainable development of Asia is not possible without the cooperation of the two countries.[98] Lan Jiansyue also makes a case for Sino-Indian relations becoming deeper with 'water resources security deserving the attention' of policy makers on both sides.[99]

The flip side to the welcome calls for cooperation is China's cautious behaviour regarding the issue of transboundary rivers. Not to be lost sight of by policy makers is China's approach to discussing the sharing of river waters with its neighbours with the Mekong River Commission (MKC) as a case in point. Comprised of four countries—Cambodia, Lao PDR, Thailand and Vietnam—the MKC has China and Myanmar as 'Dialogue Partners' and not as full members. This position gives China the flexibility to participate in the deliberations, make comments and observations and yet take no responsibility or make any binding commitments. It could be inferred—from a drastic perspective—that its river water sharing behaviour is akin to the 'Harmon Doctrine' that held that 'a country is absolutely sovereign over the portion of an international watercourse within its borders'.[100]

China's almost constant refrain about the inviolable aspects of sovereignty leads to the question of whether it is adhering to a 'Harmon Doctrine' with Chinese characteristics.

Returning to the position on 'cooperation', it is not that there is no hope and the future of Sino-Indian hydropolitics is dire. Rather, the issue of sharing river waters offers prospects for cooperation—not conflict. China and India need to initiate a comprehensive structured dialogue on water issues with the objective of institutionalizing the same by setting up a Commission that bears overall responsibility for all trans-boundary rivers flowing into India. With regard to the Brahmaputra/Yarlung Zangpo, as a downstream nation, Bangladesh needs to be part of any initiative. If one were to look for a template within the extended region the best instance of this has been the Indus Water Commission (IWC).

As mentioned by scholars before,[101] despite a dyadic rivalry, India and Pakistan have held steadfast to the Indus Water Commission irrespective of the wars they have fought with each other in the duration since the treaty was signed in September 1960. Perhaps, it could be argued that the relative success of the IWC is owing to its being 'de-securitized' and being an administrative/bureaucratic expression of managing a technical issue. In its widest form, such an instance could be theoretically framed in Anne-Marie Slaughter's terms as a 'trans- governmental network' that facilitates 'horizontal cooperation' amongst middle-to-senior level government officials—one that bypasses the 'sensitive' and 'hyperactive' nodes within and outside every government structure.[102]

In other words, the creating of an institutional structure flexible enough to accommodate a wide tapestry of stakeholders (technical experts/water-related bureaucracies, etc.) will have the effect of 'de-securitizing' a potential flashpoint and encourage much-needed dialogue custom between the participants. Encouraging signs are visible in this direction and bilateral cooperation between the two countries, though nascent, offers pointers to the future. In 2002, India signed an MoU with China for the provision of hydrological information on Yaluzangbu/Brahmaputra river in flood season by China to India. This MoU was for a period of five years. Abiding by the provisions of the

MoU, China provided hydrological information on the water level, discharge and rainfall in respect of three stations, namely, Nugesha, Yangcun and Nuxia located on river Yaluzangbu/Brahmaputra from 1st June to 15th October every year—data that helped in the formulation of flood forecasts by the Central Water Commission (CWC) and also to alert state governments along the course of the river to prepare for any exigencies. A new MoU with a validity of five years was signed with China on 5 June 2008.[103]

In June 2018, this MoU was revived during Prime Minister Narendra Modi's visit to China.

A separate MoU was signed during the visit of Wen Jiabao to India in April 2005 for the supply of hydrological information in respect of Sutlej (Langquin Zangbu) in flood season. China provides hydrological information from the Tsada station on river Sutlej. A new MoU on the supply of flood season hydrological information on river Sutlej had been agreed in August 2010 by both the countries for signature by two countries. The landslide dam that formed on the Parechu river in 2004 and its bursting in 2005 leading to sudden discharge into the Sutlej was perhaps a moment of truth for both sides. Another vestige of cooperation is the Joint Expert Level Mechanism (ELM) headed by Joint Secretary level officials to discuss interaction and cooperation on the provision of flood season hydrological data, emergency management and other issues regarding trans-border rivers existing between the two countries since 2006.[104] The ELM meets every year on a reciprocal basis.

Conclusion

Policy choices in China and India are decided at the intersection of 'economic capacity' and 'socio-environmental impact' and 'domestic consensus'. While adopting a seemingly united position on global issues like climate change, China and India need to develop deeper institutional linkages and structures to address their growing list of bilateral differences. So far, the unresolved territorial claims between the two countries have not been an impediment in cooperative endeavours related to climate change. There needs to be more ballast to the nascent cooperation between the two sides on climate change lest the commonalities end up being spasmodic and summit centric.

As China and India grow, their 'ecological footprint' is increasing and other issues—of a bilateral nature—are going to encroach upon the policy priority list. The issue of trans-boundary rivers, melting of glaciers and increase of snowmelt into rivers during summer months makes it imperative for both the countries to cooperate—not doing so is not an option. Hydropower projects proposed by China on the Yarlung Zangpo (Bramhaputra) are potential obstacles in bilateral relations especially since the two countries do not have a water-sharing treaty between them. Currently, China and India share hydrological data on the monsoonal flows of the Sutlej and the Brahmaputra. The two countries do not share any information on the melting of glaciers. There is recognition of this lacuna and to quote former Chinese premier Wen Jiabao,

> 'China takes seriously India's concern about the trans-border rivers, and we are ready to further improve the joint working mechanism'.[105]

China and India need to go beyond the corpus of agreements and statements issued on cooperation regarding climate change and need to conduct joint studies on climate change in a comprehensive manner. Cooperative technical and academic research is scant, if not absent in the public domain, and if initiated, will transform the manner in which current policymaking is made regarding climate change by providing more choices to decision-makers and stakeholders to approach this crucial issue. Scientific knowledge and data, independently and collaboratively on issues pertaining to the environment and interaction between technical and policy research institutions need to be encouraged between China and India on all aspects of climate change, especially, mitigation, funding, clean technologies, strategic impact and negotiations. A constant analytic and deliberative process between China and India on the environment has its benefits in guiding analyses, formulating problems, generating independent data and variables, providing unique theoretical models and anticipating uncertainties.

The positions adopted by China and India at global conventions on climate change and sustainable development reflect their priorities of internal economic development. The challenge facing the two countries is to create a custom of cooperation—through dialogue mechanisms and bilateral institutional forums—that ensure a delicate balance between sustainable development and continued economic growth. These conjoined existential necessities generate political goodwill in India for the government of the day and continued legitimacy in China for the Communist Party of China.

As an overlap issue, impacting the domestic political sphere and influential enough to warrant constant international pressure to comply with evolving global norms, the positions China and India adopt towards Climate Change are introducing 'game changing' aspects to their international relations. The linkages that emerge between the domestic and the external or alternately the national and the international are unmistakable.[106]

Despite different internal structures of governance, China and India coordinate positions on Climate Change since at stake are their carefully constructed programmes of national development. Politically, for both countries, agreeing to a binding treaty on Climate Change is not feasible at present and will erode the legitimacy of their respective leaderships with the added corollary of internal political impact such a decision would have.

The existence of potential benefits accruing to actors from cooperation is not a sufficient condition. China and India need to jointly identify a roadmap for cooperation on Energy and Climate Change. This will be an important step in enhancing cooperation especially since the United States and China have set a template for conducting dialogue on the environment at various levels and which is subsumed within the overall strategic and economic dialog between the two countries. This dialog with the United States complements the EU–China Energy and Environment Programme and the EU–China Environmental Governance Programme.

Negotiating climate change requires a radically different approach that the emergence of an international order of environmental governance comprised of institutional, NGOs and civil society organizations poses challenges to China and India owing to their relentless scrutiny of internal policies and governmental excesses and lapses. Inhabiting the sphere where 'sovereignty' is not a restraining feature these 'pan-sovereign groupings' are powerful stakeholders in the debate on climate change and have the necessary resources and technological skills of mobilization that do not respect territorial extremities. They make 'sovereignty' a flexible and dynamic category and accept 'sovereignty' as a 'dynamic and socially constructed' determinant with multiple meanings as opposed to the static and inflexible.[107] Countries such as China and India have the uncomfortable choice of either co-opting or rejecting these actors in the absence of a middle ground on Climate Change and the environment. To John Ruggie, this 'global ecological interdependence' is reflective of a nascent 'multiperspectival' system that while not supplanting the state, is an alternative to the hitherto single voice or perspective.[108]

While cooperation on climate change between China and India is encouraging, India needs to distinguish between the technical aspects of Climate Change mitigation efforts and the ideal type formulations it wishes to incorporate in any eventual agreement at the UNFCCC. It just might be possible that if China were to see merit in the technicalities of any eventual agreement, India should not find itself isolated.[109] If foreign policy decision-making with a slant of bilateral cooperation was there at the UNFCCC, it adds several layers to the decision-making spectrum. The next chapter moves beyond UNFCCC limited cooperation between China and India into strategic wariness, where China, India and the United States are involved in a study of respective behaviour revealing apprehensions, limitations, worldviews, politics and personalities, agreeing only when it comes to disagreeing!

Notes

1. United Nations, *Report of the United Nations Conference on the Human Environment*. Available at: UN Doc.A/Conf.48/14/Rev.1 1973, 5
2. Dr Manmohan Singh, Prime Minister of India, Speech at the Plenary of Head of States/Governments, 15th Conference of Parties (COP), Copenhagen, 18

December 2009, *India Review* (Philadelphia, PA), Vol.6, Issue.1, 1 January 2010, Embassy of India, Washington.
3. Intergovernmental Panel on Climate Change (IPCC) *Fourth Assessment Report: Climate Change 2007*. Available at: http://www.ipcc.ch/publications_and_data/ar4/syr/en/spms5.html (Accessed on 24 November 2017).
4. Wendy E. F. Torrance, 'Science or Salience: Building an Agenda for Climate Change', Ch. 2 in *Global Environmental Assessments: Information and Influence*, eds. Ronald B. Mitchell, William C. Clark, David W. Cash and Nancy M. Dickson (Cambridge, MA: MIT Press, 2006): 42–43.
5. Barry Buzan and Ole Waever, 'Macrosecuritisation and security constellations: reconsidering scale in securitisation theory', *Review of International Studies* 35, no. 2 (2009), 271.
6. United Nations Framework Convention on Climate Change (UNFCCC), Article 1, *Full Text of Convention*. Available at: http://unfccc.int/essential_background/convention/background/items/2536.php (Accessed on 30 November 2017).
7. Kelly McManus, 'The Principle of 'Common but Differentiated Responsibility' and the UNFCCC', *Climatico* (Seattle) November 2009. Available at: http://www.climaticoanalysis.org/wp-content/uploads/2009/12/kmcmanus_common- responsibilities.pdf (Accessed on 29 May 2018)
8. Sean Walsh, Huifang Tang, John Whalley and Manmohan Agarwal, 'China and India's Participation in Global Climate Negotiations', *International Environment Agreements: Politics, Law and Economics* 7, no. 1 (March 2007): (E- Journal without pagination).
9. According to the *Carbon Dioxide Information Analysis Center* (CDIAC), Department of Energy, United States in 2007.
10. See 'India: Greenhouse Gas Emissions 2007' Report prepared by Indian Network for Climate Change Assessment (INCCA) for Ministry of Environment and Forests, Government of India, May 2010, p.i.
11. See *National Action Plan on Climate Change*, Government of India, Prime Minister's Council on Climate Change released on 30 June 2008. Available at: http://www.indiaclimateportal.org/the-napcc (Accessed on 7 June 2017) and *China's National Climate Change Programme*, National Development Reform Commission, June 2007. Available at: http://www.ccchina.gov.cn/WebSite/CCChina/UpFile/File188.pdf (Accessed on 7 June 2017).
12. Veronica Ward, 'Sovereignty and Ecosystem Management: Clash of Concepts and Boundaries?' Ch.4 in *The Greening of Sovereignty in World Politics*, ed. Karen T. Litfin (Cambridge, MA: MIT Press, 1998), 82.
13. Detlef Sprinz and Tapani Vaahtoranta, 'The Interest – Based Explanation of International Environmental Policy', *International Organisation* 48, no. 1 (Winter 1994): 78–79.
14. Robert D. Putnam, 'Diplomacy and Domestic Politics: The Logic of Two-Level Games' in *International Bargaining and Domestic Politics – Double Edged*

Diplomacy, ed. Peter B. Evans, Harold K. Jacobson and Robert D. Putnam (Berkeley: University of California Press, 1993), 437.
15. Yuka Kobayashi, 'The 'Troubled Modernizer': Three Decades of Chinese Environmental Policy and Diplomacy,' in *Confronting Environmental Change in East and Southeast Asia: Eco-Politics, Foreign Policy, and Sustainable Development*, ed. Paul G. Harris (London and Stirling, Virginia: Earthscan, 2005), 94.
16. Cai Shouqiu and Mark Voigts, 'The Development of China's Environmental Diplomacy,' *Pacific Rim Law & Policy Journal* 3 (1993): S-21. China's delegation however did not sign on to the final agreement in Stockholm since it did not 'contain strong socialist statements'—a reflection of the internal churnings owing to the Cultural Revolution.
17. Maurice F. Strong, 'One Year after Stockholm: An Ecological Approach to Management', *Foreign Affairs* 51 (1973): 691.
18. Margaret Keck and Kathryn Sikkink, *Activists beyond Borders: Advocacy Networks in International Politics* (Ithaca, NY, Cornell University Press, 1998), 124.
19. Keck and Sikkink, *Activists beyond Borders*.
20. Kate O'Neill, *The Environment and International Relations* (Cambridge, UK and New York: Cambridge University Press, 2009), 51.
21. Sjur Kasa, Anne T. Gullberg and Gorild Heggelund, 'The Group of 77 in the International Climate Negotiation: Recent Developments and Future Directions', *International Environmental Agreements* 8 (2008), 114 (113–127).
22. Kobayashi, *op. cit.*, 97.
23. Chen Gang, *Politics of China's Environmental Protection: Problems and Progress* (Singapore: World Scientific, 2009), 106.
24. See Chandrashekhar Dasgupta, 'The Climate Change Negotiations', in *Negotiating Climate Change – The Inside Story of the Rio Convention*, ed. Irving M. Mintzer and J. Amber Leonard (Cambridge: Cambridge University Press, 1994), 129–148.
25. Chen Gang, *Politics of China's Environmental Protection*, 108.
26. Department of Climate Change, National Development and Reform Commission, Clean Development Mechanism in China, April 20, 2012. Available at: http://cdm.ccchina.gov.cn/WebSite/CDM/UpFile/File2854.pdf (accessed April 21, 2017)
27. UNFCCC, CDM reaches milestone: 4000th registered project, Press Release, April 12, 2012. Available at:http://cdm.unfccc.int/CDMNews/issues/issues/I_L9HTDCWQC5OT5N0A7U0L9Q97XSZB7Q/viewnewsitem.html (Accessed April 21, 2017)
28. See Sukumar Ganapati and Liguang Liu, 'The Clean Development Mechanism in China and India: A Comparative Institutional Analysis', *Public Administration and Development* 28, no. 5 (2008), 351–362.
29. Chao-lung Liu, 'China's Strategic Adoption in Climate Change', *Review of Global Politics* 37 (2012), 104.

30. Yu Hongyuan, *Global Warming and China's Environmental Diplomacy* (New York: Nova Science Publishers 2008), 78.
31. Chen Gang, *Politics of China's Environmental Protection*, p. 122. Also see 'China: developing nations should set own emissions reduction targets' People's Daily Online, 23 November 2007. Available at: http://english.people.com.cn/90001/90776/90883/6307741.html (accessed on 23 March 2017)
32. See Text of 'Agreement on Cooperation in Addressing Climate Change' Accessible at: moef.nic.in/.../India- China%20Agreement%20on%20Climate%20Change.pdf
33. Kong Fanwei (School of International Relations and Public Affairs, Fudan University), 'Qianxi zhongguo qihou waijiao de zhengce yu xingdong (The Policies and Actions of China's Climate Diplomacy)' *Xin shi ye* (*Expanding Horizons*, Beijing) 4 (2008): 94–96.
34. Amb. Shyam Saran (ret'd), The Prime Minister of India's former special envoy on Climate Change at a talk delivered at the Institute of International Relations, National Chengchi University, Taipei on 16 December 2010.
35. Shyam Saran, 'India at Copenhagen', *Seminar* 606 (February 2010).
36. Michael Grubb, Christiaan Vrolijk and Duncan Brack, *The Kyoto Protocol – A Guide and Assessment* (London: Royal Institute of International Affairs, 1999), 29.
37. 'India and China maintain primacy of UN-two track negotiations' *Third World Network*, Info Service on Climate Change, 11 March 2010.
Available at: http://www.twnside.org.sg/title2/climate/info.service/2010/climate20100301.htm (Accessed on 23 February 2017)
38. See Vaclav Smil, *China's Environmental Crisis: An Inquiry into the Limits of National Development* (New York: M.E. Sharpe, 1993).
39. John Vogler and Mark F. Imber, eds., *The Environment and International Relations* (London: Routledge, 1996), 24–26.
40. Zhang Yan, 'Bonding at Copenhagen Cemented India–China Relations' *Outlook* (New Delhi) January 18, 2010. Available at: www.outlookindia.com
41. See Text of *Agreement on Cooperation on Addressing Climate Change Between the Government of the People's Republic of China and the Government of the Republic of India*, Press Information Bureau, Government of India, 21. October 2009. Available at: http://pib.nic.in/newsite/erelease.aspx?relid=53317 and https://mea.gov.in/bilateral-documents.htm?dtl/25238/ (Accessed on 12 September 2017)
42. Erica Downs, 'China's Energy Rise', in *China's Rise in the Historical Perspective*, ed. Brantly Womack (London, Boulder, New York, Toronto and Plymouth, UK: Rowman & Littlefield, 2010), 190.
43. Planning Commission, Government of India, 'Power and Energy'. According to the time series data, one per cent increase in per capital GDP resulted in 1.08 per cent increase in per capita energy consumption in 1980–1981, but

only 0.82 over 1990–1991 to 2003–2004. See http://planningcommission. nic.in/sectors/index.php?sectors=energy (accessed April 1, 2017).
44. Kamaljit S. Bawa et al., 'China, India and the Environment', *Science* 327 (19 March 2010): 1457.
45. Matthew Paterson, 'IR Theory – Neorealism, Neoinstitutionalism and the Climate Change Convention', Ch. 4 in *The Environment and International Relations*, eds. John Vogler and Mark F. Imber (London: Routledge, 1996), 59.
46. Paragraph 11 of *Joint Communique of the Republic of India and the People's Republic of China*, 16 December 2010. The Bali Action Plan involves four specific yet interrelated climate change action plans, namely 'mitigation' (reducing and GHG emissions), 'adaptation' (building capacity to cope with climate change), 'finance' (raise resources for mitigation and adaptation), and 'technology' (transferring climate friendly technology to developing countries).
47. Daniel Yergin, *The Quest: Energy, Security, and the Remaking of the Modern World* (New York: Penguin, 2011), 511.
48. Yu Hai, 'Global Environment Change and China's International Environmental Cooperation', *International Review* 2 (2008): 16.
49. 'Project to conserve Mount Kailash launched' *The Hindu* (New Delhi) 11 April 2010. Available at: http://www.hindu.com/2010/04/11/stories/2010041156971300.htm (Accessed on 27 September 2019).

Institutions involved in this initiative under the aegis of the International Centre for Integrated Mountain Development (ICIMOD) and the United Nations Environment Programme (UNEP) are from the Indian side, the G. B. Pant Institute of Himalayan Environment & Development (GBPIHED as Lead Institute); the Wildlife Institute of India (WII as Partner Institute); and the Forest Department of Uttarakhand state as a partner organization, who bring to the project their skills and expertise in conservation of mountainous terrain. The Ministry of Forests will be the nodal partner from Nepal, and the Chinese Academy of Sciences (CAS) will be the lead partner and nodal reference institution from China.
50. Huang Liming, 'A study of China-India cooperation on renewable energy field', *Renewable and Sustainable Energy Reviews* 11 (2007): 1739–1757.
51. Pranab Bardhan, *Awakening Giants, Feet of Clay – Assessing the Economic Rise of China and India* (Princeton, NJ: Princeton University Press, 2010), 120–121.
52. Daniel Yergin, *The Quest*, 511.
53. 'Join Hands to Address Climate Change' Statement by H.E. Hu Jintao, President of the PRC at the Opening Plenary Session of the United Nations Summit on Climate Change, 22 September 2009, New York. Available at: http://www.fmprc.gov.cn/eng/wjdt/zyjh/t606275.htm (Accessed on 3 January 2012)
54. Adil Najam, 'Developing Countries and Global Environmental Governance: From Contestation to Participation', *International Environmental Agreements* 5 (2005): 304.

55. It was only in the immediate aftermath of Chernobyl accident in 1986 that a convention was signed, namely *The Convention on Early Notification of a Nuclear Accident or Radiological Emergency*.
56. On the schema of 'negotiations' see Stephen Krasner, ed., *International Regimes* (Ithaca, NY: Cornell University Press, 1983) and Deborah D. Stine, *International Environmental Decision Making* (Ann Arbor, MI: University of Michigan, 1994).
57. Gunnar Sjostedt, 'International Negotiation and the Management of Transboundary Risks', Ch.10 in *Transboundary Risk Management*, eds. Joanne Linnerooth, Ragnar E. Lofstedt and Gunnar Sjostedt (London: Earthscan Publications, 2001), 280.
58. Gunnar Sjostedt, *Transboundary Risk Management*, 281. Also see, Gunnar Sjostedt, ed., *International Environmental Negotiation* (Newbury Park, CA: Sage Publication, 1993).
59. Preety M. Bhandari, 'India: Sustainable Development and Climate Change Policy Contexts', in *Climate Change in Asia: Perspectives on the Future Climate Regime*, eds. Y. Kameyama et al. (Tokyo: United Nations University Press, 2008), 92.
60. Huang Yusong and Huang Min, 'Qianxi Yindu yingdui qihou bianhua de zhengce' (India's Policy to Address Climate Change), *Nanya yanjiu* (South Asian Studies) 1 (2010), 68–69.
61. Ibid., 76. In fact, India's current emission is only a quarter of China's.
62. See Pamela S. Chasek, David L. Downie and Janet Welsh Brown, *Global Environmental Politics*, 5th ed. (Boulder, CO: Westview Press, 2010). Also see Barry Buzan, Ole Waever and Jaap de Wilde, *Security – A New Framework for Analysis* (Boulder, CO: Lynne Rienner, 1998), 77–79.
63. Tobias Rapp, Christian Schwagerl and Gerald Traufetter, 'The Copenhagen Protocol – How China and India Sabotaged the UN Climate Summit', 5 May 2010, *Spiegel Online International*. Available at: http://www.spiegel.de/international/world/the-copenhagen-protocol-how-china-and-india-sabotaged-the-un- climate-summit-a-692861.html (Accessed on 13 June 2017). Also see, Markus Becker, 'Climate Negotiations in Durban – Usual Suspects Continue to Block Emissions Deal', 12 September 2011, *Spiegel Online International*. Available at: http://www.spiegel.de/international/world/climate-negotiations-in-durban-usual-suspects-continue-to-block-emissions-deal-a-802828.html (Accessed on 13 June 2017).
64. Lichao He, 'China's Climate-Change Policy From Kyoto to Copenhagen: Domestic Needs and International Aspirations', *Asian Perspective* 34, no. 3 (2010): 7.
65. Lichao He, 'China's Climate-Change Policy', 12.
66. *China's National Climate Change*, National Reform Development Reform Commission, 2007. Available at: http://www.ccchina.gov.cn/WebSite/CCChina/UpFile/File188.pdf (Accessed on 13 October 2017).

Apart from the NDRC, 12 other ministerial and other bureau were involved in the preparation of this report reflecting the wide spread of 'environment' as a policy issue within China's political and administrative setup. The other ministries and bureau were: the Ministry of Science and Technology, the China Meteorological Administration, the CAS, the Ministry of Foreign Affairs, NDRC, the State Environmental Protection Administration, Ministry of Education (MOE), Ministry of Agriculture, Ministry of Water Resources, State Forestry Bureau. State Oceanic Administration, the National Natural Science Foundation.

67. Zhu Xufeng, 'China's National Leading Group to Address Climate Change: Mechanism and Structure', *East Asia Institute* (Singapore) Background Brief No. 572, 22 October 2010, i.
68. See *Implementation of the Bali Roadmap – China's Position on the Copenhagen Climate Change Conference*, 20 May 2009.
69. See White Paper on *China's Policies and Actions for Addressing Climate Change*, Information Office of the State Council, PRC, November 2011, Beijing.
70. Joanna I. Lewis, 'China's Strategic Priorities in International Climate Change Negotiations', *The Washington Quarterly* 31, no.1 (2007–2008): 162.
71. Du Juan, 'China to establish climate change think tank', *China Daily*, November 22, 2011. Available at: http://www.chinadaily.com.cn/cndy/2011-11/22/content_14137549.htm (Accessed on 12 January 2018).
72. Zhang Haibin, 'Zhongguo yu guoji qihou bianhua tanpan', (China and International Climate Change Negotiation). *Guoji zhengzhi yanjiu*, (International Politics Quarterly) (Beijing) (2007): 35.
73. Wang Limao, 'Zhongguo yingdui qihou bianhua tanpan de jidian sikao,' (Consideration of China Coping with Negotiations for Global Climate Change). *Qihou bianhua yanjiu jinzhan*, Advances in Climate Change Research) (Beijing) 1, no. 5 (May): 35–37.
74. Qin Dahe, 'Quanqiu qihou yu huanjing yanbian ji duice', (The Global Climate and Environment Change and the Countermeasures). *Zhongguo keji jiangli*, China Awards for Science and Technology) (Bejing) 1: 37–38.
75. Zhang Kun-min and Wen Zong-guo, 'Zhongguo guanyu quanqiu biannuan de guandian yu duice', (China's Point of View and Countermeasures on Global Warming), *Zhongguo ruankexue* (China Soft Science) (Beijing) 7 (2011): 8–10.
76. Karen T. Litfin, *The Greening of Sovereignty in World Politics* (Cambridge, MA: MIT Press, 1998), 4.
    Karen T. Litfin proposes that if 'sovereignty' were understood as a 'socially constructed institution' varying across time and space with interpretative meanings, its relationship to the environment can be studied (p. 4).
77. Piers M. Blakie and Joshua S.S. Muldavin, 'Upstream, Downstream, China, India: The Politics of Environment in the Himalayan Region', *Annals of the Association of American Geographers* 94, no. 3 (2003): 522.

78. Nitin Sethi, 'Climate Talks: Jayanthi Natarajan Applauded for Stirring Speech at Durban', *Times of India*, 10 December 2011. http://articles.timesofindia.indiatimes.com/2011-12-10/global-warming/30501920_1_climate-talks-climate-change-small-island-countries (accessed 1 February 2018)
79. Indo-Asian News Service, 'India gets its way as climate conference in Durban closes', Hindustan News, December 11, 2011. (accessed in February 1, 2018, http://www.hindustantimes.com/world-news/Africa/India-gets-its-way-as-climate-summit-in-Durban-closes/Article1-780872.aspx)
80. Xinhua, 'China urges developed countries to take serious actions at Durban climate conference' December 7, 2011. http://news.xinhuanet.com/english/china/2011-12/07/c_122391570.htm (accessed on 23 February 2017)
81. See United Nations Framework Convention on Climate Change, FCCC/CP/2011/9/Add.1. 'Establishment of an Ad Hoc Working Group on the Durban Platform for Enhanced Action', paragraph no. 4 of Decision1/CP.17. Released on 15 March 2012.
Available at: http://unfccc.int/resource/docs/2011/cop17/eng/09a01.pdf (Accessed on 19 March 2017)
82. 'No binding pacts inked in Durban climate meet: Jayanthi Natarajan', *Times of India*, December 22, 2012. http://articles.timesofindia.indiatimes.com/2011-12-22/developmental-issues/30546288_1_binding-commitments-kyoto-protocol-climate-negotiations (accessed on 23 February 2018)
83. 'Increasing Ambition Level under Durban Platform for Enhanced Actions', Submission by Government of India, 28 February 2012.
Available at: http://unfccc.int/files/documentation/submissions_from_parties/adp/application/pdf/adp_india_28022012.pdf (Accessed on 12 April 2018).
84. 'China's Submission on Options and Ways for Further Increasing the Level of Ambition'. Available at: http://unfccc.int/files/documentation/submissions_from_parties/adp/application/pdf/adp_china_08032012.pdf (Accessed on 12 April 2018).
85. Stephanie Beyer, 'Environmental law and Policy in the People's Republic of China', *Chinese Journal of International Law* 5, no. 1 (2006): 188–189.
86. Piers M. Blakie and Joshua S.S. Muldavin, 'Upstream, Downstream, China, India', 533.
87. Yohei Harashima, 'Environmental Governance in Selected Asian Developing Countries', *International Review for Environmental Strategies* 1, no.1 (2000): 195.
88. Piers M. Blakie and Joshua S.S. Muldavin, 'Upstream, Downstream, China, India', 533.
89. The exact status of the APP is in doubt since many of the projects initiated by it to create clean energy technologies have stalled and its critics point out the lack of a cap on emissions.
90. See *EU and China Partnership on Climate Change*, Memo/05/298, Brussels, 2 September 2005. Available at: http://europa.eu/rapid/pressReleasesAction.do?reference=MEMO/05/298 (Accessed on 8 November 2017)

91. See *Australia–China Partnership on Climate Change*. Available at: http://www.climatechange.gov.au/government/initiatives/bilateral-cc-partnership-program.aspx (Accessed on 8 November 2017).
92. The G77 is not to be interpreted as a monolithic whole with one fixed position. It has more than 130 members and comprises sub-clusters with the OPEC countries having different perceptions and the AOSIS having a separate agenda. The newly industrialized countries (NICs) and the BRICS have their respective agendas too.
93. For a detailed exposition on the subject, see P. K. Gautam 'Sino-Indian Water Issues', *Strategic Analysis* 32, no. 6 (2008): 969–974 and 'Climate Change and Environmental Degradation in Tibet: Implications for Environmental Security in South Asia', *Strategic Analysis* 34, no. 5 (2010): 744–755.
94. Mats Eriksson, Xu Jianchu, Arun Bhakta Shreshta, Raman Ananda Vaidya, Santosh Nepal and Klas Sandsttrom, *The Changing Himalayas: Impact of Climate Change on Water Resources and Livelihoods in the Greater Himalayas*, The International Centre for Integrated Mountain Development (ICIMOD), Kathmandu, Nepal, 11 December 2009, 15.
95. Paul G. Harris, 'Peace, security and global climate change: the vital role of China', *Global Change, Peace & Security: formerly Pacifica Review: Peace, Security & Global Change* 23, no.2 (2011): 143.
96. Mohan Malik, 'India–China Competition Revealed in Ongoing Border Disputes', Power and Interest News Report (PINR) 9 October 2007. Available at: http://www.worldsecuritynetwork.com/showArticle3.cfm?article_id=14981 (Accessed on 14 April 2019).
97. Zhang Jincui (Office of Military Studies, Shanghai University). 'Yingduei shueizihyuan jhengduan:jhong yin celyue de boyilun fensi (Sino-Indo Strategy Game on Water Resource Dispute)'. *Nanya yanjiou jikan* (*South Asian Studies Quarterly*, Chengdu) 4, (2010): 19; 15–21.
98. Wang Bin (College of Law, Qingdao University). 'Shilun zhong yin huanjing hezuo wenti (The Issues on Sino-Indian Environmental Cooperation)'. *Shangqiu shifan xuebao* (*Journal of Shangqiu Teachers College*, Henan: Shangqui) 24, no. 4 (2008): 65–66. Also see Li Xiangyun, 'Cong yindu shuizhengce kan zhong yin bianjiexian zhong de shui wenti (Analysis on the Water Issues Along the Sino-Indian Border: From the Perspective of India's Water Policy)' *Shuili fazhan yanjiu* (*Water Resources Development Research*, Beijing) 10, no. 3 (2010): 68–70.
99. Lan Jiansyue (Centre of South Asian Studies, China Institute of International Studies). 'Shueizihyuan anchuan hezuo yu jhong yin guansi de hudong' (The Cooperation on Water Resource Security and The Interaction of Sino-Indian Relations). *Guoji wunti yanjiou* (*International Studies*, Beijing) 6 (2009): 37–43.
100. Stephen C. McCaffrey, 'The Harmon Doctrine One Hundred Years Later: Buried, not Praised', *Natural Resources Journal* 36, no. 3 (1996): 549. Attorney General Judson Harmon had issued a statement that the United States has no

obligation towards Mexico over the use of waters of the Rio Grande since the former held absolute sovereignty over the river's waters within its territory. I wish to thank Sebastian Biba for raising this detail on natural resources law.

101. See B. G. Verghese, 'Political Fuss Over The Indus – 1,' 'Peace Promise of Indus – 2', *The Tribune* (Chandigarh) May 24–258, 2005; 'New Charter for Water' *Hindustan Times* (New Delhi) July 2009. Available at http://www.bgverghese.com/articles.htm#water (accessed on 8 April 2019)

102. Anne-Marie Slaughter, 'The Real New World Order', *Foreign Affairs* 76, no. 5 (September-October 1997): 183–185. Also see, James Kraska, 'Sharing Water, Preventing War—Hydrodiplomacy in South Asia', *Diplomacy & Statecraft*, 20, no.3 (2009): 515–530.

103. 'India–China Cooperation' Ministry of Water Resources, Government of India. Available at: http://www.wrmin.nic.in/printmain3.asp?sslid=372&subsublinkid=290&langid=1 (Accessed on 23 April 2018)

104. See 'Water Sharing Relations with China' Rajya Sabha Unstarred Question No. 3910 by Kumar Deepak Das, 8 September 2011, Ministry of External Affairs, Government of India.
Available at: http://mea.gov.in/mystart.php?id=220118234 (Accessed on 23 April 2018)

105. Wen Jiabao, *Working Together for New Glories of the Oriental Civilization*, Special Address delivered to the Indian Council of World Affairs (ICWA) on 16 December 2010.

106. See, James Rosenau, '*Toward the Study of National – International Linkages*', in Linkage Politics: Essays on the Convergence of National-International Systems (New York: Free Press, 1969).

CHAPTER 4

China, India and the United States
Wary Trio?

Introduction

China, India and the United States are nations proud of their histories and contributions to 'globalism' where the national interests effortlessly blend into creating an aura of goodwill for all. In the case of China and India, their civilizational continuity and expressions have created an image where IR as a field of interest and studied interpretations repeatedly characterize these countries as 'spheres' of interest. The usage of the noun 'sphere' encompasses the range, domain, scope, realm and interest emanating from their influence globally. The aspect of influence straddles political, economic, security, culture and other heuristic aspects, situating interrogative postulates on the speculative aspects of the relations, the three countries share or otherwise. This chapter attempts to determine the integrative and non-integrative facets of the relations between the three countries. To social scientists and area study scholars, examining these three countries poses challenges, as the conventional basis of studying and interpreting 'bilateral' gets complicated by adding 'trilateral' dynamics.

Interpreting the three countries and their *modus vivendi* (mode of living/way of life) involves the study of research material covering a vast scope of epistemic enquiry. To systematize the findings, this chapter adopts the theoretical framework of 'constructivism' to analyse, construct and deconstruct the integrative and non-integrative aspects of the relations among the three countries.

Theoretical Frame—Constructivism and the 'Trilateral'

A conundrum facing scholars and analysts studying area studies is the challenge posed by empirical–theoretical problems, conflicting with political theory and practice. Globalization as a new template in IR has been accompanied by newer problems that pose more questions and few answers. In contemporary politics—domestic, regional and international—themes highlighting cooperation and conflict assume a centrality, depending upon the 'values' identified and extrapolated by the polity at the helm in a sovereign state.

In the mid-to-late 1980s, questions began to be raised about theories and scientific methods of IR and the extent to which they were implicated in the production of international power. Assumptions determining studying IR emerged during the Cold War when realism was the dominant approach to lend and create a framework enquiring into aspects—variables and determinants—keeping the United States and the Union of Soviet Socialist Republics (USSR) a hair-trigger away from global conflagration. With the end of the Cold War, IR theoreticians were left wondering why the field of IR had failed to identify lacunae, leading to the implosion of the USSR and the emergence of new states in Eastern Europe and Central Asia. These questions led to the evolving nature of reinterpreting IR from a framework posting social construction as the bedrock of relations between countries. This fresh approach was dubbed 'constructivism' and it goes beyond the restrictions of realism and neo-realism where 'power' was the leitmotif of nation state interactions and arrangements.

Constructivism is of the view that:

The typologies with which the material world is shaped by human action and the multiple interfaces that evolve from vibrant normative and epistemic elucidations determine the centrality of social actors.

Constructivists believe that 'human capacity for reflection or learning has its greatest impact on the manner in which individuals and social actors attach meaning to the material world and cognitively frame the world they know, experience and understand'.[1] IR, to Constructivists, consist primarily of social facts, which are facts only by human agreement.[2] In a radical departure from the overwhelming fixation towards power and its attributes, the social triumphs over the material. A social structure leaves more space for agency, that is, for the individual or state to influence their environment, as well as to be influenced by it. The title of Alexander Wendt's famous article (Anarchy Is What States Make of It)[3], captures this idea. To Constructivists, enmity and egos are passé. The constitutive aspects of norms and a shared understanding make for creating an agency and structure to any relationship between nations.[4]

By accepting a positivist epistemology, constructivists gained theoretical acceptance to a new theoretical line of reasoning beginning with the writings of Nicholas Onuf.[5] There are three arguments motivating the adoption of constructivism as a theoretical frame to situate the as-yet inchoate trilateral of China, India and the United States.

First, social structures are defined, in part, by shared understandings, expectations or knowledge.[6] What makes ideas (and structure/s) 'social', is their intersubjective quality. In other words, sociality (as opposed to 'materiality' of realism and neo-realism, and the centrality of immense physical capabilities), is countered by constructivism articulating shared knowledge.

Second, 'social structures include material resources like gold and tanks'.[7] Constructivists argue that material resources acquire relevance for collective action through the embedded nature of shared knowledge in which they are embedded. Constructivism is cognizant of changes and shifts in material power affecting social relations between nations.

Third, social structures exist in practices. The UNFCCC is an illustration of the constructivist view where the challenge is more than just pure security. Climate change is a social, political, economic and political reality. Global climate and evidence of its changing respect no sovereignty or material progress.

Simply put, what is real are social structures depending on shared knowledge for objectivity, setting aside the dominance of 'power' and 'interests' negating or relegating other aspects to a secondary level. Do the countries that are the focus in this paper, have the social structures to determine and map global influence with minimal rancour as a necessary feature? The next section is a brief overview of China–United States relations more than two centuries ago. Beginning with their bilateral history is an attempt at constructing a social endeavour with economic variables.

China and the United States: Some Historical Issues

Less than a decade after the 1776 revolution leading to the creation of the United States, the merchants of Boston in December 1783 sent 'Harriet', a 55-ton sloop[8], carrying a cargo of ginseng to China. On learning of this 'economic adventurism', the British East India Company purchased the cargo at double price.[9] This was to prevent the emergence of a rival in commercial terms who could evolve into becoming a rival dislodging the 'empire where the sun never sets'. Revealing a spirit of resilience, efforts to trade with China continued with the 'Empress of China' leaving New York in February 1784, arriving in Macao and Canton in August 1784, becoming the first instance of bilateral trade between the two countries. Success of the 'Empress of China' commercial endeavour, and profits made, led to a 'China fever' with products from China such as tea, silk, spices, cotton fabrics and porcelain finding a market in the United States.

With the successes in trade, it was only several decades later that religion followed. In 1830, the first missionaries from the United States came to China. Perhaps, the first book on China written by an American was Samuel Wells Williams' *Middle Kingdom* (New York: Wiley and Putnam) in 1848. Prior to even the missionaries, was The Canton Register published by William B. Wood. The fascination for China and the Chinese things continued with Wood publishing *The Chinese Courier and Canton Gazette* in 1831 to promote knowledge on China to westerners based then in Canton (Guangzhou), a trading port. If interest in the United States on China was increasing, it was the turn of Chinese students to want to know more about the country becoming known as the 'land of the free'. Yung Wing, Wong Sheng and Wong Fung were the first group of Chinese students in the United States to study at the Monson Academy, Massachusetts in 1847 with Yung Wing graduating from Yale in 1854.

Diplomatic relations between the countries were established in 1786 with a consul for Canton appointed by the United States. In 1844, the first Sino-American Treaty was signed in Wanghia, also called the Treaty of Wanghia, the then Portugal-controlled Macau, since the insular Qing dynasty was unwilling to recognize a foreign power. The Treaty of Wanghia—a treaty of peace, amity and commerce, with tariff of duties—was a diplomatic agreement signed between the Qing dynasty of China and the United States, on 3 July 1844, in the Kun Lam temple located in northern Macau. The agreement was ratified by President John Tyler on 17 January 1845 after being passed by the US Congress. This agreement remained in existence formally until the 1943 'Sino-American Treaty for the Relinquishment of Extraterritorial Rights in China'.[10]

The Treaty of Wanghia was reflective of the public opinion in the United States against the trade in opium reflecting the domination of trade in those days by countries with colonies and markets where economic development was very rudimentary and mostly involving subsistence farming and outdated skills that were an anachronism, requiring correction by a country that rid itself of colonial influence and advanced its credentials as a welcome and benign entity supportive of overthrowing colonialism everywhere. An indication of soft power, even before it was termed as such, was the role played by the Church in encouraging education in China. Tsinghua (Qinghua) University was created after the Theodore Roosevelt administration reduced the amount owed by the Qing after the Boxer Uprising. The United States at that time felt that the war reparations were in excess and this excess was to be channelled into education. This university is now known for filing more patents than Harvard University. Another instance is the Yenching University, which was primarily established by the Methodist Episcopal Church of the United States in 1890.

These ideals, stemming from civil initiatives, morphed over time, into becoming the spirit behind the United Nations a century later.

The influence of the United States in educational and religious terms found a socially fertile China in the first two decades of the last century owing to the slow political implosion of the Qing and a rapid descent into ideological politics. This came to the forefront after the success of the 1917 Soviet revolution painting political canvas with the colour red representing progress, modernization and equality. To the Chinese, especially intellectuals and traders, the United States was a distant land representing new processes of political and economic dynamism after overthrowing feudalism and colonialism—ills plaguing China at that time. The term for the United States in China is 美国 (mei guo/beautiful country). This term also stemmed from the United States projecting an image of being welcomed to all fleeing oppression. The new country was also attracting non-Americans as the growing economy was dependent on immigrants to sustain its agriculture and manufacturing sectors.

The Cold War decades witnessed the politico-strategic dominating bilateral relations between the United States and China. The frictions in the 'socialist camp' were utilized by hard realists exemplified by Henry Kissinger to make overtures to Beijing. This aspect witnessed the Nixon visit to China to meet ailing Mao Zedong and kick-start a bilateral economic relationship that close to five decades has benefitted both. Current, sanctions and trade limitations in the bilateral are to be juxtaposed with many factors, primarily domestic in the United States. The next section moves to situate the China–United States bilateral in the reform period in China since the 1970s.

China and United States—The Years since the 'Open Door' Policy

'A country's national self-image reflects not only its basic political values and ideals but also its responses to how others perceive it'. [11]

On 27 February 1972, the Shanghai Communique was signed between the United States and China. The two sides agreed on the 'one China principle' in which Taiwan was 'China's internal affair in which no other country [had] the right to interfere'.[12] On 1 January 1979, a Joint Communique on Establishing Diplomatic Relations was signed with the United States recognizing the People's Republic of China as being the sole legitimate government of all China.[13]

The United States has a policy towards China mediated by several actors. These are:

1. The President and his advisors giving the White House the 'yea' or 'nay' on China.
2. Policymakers in the State Department and Defense comprising diplomats, policymakers and implementers.
3. Activist legislators on bi-partisan basis in Congress, united when it comes to China.
4. Special interest groups reflecting civil society debates and on China-related issues.
5. The mass media and public opinion.

These actors have not always been in synchrony, and appear at times to be having differences. That is bound to happen in any long-standing democracy. In China, when the civil war between the Kuomintang (KMT) and the Communist Party of China (CPC) was at its peak in the mid-1940s, George Catlett Marshall, known more for his Marshall Plan in the post-World War II years, was sent as a mediator by President Harry Truman to encourage the two belligerents to form a coalition. He was rebuffed.[14] Economics plays a central role in the United States foreign policy and this has been evident since John Hay's time as Secretary of State from 1898 to 1905, during the Presidencies of William McKinley and Theodore Roosevelt. He is known to have enunciated 'Open Door' principles for global trade with China, arguing for free and open markets providing opportunities to traders from all countries.[15]

Even prior to the current spat between the United States and China there was a strand of hostility regarding China's economic success and the beginnings of an investment agenda involving loans to the underdeveloped countries, many of them resource-rich. Hence, Chinese foreign investment schemes have been called a 'Chinese Marshall Plan'.[16] China policy had played an important role in the United States since the years of the Cold War. Democrats and Republicans have in the past coalesced on issues such as non-proliferation and human rights. These days, the sanctions imposed on China by former president Donald Trump have quiet acceptance from the Democrats under Joe Biden, who feel China's trade surplus with the United States has eroded competitiveness and innovation, aspects that marked the economy since the end of the World War II.

To the United States, China is not a single political issue (communism/socialism) but congeries of various issues (trade/human rights/environment/copyrights/nuclear proliferation/arms trade to sanctioned countries/Taiwan/Korean peninsula/Iran/South China Sea to mention a few). The United States has an approach where problems are identified, with a considered view to solve the issue/s. China, in contrast, identifies problems as being 'manageable.'[17] The current trade war between the two countries has been sequestered into a bilateral issue with talks and sanctions dominating headlines without any resolution in sight. The two countries assess one another as 'spoilers' with the United States being at the forefront in slapping sanctions on China for manifold reasons (increase in the bilateral trade deficit for a couple of decades/protectionism practiced by China/manipulation of foreign exchange rates to benefit Chinese exporters/violation of intellectual property rights, etc.). To China, the United States is behaving in a manner reflecting insecurity stemming from an economy that has perhaps seen better days.

Cooperation and issues promoting or retarding a commingling of interests depend on the 'values' articulated by the respective political elites at the helm of political culture. The 'Open Door' policy initiated by Deng Xiaoping was a process of introducing market reforms under the leadership of the Communist Party-State leading to 'socialism with Chinese characteristics'. The success of economic reforms in China was in many ways possible owing to the 'encouragement' provided by western powers especially the United States. The confidence shown by the United States in China's vision of creating an economy where market logic will be welcomed, led to the 'rapprochement', heralded by the week-long Richard Nixon visit (21–28 February 1972). For the

US government, China was a strategic partner owing to the Cold War and tensions with the erstwhile USSR and for the American corporate sector, China had enormous potential as a market with more than 600 million consumers at that time.

By setting aside close to two-and-a-half decades of 'diplomatic freeze,' China was acknowledged as the lesser evil during the Cold War. The intensity of the China–United States bilateral has evolved from a methodology of Cold War necessity in the 1970s and 1980s to a necessity determined by globalization and its myriad attributes, primarily determined these days by technology flows. The United States also prevailed upon the global order when it lobbied for China's joining the World Trade Organization (WTO) in 2001 and granting the most favoured nation (MFN) status in December that year. In the four decades of intense bilateral trade, China has emerged as the global producer of manufactured goods/electronic goods/electrical machinery/textiles/clothing/footwear/agricultural products/chemicals/high-end medical gadgets and multifarious aspects explicating the intense supply chains prevalent in international trade.

From a bilateral trade of around USD 2 billion in 1979, when the 'Open Door Policy' became a template in China for economic development, by 2017, the two countries had trade totalling USD 636 billion. After trade sanctions imposed by former US President Donald Trump, bilateral trade in 2020 was around USD 560 billion, with US exports to China being USD 124.6 billion and imports from China being USD 435.4 billion. Enshrining the bilateral was the strength of the US dollar with China holding US Treasury securities to the tune of USD 1.1 trillion in March 2021. These statistics alone reveal US economic insecurities regarding China, in amassing massive trade surpluses and investing in US domestic debt, making Republicans and Democrats, in agreement on something to be done about China. Perhaps, too little and too late!

Situating Sino-Indian Relations

This section in the chapter details the China–India bilateral by identifying and isolating variables. I begin this section by arguing that there are perhaps no set frameworks to examine Sino-Indian relations in their entirety. One can surmise that this 'vacuum' exists as contemporary IR theory is very narrowly focused on 'power' and its myriad attributes.[18] Space for ideas, beliefs and values do not exist since the altar of 'realism' (imagined and otherwise) constricts other approaches and negates attempts to examine issues from other perspectives. Sino-Indian relations and the discourses surrounding their bilateral relations are more often than not reflective of a predetermined postulation that is stubborn to newer approaches and fresh perspectives.

Ontologically, a deconstruction of Sino-Indian relations to its essentials is a project that awaits its day. Categories that go into this bilateral relationship are more than what is academically discussed and written. For instance, six decades ago when the two countries had 'arrived' on the global stage as new entities shaking-off colonialism and civil war they had more in common with each other—large population, abysmal social indicators, shattered economic infrastructure, weak governance structures and the need for external aid to stimulate domestic economic production. Today, the only similarity the two countries share—apart from large populations—is the focus on their domestic needs of development. Even this 'commonality' is not without its departures. By every other measurable indicator and variable, China and India have less in common with each other in 2011 than in 1949.

I supplement the above arguments by listing out a few variables for both the countries and these are to be juxtaposed with their six-decade-old bilateral relationship as the constant. These listed variables are neither exclusive nor comprehensive but are to be seen as contributing to the making of 'categories' that could be used to frame an ontological approach to study Sino-Indian relations.

Politically, China has transited from individual totalitarianism to collective authoritarianism. This shift in political temperament has coincided with China's reform program and is to be seen as a pragmatic choice made by the CPC to retain its relevance and legitimacy. As a political system, India began its newly independent journey with experienced individuals who strived to build institutions. These ideas got blurred when in the realm of foreign FPDM in its early decades, India made choices that reflected 'individualism' over 'institutionalism.' As a system, democracy has entrenched itself over the decades and the country has been governed by coalitions that offer alternating periods of crises and stability.

Economically, China has moved from a centralized command economy model to one where entrepreneurship—by the state and the individual—is valued. India has effected a transition—arguably, still underway—from Nehruvian socialism and a 'mixed economy' to that of a largely free market where regulatory mechanisms function as 'referees.' It has to be added, though that individual entrepreneurship in India was never formally constrained by the state.

Development wise, China has forged far ahead of India in every possible manner—manufacturing, infotech, start-ups, life expectancy, education, primary health care, access to amenities, etc. and India faces the ignominy of being one of the 'underperformers' stalling the noble aims of the UN's Millennium Development Goals.

In ideological terms,[19] China has abandoned the doctrinaire postures it had adopted in the first few decades of its existence and adopted a more or less agnostic approach designed to derive benefits, both domestic and external. In the realm of foreign policy; however, this agnostic temperament morphs into the arbitrating of power and influence. India has made the transition where it underplays its past foreign policy shibboleth—'Non-alignment'—but is cautious to not be labelled as a 'camp follower' in the prevailing order largely described as 'liberal institutionalism.' 'Autonomy' in decision-making is India's new framework of practicing foreign policy.[20]

Globally, China is one of the pillars of the international structures of governance and has the necessary heft and voice to have its interests accommodated. India, on the other hand, is an aspirant to those very forums where heft counts, yet falls short primarily owing to its own lack of economic standing and a perceived lack of clarity as to what it wants.

Psychologically, China behaves as an 'actor' well-conditioned to the ways of the international system and assiduously prepares itself to be part of constructive solutions and leads the way in creating new institutional structures—One Belt One Road (OBOR), Maritime Silk Road Initiative (MSRI), New Development Bank (NDB), Shanghai

Cooperation Organization (SCO)—to ensure stability and spread its influence. India, by contrast, follows an approach where it seeks to maximize its influence at global forums and its views are generally taken seriously. Nonetheless, in its bilateral relations with China, the catharsis of 1962 forms a rubric motivating and dominating its policymakers.

Epistemologically, Sino-Indian relations need to define or ascribe 'values'—to themselves, each other and the rest—and this kind of approach is most suitable while examining specific issues, such as their respective political systems. Challenging as it is to locate Asia's two largest countries within a theoretical framework, this chapter attempts to base itself by adopting the Constructivist approach, interpreting Sino-Indian relations by delineating 'categories' in the narrative on the two countries. Social constructivist methodologies also require 'discourse' to be empirically dissected within its social context.[21]

In addition, the above-discussed variables display a tendency to morph into intervening variables. As is evident, there is no absolute and all-encompassing theoretical approach for a dynamic social-science discipline like IR. Hence, supplementing this approach, the importants correlates influencing the discourse on Sino-Indian relations are 'historical dimensions', 'socio-political contexts', 'ideological bases', 'power relations,' 'domestic politics' and 'economic performance.' These are in evidence as a constantly running sub-script in the analysis of India–China relations.

India and the United States

For India, unarguably, bilateral relations of *gravitas impetum concitati* (overwhelming gravity) with the United States are the most important component of its foreign policy. This is determined by a necessity stemming from more than seven decades of interactions not exactly satisfactory to both sides. Irrespective of who is in the White House, a Republican or Democrat, for India, institutional relations with the State Department, Department of Defense at the Pentagon and the Department of Commerce are paramount. In India, every government has kept the United States as a template of global order and in the past during the old War, disorder!

Beginnings of India–United States bilateral are to be seen since October 1949. From 11–15 October 1949, Jawaharlal Nehru made his first official visit to the United States, the first foreign visit he made after becoming India's Prime Minister. Was his visit an indicator of a 'lean to the west' with Indian grammar? His visit was epochal and generated a lot of adulation in the media with newspapers and journals highlighting the role India will play at a time when the People's Republic of China had turned Communist with the Chinese Communist Party in power after a brutal and long civil war with the KMT who 'relocated' to Taiwan. The media in the United States had quoted India as being the 'heartland of Asia' (New Republic), 'great Indian experiment in democracy' (Newsweek), 'India offers the best hope of holding back the tide of communism flowing south through Asia' (The Nation). A common refrain in the United States was that this was a fortuitous moment where India should not be allowed to become a Communist appendage and the United States should use its power and influence to pre-empt such a development.[22]

Nehru's visit to the United States did have its tense moments with George McGhee, the assistant secretary for South Asian affairs finding an uninterested Nehru when it came to stitching together an anti-communist alliance. On pointing out that an unresolved boundary with China would lead to aggressive behaviour by the Chinese, the opinion he heard was that China will be engrossed with its internal matters to handle for more than a decade. Nehru said that whatever the Commonwealth did, after naming China as an aggressor and involved in comprehensive rearming, India will decide its foreign relations basing itself on traditions. Missing was a realist streak, thanks to Hans Morgenthau's 'Realism in IR,' discomfiting to McGhee and others in the State Department.[23] This visit by the then Indian Prime Minister was perhaps the beginnings of a bilateral relationship which is two-faced—personality and popularity preceding institutional and diplomatic commingle over shared perspectives.

What one cognizes is that democracy in the United States is deeply entrenched with a libertarian streak that would be difficult to replicate by other democracies. An instance is that of the Anti-Communist Bill. On 24 August 1954, the Communist Control Act was passed and was a successor to the Internal Security Act of 1950. Harry Truman, then President had opined on the introduced bill and implored Congress not to pave the way for 'thought control' that would constrict the American way of life. The US Congress passed the bill despite objections raised by the President, revealing the post-war phase of a 'red scare' permeating through the body-politic.[24]

Domestic political change does play a role in foreign policy. India for long subscribed to a foreign policy termed as 'Nehruvian' which crafted a non-aligned policy during the Cold War years. Post-1991 with economic reforms undertaken, India was at the forefront to prepare for a world where multilateral credentials were to be matched with economic finesse. Globalization played the role of being a vehicle for multilateral behaviour in shaping a new world where trade is the determinant beyond ideological moorings. A few limited dissenting noises in India on joining the World Trade Organization (WTO) gave way to a broader approach on trade, tariffs, technology and various aspects of global monetary flows, investments, etc.

The late 1990s marked a significant political change when the BJP came to power. With an economic ideology advocating privatization and apolitical ideology of nationalism, the BJP had a stint of five years led by Atal Behari Vajpayee as Prime Minister. His foreign policy was not doctrinaire and slowly moved India's foreign policy away from being anchored to Cold War relics of a difference like the NAM. To Washington, India possesses the potential to swing regional balance against China, owing to New Delhi's pathos of 1962 defeat. The view of Democrats and Republicans alike is that the end of the Cold War opened India not just on economic terms, but also on the strategic front, where decades of self-imposed strategic autonomy was a feint with extremely close relations with the former Soviet Union. These close relations were on exhibition every year at India's Republic Day parade on 26 January, when Soviet gadgetry was displayed to the audience present and on television.

In constructivist terms, India has a long way to go, before being considered intrinsic to US preponderance in strategic matters. New Delhi portrays itself as being an 'indispensable element' to the balance of power in Asia, without taking into consideration through consultations and military/naval exercises with other countries in Southeast Asia, what they think of a larger role and profile for India in security matters of the region—mostly maritime.

China: Commonality of Convergence or Divergence?

This chapter strives to introduce constructivism as a veneer to China, India, the United States differing and contesting worldviews (*die weltanschauungen*). Constructivism posits the salience of determinants influencing foreign strategic policy beyond the institutional. In the case of the United States, Hollywood, for instance, advertises, markets, highlights, peddles and sells to a universal audience what the United States is and is not. If this is not soft power constructing an identity of a country then what is 'soft power' and its attributes?

This is where India–US relations need to be introspected upon with a criticality that attempts to construct a syllogism where two propositions arrive at a middle ground with both the sides retaining their 'identity' with internal transfigurations.

Largely, India–US relations have over seven decades, oscillated from optimism to pessimism with scepticism being a constant. To the United States, the appeal of India has depended on the President in White House at a given frame of time. Franklin Delano Roosevelt (FDR), President of the United States from 1933 to 1945, was a Democrat who made his perceptions of India becoming independent clear to an unhappy Winston Churchill during the Atlantic Charter in 1941. In the decade after India's independence, the United States and India initiated a stronger bilateral relationship with defence being the determinant. The 1962 war India had with China led to a defence agreement with the United States in July 1963 where arms sales and air defence were central. This agreement was farsighted with joint training exercises between the United States, British and Indian armed forces within India, with a rider that consultations would take place if there were to be an attack by China.[25]

At this juncture, complicating the Cold War, was a nuclear test conducted by China on 16 October 1964. This test was conducted at Lop Nor, in Xinjiang (formerly East Turkestan).[26] Rather quickly, on the same day, in an unprecedented manner, US President Lyndon Johnson, emphasized US defence commitments in Asia. He added that China's nuclear test 'would have no effect upon the readiness of the United States to respond to requests from Asian nations for help in dealing with Communist Chinese aggression'.[27] Reactions to China's test were many, some alleging a Sino–Soviet ideological split, domestic crisis within the CPC, the emphasis on scientific progress woven to ideological aspects, etc. Very presciently, reports had come in the United States, that India would test a nuclear device in 1972 and that the government was in the process of a program to test a 'peaceful nuclear explosive'.

Whether India had kept the United States briefed on its nuclear program or the latter had inside ingress (more plausible) to the program have not been made clear as opacity prevails.[28]

The end of the Cold War with the implosion of the Soviet Union led India to a quandary as to how to deal with the new realities and importantly, the supply of arms from the former Soviet Union. Until the beginning of this century, Indian armed forces were equipped largely by Soviet weaponry. The few exceptions were mostly European, with French, British and Swedish air and field artillery. During the post-Cold War phase, India gradually replaced its arms vendors and the United States was then emerging as the valued supplier of advanced weapons systems. To India, this was a phase of entrenched interests on both sides with Bill Clinton after years of opprobrium at India's nuclear tests of May 1998 yielding way to a purposeful bilateral engagement straddling many facets.

In contemporary times, with a Republican President, Donald Trump at the White House, bilateral relations between the two countries became stronger, thanks to the personal connection between Prime Minister Narendra Modi and Donald Trump. The Joseph Biden years are to be watched, whether there is continuity or stalling in the bilateral. There are layers to the bilateral, with the United States wanting access to India's market to sell among other things, its expensive medical equipment with riders attached—proprietary software, no transfer of technology, no duplication or replication of medical equipment—that lends some discomfort to the commercial ties. In 2019 bilateral trade between the two countries was estimated at USD 146.1 billion. With the US imports from India at USD 87.4 billion and exports at USD 58.6 billion, the trade deficit was around USD 28.8 billion[29]—an issue rankling the White House. From a bilateral trade of less than USD 20 billion in 2000 to current figures reveal various processes of constructing tangible economic gravitas to much-required duumvirate—one prevailing over the Atlantic and Pacific oceans, and the other wanting to dominate the Indian ocean. The India–US bilateral trade is modestly low, in comparison to China–US trade in 2018 being USD 659.8 billion and the United States with a trade deficit of USD 419.2 billion, a figure resonating in former President Donald Trump imposing widespread trade sanctions on China.

Trade, though not very large, is a significant determinant, and Indian foreign policy towards the United States could be termed as 'economic diplomacy' accompanied by a strong defence calculus where the Pentagon is an advocate of stronger institutional relations with India and defence material play a role in deepening the bilateral.[30] The Pentagon is wanting deeper relations with India as an ally in Asia, with India's geographical centrality an 'asset' not wanting to be an appendage of China. An intensive defence relationship has its commercial calculations with the United States wanting India to not rely excessively on defence materiel from Russia. The military–industrial complex in the United States appears to be satisfied with the state of affairs and is playing the role of facilitator of ties while assuaging the concerns of other departments, wary of India's 'stand-alone' approach. 'Defence diplomacy' with India goes hand in hand with 'economic diplomacy.' The presence of a large workforce with the requisite skills could act as an incentive to the US defence industry, to base some of its production of arms and ammunition in India. As a norm player, India will find providing space to defence manufacturers of the United States in India translating into the country being welcomed into the Nuclear Suppliers Group (NSG), a 48-member group, that seeks to prevent the proliferation of nuclear and fissile material. India's relations with all members of the NSG are cordial, with the exception of two—China and Turkey. These two countries can create hurdles and obstruct India's entry into the NSG.

Complications in the bilateral arise when it comes to Russia. Indian foreign policy has tried to impress upon the United States that their advanced defence products are expensive and that Russia and India have agreements of bilateral exchange of information regarding technology while the United States cocoons its arms exports by arguing that corporate secrets cannot be arbitrated when it is a buy-and-sell transaction. A challenge Indian diplomacy faced was when the United States wanted to enforce Countering America's Adversaries Through Sanctions Act (CAATSA) for signing an agreement with Russia to buy S-400 Triumf air defence missile system. India's diplomacy with the United States is currently going through a phase where a 'personal' connect at the highest levels has not translated into deeper institutional links owing to the past when India was a firm adherent to NAM. This adherence however was with embedded inconsistencies as arms sales from the erstwhile Soviet Union kept our armed forces in fine fettle and the links continue.

At a time when Washington has walked out of international agreements and arrangements like the Paris Agreement (signed 2015 and opting out in 2017) and as a consequence the UNFCC as also the Trans-Pacific Partnership (TPP) in 2017, a question uppermost is whether the United States is an 'irrational actor'? The United States pulling out of international covenants came as a shock and welcome development to Beijing, as it sees a vacuum that needs to be filled by a 'responsible' and 'law abiding' nation! To India, these developments are with portents of how the world order is changing fast and how can it leverage an advantageous position for itself. Our foreign policy cannot replicate China's 'dollar/renminbi' diplomacy and extend loans on extremely soft terms (Sri Lanka an instance is a later chapter) to create the infrastructure that a growing Chinese economy needs to utilize in the coming decades, to emerge as the world's largest economy with the commensurate clout in strategic terms.

Analysis

For constructivists, decisions of political leaders that is, the foreign policy of China, India and the United States, are known for their stolid policy-framing and making process. In the case of the United

States, the State Department is at the fulcrum, with the Department of Defense, Department of the Treasury and the Central Intelligence Agency playing very important roles with the final word coming from the President. In China, foreign policy is coordinated by the MFA, with substantial inputs from the Ministry of Commerce (MoCOM). The role of intelligence agencies is to be expected but without much fanfare. The case of India is unique. The Ministry of External Affairs presides over a foreign policy that has minimal interface with other ministries, especially the Ministries of Defence and Home. This exclusivity has at times led to a quarantining of issues, leading to delayed decisions. A very important determinant in the FPDM in the three countries is the role of personalities at the very apex. Donald Trump, when as President used the electronic medium of Twitter to announce foreign policy. Xi Jinping does not use Twitter as it is an American platform for the current age. China has its own knock-down versions of Twitter. India's Prime Minister, Narendra Modi is on Twitter with millions of followers. He has however not announced important foreign policy decisions through this platform.

China's national interests are characterized by a very realistic strand in the pursuit of those interests, but in their official proclamations, they are also interpreted as being flexible.[31] This is not to say that wavering is what matters in Chinese foreign policy but rather the apposite. The world is naturally multipolar.[32] History is evidence enough. The unilateralism promoted by the United States rides over the multilateralism espoused by its foreign policy practitioners and theoretical experts. Optimists in the United States assess China as going through a process of economic modernization exemplified by the development of an economy determined by market forces—socialism with Chinese characteristics—as ideology spin goes in Beijing. Unlike democratic polities, the (socialist) market forces in China follow dictates issued by the state. The optimists also opine that the political leadership in China, though autocratic, is not immune or sequestered from the economic transformation over past four decades with societal changes necessitating political adaptability.[33]

China's quest for economic modernization has been accompanied by a decisive orientation that seeks to transform the geopolitics of the world. Joining global processes of stewardship, especially economic, is to create a causal pattern where apart from multilateral processes, strong institutional bilateral arrangements are preferred by Beijing. The China–US bilateral is an illustration of a relationship around five-decades old after the Nixon visit in a post-World War II setting. The historical variables mentioned earlier assist in creating a template still being constructed. In an age where technology is driving the economy of most countries, it is a natural corollary to witness a wider audience having opinions on issues sequestered earlier by ossified bureaucracies. In the case of China, online opinions are at that phase where foreign policymakers are not pretending they do not consider wider public opinion. The recent incidents in Hong Kong were 'manufactured' in China as being a 'western plot' with online forums adopting strident tone in encouraging the authorities in Beijing to take a hard stance against 'splittists.'

To observers, the United States has anchored its *Weltanschauung* to a rational evaluation and calculation of self-interests that stem from a domestic–external symbiosis. These 'rational' attributes are exemplified by a quote by Richard Snyder, a neo-realist.

> ... it is difficult to see how we can account for specific actions and continuities of politics without trying to discover how their operating environments are perceived by those responsible for choices, how particular situations are structured, what values and norms are applied to certain kinds of problems, what matters are selected for attention, and how their past experience conditions present responses.[34]

To India, the United States poses several parameters for reflection and deep introspection. These parameters are not categorical and attempt to contribute to 'constructing' a deeper and more valuable bilateral.

In political terms, the United States is a successful democracy, that for close to two and half centuries has inspired the rest of the world. India has been a democracy since 1947 with a brief period of 'Emergency' from 1975 to 1977. Elections after, revealed the strength of Indian democracy by voting out the government of Indira Gandhi who introduced this *'harakiri'* (ritual suicide) on Indian democracy. As a multi-party democracy, many Indians are mystified by the United States being a democracy with two major parties for more than 150 years administering the country. The Election Commission of India recognizes 8 national parties, 52 state parties and 2638 unrecognized political parties, making the country world's largest democracy.

The economic strength of the United States is what others envy and wish to emulate. India has managed to succeed in a few fields like software where Indian engineers in the United States are considered to be deeply entrenched in the miraculous transformation of the global economy. India aspires for an economic centrality in Asia where democracy and a free market are synonymous. India's recognition of being a pharmaceutical supplier recently by the United States at a time of the Coronavirus (Covid-19) pandemic was quietly appreciated in India. This appreciation had to be underplayed, since Covid-19 spread to every part of the country, forcing India to import antivirus vaccines.

Security is a central vector in the bilateral where India wants closer symmetry with the United States, not at the expense of its sovereignty. Every government in India has been proud of its sovereign status and independence which at no cost can be challenged by external or internal forces. Since the visit of Jawaharlal Nehru to the United States, there has been strong support for India and its unique multi-religious, multi-ethnic democracy succeeding in a geographical region where monarchies, feudal oligarchies, military politics and ethnic dominance had prevailed. India, to most US decision-makers is different. It is. A resistance in the United States towards India and closer relations comes from the State Department, yet to go beyond a mindset with strong Cold War fundamentals, typifying India as a closet member of the Eastern bloc with the Soviet Union as a behemoth. Times have changed and so have attitudes, leaving only a few in a realm with fewer adherents. Is China changing that?

Culture is a sphere where the two countries understand each other very well with reciprocity very strong. Traditional art forms from India, civilizational expressions such as yoga, rock and rap music from the United States, all strike a chord between the two countries especially younger generations.

Education is a very crucial aspect the two countries need to focus on. Hundreds of thousands of Indian students are studying in the United States and many of them do not want to return leading to charges of 'brain drain' with India coming out as the laggard. Education standards between the countries are different. Some Indian schools and universities are rated very highly, yet a wide gap exists internally which in educational terms are as in economics between the 'have's' and 'have not's'! Students in India wanting to study in the United States spend a lot of time and resources to prepare for Graduate Aptitude Test in Engineering (GATE) and Graduate Record Examinations (GRE). An apparent frailty is in the lack of any educational, enabling grade/percentile or educational quality similarities for aspirants to adhere and follow.

Institutional convergences between the two countries are reserved as the last parameter. Why? The institutions of foreign policy in both countries are similar in their obstinacy to acknowledge the change. For the United States, India's NAM was a smokescreen for closer relations with the Soviet Union. The NAM to the United States was a softer version of socialism as its founding personalities—Jawaharlal Nehru, Josip Broz Tito of Yugoslavia and Gamal Abdel Nasser of Egypt—were impressed by advancements made by the Soviet Union in creating state-owned and managed enterprises, comprehensively dominating economic sphere, making private capital and investments, expressions of capitalism ... something which did not endear NAM to Washington.

The Cold War is over, what remains is a mindset where India's foreign policy leads to consternation in Washington. To India, the United States is a deal maker, where the deal is decided without any consideration for the other side and its opinions. The upholding of United Nations Convention on the Law of the Sea (UNCLOS) by United States as a barometer to be abided by all nations to enable maritime freedom on the seas, is seen by several in India, as a flag of convenience for the United States to enable its navy to move without any restraint, while others face constraints imposed. The United States while insisting all nations to sign the UNCLOS has itself not done the same! That duplicity confuses India. On the parameter of multilateralism, India appears to be lagging behind with the last decade having witnessed the gradual eclipse of NAM and the stasis calling itself the SAARC, where India has allowed itself to be pushed around by a quasi-military state—Pakistan.

As the bilateral deepens itself, more parameters would reveal themselves for genuflection.

Conclusion

A wary trio indeed!

China, India and the United States are actors with heft in the international system. The heft these countries possess stems from economic strength, capabilities and the adoption of strategic policies that enhance domestic economic strength further. In this aspect, India needs to generate more gravitas by convincing the domestic political spectrum to look at foreign policy as a national strategy going beyond calculations that are only up to the next elections—state or national. When domestic politics begins to identify with issues that have domestic and international similarities, the domain of foreign policy expands to include more voices with perspectives that may differ yet conclude by enriching democracy and its associated variables and determinants.

A state makes and implements decision taken by the political executive after due deliberations with an elected and nominated assembly/parliament members. In matters pertaining to foreign policy and security interests, negotiations have a seamless strand of continued emphasis on legitimacy, territoriality, society and economy as beams of an edifice—the State. The three nations constantly reveal, reiterate and refuse any word, phrase or legalese infringing on the four beams. It is here that one is tempted to ask the question, what if the known and accepted rationales of contemporary times are yielding to new schema, not scripted by the United States and its allies, but by Beijing? This question arises, as China is at the cusp of becoming the world's largest economic power. This will be at the expense of the United States displaying a truculence by labelling everything negative happening in China. Maybe, the Cold War is over, but the mindset is preparing itself for another Cold War (a Hot War?) with China at the crosshairs of the United States.

To conclude, constructing a layered perspective on foreign policy with China, India and United States is a complex task. Similarities are there and so are dissimilarities. Opportunities present themselves for fleeting moments before erstwhile methods impose themselves hence scuttling new openings and ideas. The optimism for China, India and the United States, lies in attempting to graft the 'social' in constructivism with the 'rational.'

Notes

1. Emanuel Adler, Communitarian International Relations: The Epistemic Foundations of International Relations, (London and New York: Routledge, 2005), p. 92.
2. Steve Smith, "International theory and European integration" in Morten Kelstrup and Michael C. Williams (eds.) International Relations Theory and the Politics of European Integration – Power, Security and Community, (London and New York: Routledge, 2000) p.38.
3. See Alexander Wendt, "Anarchy is what States Make of it: The Social Construction of Power Politics," International Organization (Cambridge), Vol. 46, No. 2 (Spring, 1992), pp. 391-425.
4. Emanuel Adler, Communitarian International Relations: The Epistemic Foundations of International Relations (London and New York: Routledge, 2005), p.90.
5. KM Fierke, "Constructivism" in Tim Dunne, Milja Kurki, and Steve Smith (eds.), International Relations Theories – Discipline and Diversity, Third Edition, Oxford: OUP, 2013 pp. 187-20.
6. Alexander Wendt, "Constructing International Politics," International Security (Harvard), Vol. 20, No. 1 (Summer, 1995), p.73.
7. Alexander Wendt, ibidem p.73.
8. A sloop is a sailing boat with a single mast ahead of the main mast and a second mast behind the main mast.
9. Ta Jen Liu, A History of Sino-American Diplomatic Relations, 1840-1974, Chinese Culture Series 2-2, (Taipei: China Culture Academy, 1978. p.12.
10. Ta Jen Liu, Ibidem pp. 20-21.
11. Lucien W. Pye, Ch. 9,"China's Self-Image as Projected in World Affairs" in Gerrit W. Wong and Bih- Jaw Lin, Sino-American Relations at a Time of Change (CSIS-Washington and IIR-Taipei, 1994), p. 157.
12. Shanghai Communique, Paragraph 11, 28 February 1972.
13. See Joint Communique On The Establishment Of Diplomatic Relations Between The United States Of America And The People's Republic Of

China, January 1, 1979. Accessible at: https://www.ait.org.tw/our-relationship/policy-history/key-u-s-foreign-policy-documents-region/u-s-prc-joint-communique-1979/ (Retrieved on 20 May 2019).
14. Benn Steil, The Marshall Plan – Dawn of the Cold War (New York: Simon & Schuster, 2018), p.56.
15. Benn Steil, ibidem, p.88.
16. Benn Steil, ibidem, p.374.
17. See Mark Pratt, Ch.2, "The Future of Sino-American Policy: The Issues" in Gerrit W. Wong and Bih- Jaw Lin, Sino-American Relations at a Time of Change (CSIS-Washington and IIR-Taipei, 1994).
18. The classic texts on 'realism' and 'neo-realism by Kenneth N. Waltz, Theory of International Politics (Reading, MA: Addison-Wesley, 1979); John J. Mearsheimer, The Tragedy of Great Power Politics (New York, NY, Norton, 2001); Stephen M. Walt, The Origin of Alliances (Ithaca: Cornell University Press, 1987) are illustrations of this approach.
19. See Chih Yu-Shih, The Spirit of Chinese Foreign Policy – A Psychocultural view (New York: Palgrave Macmillan, 1990); Tang Jiaxuan, Heavy Storm and Gentle Breeze – A Memoir of China's Diplomacy, First edition (Beijing: Foreign Languages Press, 2011).
20. C. Raja Mohan, "India: Between "Strategic Autonomy" and "Geopolitical Opportunity", Asia Policy (NBAR Seattle: Washington) No.15, January 2013, pp.21-25.
21. "[a] discourse captures a particular way of talking about and understanding the world (or an aspect of the world)." Marianne Jørgensen and Louise J. Philips, Discourse Analysis as Theory and Method (London: Sage, 2002), p.1.
22. H. W. Brands, "India and Pakistan in American strategic planning, 1947–54: The commonwealth as collaborator," The Journal of Imperial and Commonwealth History, 15:1, 1986, 41-54.
23. Summary of South Asian conference, 26 Feb.-3 March 1951, box 2, McGhee papers, Truman Library. McGhee's later account of the conference can be found in his memoirs, Envoy to the Middle World (New York, 1983), 277-89 as cited in pp. H. W. Brands 41-54.
24. Amlan Datta, "Culture and War" The Economic Weekly (Bombay), April 14, 1951, p.371.
25. For content of the air defence agreement, see "Telegram from the Embassy in India to the Department of State," July 10, 1963, in Foreign Relations of the United States [FRUS]: 1961–1963 (Washington, D.C.: U.S. Government Printing Office, 2000), Vol. 19, item 307, http:// history.state.gov/historicaldocuments/frus1961-63v19/d307.
26. Andrew B. Kennedy, "India's Nuclear Odyssey – Implicit Umbrellas, Diplomatic Disappointments, and the Bomb," International Security, Volume 36, Number 2, Fall 2011, p.124.
27. Andrew B. Kennedy, Ibid. p. 128.
28. State Department Bureau of Intelligence and Research Intelligence Note, 'India to Go Nuclear?'," January 14, 1972, History and Public Policy Program

Digital Archive, National Archives, Record Group 59, "SN 70-73, Def 18-8 India. Obtained and contributed by William Burr and included in NPIHP Research Update #4. Wilson Center Digital Archive, International History Declassified.
29. Office of the United States Trade Representative, Executive Office of The President, 2 October 2020. Accessible at https://ustr.gov/countries-regions/south-central-asia/india (Retrieved on 3 December 2020).
30. See U.S. Relations With India – Bilateral Relations Fact Sheet, Bureau of South and Central Asian Affairs, U.S. Department of State (Washington), June 21, 2019.
31. Yufan Hao and Lin Su, "Influence of Societal factors: A Case of China's American Policy Making" in Yufan Hao and Lin Su (eds.) China's Foreign Policy Making: Societal Force and Chinese American Policy (Aldershot: Ashgate, 2005), p.2.
32. Daniel C. Lynch, Rising China and Asian Democratization – Socialization to "Global Culture" in the Political Transformations of Thailand, China and Taiwan (Stanford: Stanford University Press, 2006), p. 93.
33. Ramon H. Myers, Michel C. Oksenberg and David Shambaugh (eds.) Making China Policy – Lessons from the Bush and Clinton Administrations (Lanham, MD: Rowman & Littlefield, 2001), p.2.
34. Richard C. Snyder, H.W. Bruck and Burton Sapin (eds.) Foreign Policy Decision-Making: An Approach to the Study of International Politics (New York: Free Press of Glencoe, 1962), p.5.

CHAPTER 5

New Variable for India in Its Tenuous Relations with China
Taiwan

Introduction

China and India are countries with deep historical traditions and contributions to humanity before they evolved into Westphalian expressions of nation states after the vicissitudes of colonialism and its often-violent after currents. For China and India, colonialism and its manifestations came as a long interregnum to their civilizational existence sowing deep seeds into local histories and the body politic, not necessarily in their Westphalian temperament and expression.

As civilizational states, China and India have throughout history contributed to philosophy, science, music and arts. Mathematics and yoga from India, the magnetic compass guiding ships on voyages and also Taichi from China have a history and resonance, which cannot be dated or even patented! Yoga and Taichi have seamlessly fused to become expressions of civilizational attributes going beyond narrow restrictive national expressions. Belonging to all humanity, these instances are illustrations of the refined repository of both these civilizational entities. The epics and historical stories in China and India, oral narratives of history, philosophy, poetry and ballads have an interminable resonance predating their Westphalian expressions of today.

It is, perhaps, the Westphalian interpretation of a state that constricts civilizational political expressions of these two countries with their adopting and adapting to a political schema, from the occident—Communism for China and Democracy in India.

The contribution made by these two 'civilizational states' has not been comprehensively chronicled or jointly studied by the bilateral—lacunae that need redressal. It is precisely the timeless contribution made by these two 'civilizational states' that makes it imperative for them to coalesce and cooperate by enriching and expanding current interaction to include a wider panoply of interests motivating and guiding the bilateral to a direction where national interests are revolving around societal aspirations and stellar erstwhile contributions.

This chapter is to examine the deep schisms in China–India bilateral while examining the growing role of a new variable—Taiwan. Foreign policy decision-making between the two countries gets one more variable with Taiwan emerging as an archetype of how New Delhi wishes to enhance its profile in East Asia, not circumscribed by China. The Taiwan–India aspect has played an additional role when China–India relations appear to be at the brink of comprehensive rupture, exemplified by repeated skirmishes on the high Himalayas where the absence of a firm border between the two countries makes the pre-Westphalian period an improbable past.

Arguments and Methodological Approach

I have chosen four arguments to situate the chapter through prisms critical in tone finding extrapolation in text. The methodology adopted is taking a critical look into constantly shifting power loci in the region, where at an expanded prism, the United States is 'retreating' owing to domestic politics of 'localism' taking the front stage over 'globalism'. In India too, the 'domestic' has emerged as the only constant with 'external' becoming a stage where India's opinions and erstwhile positive value features are not in synchrony with changes at the international level. Still, it is the international level, where the country aspires to a bigger role not circumvented by its position in South Asia as a long-standing democracy, as civilization with a tradition for quietude and not prone to lambasting other political cultures or exporting its innate political values through the prism of power—soft or hard.

Four arguments motivating this chapter are:

Argument 1
To Beijing, India presents a frame of being hostage to the very region it is located in with little room for policy flexibility owing to domestic politics.

Argument 2
For China, economic incentives—OBOR and MSRI are eco-strategic overtures to the region to keep India strategically isolated and economically quarantined in its region acting as a brake to India's highly advertised geopolitical ambitions.

Argument 3
OBOR and MSRI stem from the powerful domestic rationale for domestic and near regional economic development as the next stage of internal economic development that will include its economically neglected western and south-western provinces that abut South Asia.

Argument 4
Increasing tensions on the line of actual control (LAC) between China and India have encouraged India to create space for deeper engagement with Taiwan, making Beijing displeased.

To situate the above, a critical tone is adopted, examining the manner in which China has expanded its influence and the gradual strategic/geopolitical reverse India faces. Staying the course of undertaking a critical academic evaluation of the topic, this chapter strives to stimulate a debate on the subject.

China and Weltanschauung

'Tianxia' is a concept adopted by episteme to typify world order/disorder through China's civilizational lens. For more than two millennia, empires in China subscribed to tenets of governing the realm by articulating rise in a peaceful manner.[1] 'Tianxia' succeeds in articulating a strategic positioning of China through a discursive methodology where the Confucius Institutes (CI) are to be seen as a civilizational expression utilized by a template where the Communist Party of China is to be seen as a continuum, in post-modern terms. As a template, 'Tianxia' has geographical, psychological and institutional meanings striving to differ from existing Westphalian expressions.[2]

As an example of 'communist modernity', the CPC subscribes to an ideology where a one-party state embodies unity and resolve. In synchrony with globalization processes, where economic decentralization was the global objective, China differed by staying the course of 'economic centralism' with CPC dominating economic agenda and state enterprises driving market processes since the late 1970s. A booming economy did influence subtle changes within the polemical expressions of the CPC. In 2004, the legitimacy of the CPC was acknowledged as not being anchored to the revolution of 1949.[3] For Yasheng Huang and Dali Yang, the Chinese state represents legitimacy by shifting contentious political issues into a 'neutral' administrative zone where professional and non-coercive institutions comprise a spectrum, ever visible in China since yore.[4] The 'Neutral' and 'non-coercive' are not to be conflated with today's China where the only prevailing methodology is what Xi Jinping, General Secretary of CPC, President of People's Republic of China (PRC) and Chairman of CMC wants.

China and India—Permanent Stasis

Before moving on to India–Taiwan relations, the *dramatis personae* China and India require some explication adding to earlier chapters. They are the world's largest countries in terms of population. They are at that historical juncture when these two civilizational states are going to emerge as the top two economies. Already the world's second-largest economy, China is striving to become the largest and reclaim its historic position as being central to trade—domestic and global. India is the world's fifth-largest economy prior to the Covid-19 pandemic. With its economic fundamentals retreating, India has a long way ahead before becoming the world's third-largest economy. Strangely, the two countries are remote from each other owing to historical reasons and political animus. Geography too has kept them apart with the Himalayas becoming a natural demarcation. It is the Himalayas that are going to determine for the two countries, civilizational connect or disconnect in the decades ahead.

Long festering boundary dispute, different political cultures, foreign policies and geopolitical rivalries are a template to a bilateral, existing more in words, than actuals. A closer relationship can only manifest itself if fractious events of the past are settled in a manner where neither side feels embittered.

It has been argued that democracies find it difficult to resolve boundary disputes, and India has miserably fallen short in settling its border disputes with its neighbours.

For India, the war of 1962 with China, circumscribes policymakers arriving at a solution and the methodology—if any adopted—has quarantined the issue to a long-drawn stalemate with periodic flare-ups on the high Himalayas. After three decades of economic reform since 1991, India's foreign policy and more importantly, the constituents of its decision-making process, display new facets that need to be cognized. As the central anchor of South Asia, India does face several existential challenges within its immediate neighbourhood in the form of unresolved security issues. The unsettled nature of security issues in South Asia has at their root a few determinants and most significant of these are boundary and water disputes amongst the three principal states of the region—India, Pakistan and Bangladesh.

To date, Indian foreign policy towards China has operated along certain cardinal principles, chiefly, the Five Principles of Peaceful Coexistence and a desire to remain an independent voice, not circumscribed by being part of any alliance, formal and informal. These principles lay an overarching framework that are primarily directed 'outwards' and neglect internal stimuli influencing foreign policymaking. A more weighty section on China–India bilateral is in the Critique section of the paper.

China and Taiwan—Ideology and Economics

'The new (CPC) party leadership will continue to promote the peaceful development of cross-strait relations and push for the peaceful unification of the two sides ... for the well-being of people on either side of the Taiwan Strait'.[5]

What unites politicians, irrespective of their adherence to proclaimed ideologies are to make statements assuaging concerns, initially. Xi Jinping, after Hu Jintao was considered to be a relatively high-level party cadre in China assuming higher levels with the CPC owing to family pedigree! His father Xi Zhongxun was considered to be part of the first generation of leaders in the party. Known for his ideological adeptness, he experimented with early economic reforms in southern China. The statement made by Xi Jinping was initially welcomed in Taiwan as representing a new continuity in the Mainland's policy towards Taiwan. It took a couple of years before, Xi Jinping, revealed his renewed attributes of political orthodoxy and placing centrality of CPC (and himself) in everything that made China what it has evolved into becoming in the last four decades. History, in political literature, plays a role in the behavioural traits exhibited by Xi Jinping.

The civil war between the KMT and CPC in the late 1930s and 1940s, revealed deep ideological departures with KMT sworn to market dynamics, while the CPC wanting to replicate the then Soviet Union, forcefully declaimed capitalism as an evil ideology. To attract hundreds of millions to their ideology, the CPC announced that land belongs to the tiller. This was attractive and successfully persuasive to many facing depredations of KMT, stubborn landlords, inflation, and large-scale economic deprivation owing to regular crop failures and civil war.

The defeat of the KMT and its 'relocation' to the island of Taiwan, echoed in the Cold War years as a potential flashpoint with civil war rhetoric maintained by both sides. In China, the CPC was dominated by Mao Zedong while Taiwan had Chiang Kai Shek. The First and Second Taiwan Straits Crises of 1954–1955 and 1958 nearly led to a wider conflagration including KMT commando raids in south China. The end of the Cold War brought in a relative easing of tensions but for the Third Taiwan Straits crisis in 1996. At a parallel level, two erstwhile determinants—political and economic/strategic—conspired to initiate change in cross-strait relations. The political determinant was the passing of the revolutionary era on both sides and their successors initiating systemic changes whose impact is still felt. The 'Open Door' policy adopted by China in 1979 brought the curtains down on the Maoist phase of China's political temperament and presented economic opportunities to Taiwanese businesses through the medium of Special Economic Zones (SEZs) that were initially set up in the coastal regions adjoining Hong Kong and Taiwan. The author of this new political script that highlighted economic growth and modernization was undoubtedly Deng Xiaoping, who had the flexibility and ultimate decision-making power to re-orient China towards a progressive direction and not a regressive and isolationist one. In Taiwan too, change was on the anvil with Chiang Kai-shek's authoritarian rule giving way to democracy, ironically introduced by his son and successor Chiang Ching-kuo, following three decades of sustained economic growth that had whetted the appetite of Taiwan's nascent civil society and entrepreneurial class in the direction of subscribing to a political system that exemplified freedom of choice, respect for liberty and justice and provided space for civil society to play an active role. In effect the martial law in force since 1949 was repealed in 1987 inaugurating a new epoch for Taiwan. These systemic shifts ensured that the economic/strategic determinant was no longer decided by the rhetoric of political ideology, but rather by the need for existential accommodation of economic interests in cross-strait relations.

It was in the mid-1970s after the demise of the two megalomaniacs, a relatively quiet phase emerged with Taiwan's economic success sought to be replicated in the SEZs following Deng Xiaoping's policy of 'Four Modernizations', a theme for economic vibrancy outlined by Zhou Enlai in the mid-1960s and early 1970s. China's quest for technological strengths, modern managerial processes, scientific technocracy within CPC and in strategic terms control of maritime domain made Taiwan an interesting difference, at odds with China and yet appealing. The Pacific ocean on which Taiwan's eastern coast is located was and is the cynosure of strategic planners, in Beijing. In the last decade, Cross-strait relations between China and Taiwan indicate worrying traits exhibiting political ideologies confronting and stepping behind from economic commingling in the last decade.

The commingling in economic terms between the two sides of Taiwan Straits was exemplified by the debates in Taiwan over the Economic Cooperation Framework Agreement (ECFA) during the KMT under Ma Ying Jeou (2008–2016). These debates—stormy and accommodative to local concerns—revealed an impressive healthy democracy, Taiwan, assiduously fulfilling its adherence to a culture where politics being loud and noisy did not retreat to a cocoon where transparency is the first casualty. As an instance in political theory, Taiwan is a case study of how totalitarianism under Chiang Kai Shek, moved to authoritarianism under his son, Chiang Ching Kuo, and democracy within five decades. Revealing a shift from ideological contestation, military competition to economic commingling, ECFA became a neutral arena where differing interpretations on both sides of Taiwan straits were filtered.

The ECFA was negotiated by Taiwan in earnest to prevent being marginalized as just one of the several economic success stories in East Asia. The aim of ECFA was to lend a semblance of order to a contested relationship between two sides of Taiwan straits. It involved making the zone an arena where the transiting of shipments was becoming more expensive owing to tensions in the Taiwan Strait more sanguine. The fear of hostilities breaking the supply chain affecting international trade was a real concern with shipping insurance and re-insurance rates rising. For Taiwan, where the economy is largely dependent on foreign trade, ECFA was the balm to soothe contested politics with ideological hues stemming from the civil war era of the 1930s and 1940s. As Paul Papayonau had opined, 'when there are differences in economic salience for two sides in a commercial relationship, what is consequential for their strategic interactions becomes determinant;.[6] For Beijing, 'domestic' rationale wanting to propel economic relations with Taiwan assumes broader and deeper trade with a 'rebellious province' as starting point when economic ideologies could match political ideologies?

For Taiwan, its previous President Ma Ying-jeou of the KMT was known for his being closer to leaders of the CPC and instrumental in pushing ECFA, leading to a quasi-acknowledgement of Taiwan as a different entity by Beijing. When he left office, after two consecutive terms, in 2016, Ma Ying-jeou had said:

> Since I took office in 2008, I have staunchly maintained the status quo of 'no unification, no independence, and no use of force', in accordance with the framework of the ROC Constitution. I have also promoted peaceful development across the Taiwan Strait based on the 1992 Consensus of 'one China, respective interpretations'. Taiwan and mainland China have signed 23 agreements to date, and ministers from each side in charge of cross-strait affairs have met on seven occasions, addressing each other by their official titles.[7]

The KMT under Ma Ying-jeou was acceptable to CPC as these were indications of a thaw between the two erstwhile civil war adversaries. With Democratic People's Party (DPP) headed by President Madame Tsai Ing-wen in power in Taiwan since 2016, Beijing has ratcheted tensions, since mainland China does not entertain ideas of transforming China into a democracy like Taiwan, as CPC could do without any erosion of its legitimacy. Cross-strait relations are hence, a feature of international politics posing insecurity to the Asia-Pacific.

India and Taiwan: The Past and Contemporary

India and Taiwan are in the process of reaching out to one another for two reasons—economic and strategic. Economic reasons are motivated by Taiwan's 'Go South' policy wanting to build deeper linkages with India. The 'Act East Policy' of India grafting a new layer over the erstwhile 'Look East policy' wants to build a relationship with Taiwan, where economics is the foundation to strategic cooperation. Taiwan sees India as a market and production base where it could locate its high-technology industries away from China. India while welcoming initiatives from Taiwan is also trying to convince Taipei to establish high-technology training schools where manpower with limited technical skills could be upgraded. Both sides realize that the 'ghost at the banquet' is China!

The current strong bandwidth between Taiwan and India comes after a couple of decades of Taipei wanting to establish economic connectivity with New Delhi. It has been the institutional short-sightedness in New Delhi preventing closer economic relations. Since India recognizes 'One China' with Taiwan being part of China, the establishment of relations with Taipei took a step forward in 1995 when the India–Taipei Association (ITA) was established as de facto embassy. When the United States after Taiwan Relations Act of 1979 maintained American Institute as a conduit for diplomacy, and United Kingdom has British Office in Taipei, India with its economic liberalization process initiated in 1991, felt relations with Taiwan are required.

Taiwan in India has the Taipei Economic and Cultural Center (TECC) based in New Delhi as a counterpart to ITA. TECC and ITA by the lax standards of foreign policymaking in New Delhi are expressions of domestic economic agendas coalescing. India's 'Act East' policy is an improved version of the erstwhile 'Look East' policy. To foreign policy practitioners in Taipei and New Delhi, 'Go South' and 'Act East' are magnets with the same polarity as both are democracies abiding by international law predicates. Taiwan is a member of the WTO as Separate Customs Territory of Taiwan, Penghu, Kinmen and Matsu (Chinese Taipei).

For several decades, India was wary of Taiwan, formerly the Republic of China (ROC), a member of the United Nations Security Council (UNSC) until October 1971 as one of the founders of the United Nations in 1945. India's wariness was owing to international opprobrium against Taipei, stemming from China's continued criticism of the ROC as being 'renegade', 'splittist' and 'illegitimate'. Defeated by China in 1962, the border conflict created a paranoia of anything to do with China and its 'expressions'. Another reason for political and institutional myopia was the 'Kashmir Princess' accident.

On 11 April 1955, the Air India aircraft 'Kashmir Princess' en route to Jakarta from Hong Kong, crashed into the South China Sea following a bomb explosion on board. The explosion was targeted at China's premier Zhou En Lai who was to go to attend Afro-Asian

Conference at Bandung. He 'missed' the flight owing to 'medical emergency'. The loss of lives and bomb explosion inside aircraft was alleged to be intricacies of KMT and CIA wanting to eliminate the Premier of China. This sorry episode for India was an illustration of Cold War targeting innocent people for ideological glory.

Over time, that episode has become a historical footnote. However, Air India does not fly to Taipei while China Airlines from Taipei has had regular flights to New Delhi. Succinctly put, Taiwan–India relations are going through a phase of establishing institutional links to deepen bilaterally. It has also increased with DPP at the helm in Taipei, wanting to develop multi-layered engagement with India. The growth in bilateral trade from millions to billions is an indicator. In 2020, bilateral trade was 4.79 billion USD, a paltry figure when compared with China–India bilateral trade. In 2018, Taiwan–India trade had crossed USD 7 billion. Fluctuating bilateral trade figures impinge on investments being made by micro-electronics companies in India, who want to shift away from China.

Taipei, with the strategic lens in place, expects India to be the shepherd at World Health Organization (WHO) where it is Chair of Executive Board. Taiwan has not been allowed to be a member of WHO owing to China's strenuous protests. The world would be a loser from not learning how this island managed to avoid the Covid-19 pandemic and had very few cases. India, to the discomfiture of China, wants to learn from Taiwan how to create and manage a comprehensive health system. To China, the pro-active initiative taken by India in the last few years to stitch a quadrilateral with Australia, Japan and United States, is a feint creating an Asian North Atlantic Treaty Organization (NATO). As democracies, to Beijing, Quadrilateral poses apprehensions of Taiwan being used as 'proxy' to control the South China Sea and give the island a different political stature 'legitimacy' derailing 'One China' policy and concept—central shibboleth of the CPC.

For commercial reasons, however, China does not object to Taiwan being a member of the WTO as 'Separate Customs Territory of Taiwan, Penghu, Kinmen and Matsu (Chinese Taipei)'.

Critical Analysis of China–India Bilateral and Taiwan

Even as this chapter is on India–Taiwan relations, the shadow of China is present overwhelmingly! Beyond, China–India relations being a cause for global concern, owing to episodic 'undefined boundary/border' exuberance from China, undeniably there are strong shades of emerging 'linkages' in India's federal polity, regarding the conduct of foreign relations with neighbours. How far these linkages dovetail with James Rosenau's 'Linkage Politics' is a moot question.[8] For Rosenau 'linkages' were the basic unit of analysis but I wish to argue that in the Indian context the basic unit—linkages—is a highly contested domain where individual and institutional actors arbitrate, negotiate and adopt postures that may be at variance with overall national interests. Clearly China–India relations display several delineations that have a gradation of sorts. Some of these 'gradations' in the conduct of foreign relations are as follows:

The first gradation is witnessed in bilateral relations with shades of the 'domestic' beginning to play an important role. India's relations with China have to factor in the postures adopted by domestic states bordering that country, especially states and union territories of Arunachal Pradesh, Sikkim, Uttarakhand, Himachal Pradesh and Ladakh. These states and union territory of Ladakh have a population largely of Tibetan ethnicity, residing in India for many centuries.

The second gradation that is to be perceived is of core issues of national security such as India's boundary policy and development of infrastructure being largely beyond the purview and influence of the provinces. The very salience of these two issues makes them an agenda to be exclusively dealt with by institutions with experience, capacity and capability flowing through several decades of over-centralized management of decision-making. Interestingly, the map in Taiwan of India is similar to that of China! The legacy of the KMT continues here.

The third gradation is that of the armed forces and their role in defending the territorial extremities and sovereignty of the country remaining a subject where the centre prevails with union territories and states bordering China having little room for expressing opinions to the contrary.

The fourth gradation exists from an overarching perspective. While India is assuming a greater profile internationally, its domestic space for influencing foreign relations with neighbours is opening up with domestic actors not hesitating to display their perceptions. From available literature on the subject, Kripa Sridharan is of the opinion that Indian states are on the ascendant regarding foreign policy advocacy owing to two trends—increasing regionalization of Indian politics with coalition governments becoming the mainstay in some states, and economic liberalization encouraging states to become more pro-active vis-a-vis their neighbouring countries.[9]

There is thus space for new variables to enter into the foreign policymaking arena in India, where ideational variables and practical necessities jostle with each other. In the words of Vipan Narang and Paul Staniland, '…there is significant space for ideational variables to play an important role in shaping the trajectory of Indian foreign-security policy'.[10]

If one were to place strict categories in dividing international relations/security concerns into traditional and non-traditional security issues, it is interesting to note that in India's case, traditional security concerns are—constitutionally speaking—the domain of the centre while non-traditional security issues give ample scope for state governments to voice their opinions. As a consequence, a perceptible gap emerges between what the central government wishes to exercise in national interest/s and what the state government interprets as harming local interests. This apart there needs to be a clear demarcation of powers that impinges upon foreign relations.

The firm resolve displayed by India in the Doklam and Galwan crises revealed a hitherto new facet of Indian FPDM. Belligerent provocation from Beijing on the LAC made Beijing paint itself as an actor with irrational behaviour not behooving a member of the P5. Domestic factors may have conditioned Beijing's crude rhetoric—a legacy of the Cultural Revolution perhaps—and bullying that impressed none save captive audience at home.

For China, Beijing's limitation is still characterizing Indian foreign policy as being Nehruvian while in reality, the Doklam episode brought to light to many in India the Maoist sloganeering (Version 2) in Chinese foreign policy! Nehru indeed left an indelible stamp on India's foreign policy, but a stamp where the 'person' prevailed over 'process' that is withering with every passing year and change in popularly elected governments in New Delhi—a prospect beyond the arrested and captive imagination of those in Zhongnanhai!

To New Delhi, China poses a trilemma! When it comes to politics, the world's largest democracy is a contrast to the world's largest socialist/communist entity. Regular electoral mandates internally organized by an independent Election Commission are the opposite of authoritarianism morphing into totalitarianism in China. In economics, China is a success at fine-tuning itself to emerge as a shop floor to the rest of the world. Emergence of technology as the determinant has witnessed a nimble footedness by China, constantly adapting and innovating. For Asia's two largest countries, bilateral trade is a chimera as the two countries do not want to evolve into becoming G2 and show the political sagacity and institutional flexibility to sidestep the past and not allow past events to be a constant template. Strategic developments have China investing in creating the OBOR and MSRI with NDB and AIIB providing financial expertise. These new institutions reveal economic and financial architecture aiming to supplant the World Bank and International Monetary Fund over time. India has been caught flat-footed here!

India's foreign policy in contrast to China is seemingly outdated. The SAARC was envisioned as a multilateral initiative bringing the region closer. There were airy explanations regarding potential free trade in the region. The members of SAARC today are more distant from one another than three decades ago. India–Pakistan bilateral disputes played the role in relegating a promise to a nightmare. The question that emerges is ... was SAARC allowed to fail?

India's conduct of foreign policy comes across as a puzzle. With a reflex mechanism of 'stalling' and 'obfuscating', the Ministry of External Affairs with its statements is akin to being an ImaginationLimited.com! This in a country known for its prowess in writing software and creating an environment for start-ups worth emulation by others. This leads to stasis as a template in foreign policy. Relations with China are stuck with a mindset yet to expunge 1962. On a larger frame, democratic exuberance internally has yet to translate itself with international resonance.

If India's foreign policy was to be seen critically as a pantomime, it is owing to the limited discourse of external affairs in the country. Election manifestos by main parties before general elections are revelatory as mention of foreign policy is usually in the last pages of election manifestos. What is mentioned in the manifestos on foreign policy reveals a verbosity with oblique adjectives flowing from an earlier era. To complicate India's foreign policy are the limited discussions in parliament on external issues. Think tanks as repositories of epistemic discourse are mostly funded by the state and headed by retired diplomats who instill 'epistemic discipline' by parroting official statements. A casualty has been the failure of creating new theoretical premises and arguments in foreign policy/international relations by scholars in India.

For a democracy to be constricted in debating opinions and threshing out ideas is worrying, restricting and self-defeating. Domestic discourse on foreign policy in India is largely a narrative without introspection or prognosis making an elite and cabalistic temperament, the only actor. Overall, what factors influence China–India bilateral are as follows:

First, the growing symmetry between Taipei and New Delhi has not been welcomed by China. Several reasons are … First, Beijing's pique on New Delhi being inflamed further by India's MEA statement on the Arbitral Award Tribunal on the South China Sea under Annexure-VII of UNCLOS.[11] India has been at the forefront in supporting the freedom of navigation and unimpeded commerce and overflight predicated upon the principles of international law. The UNCLOS remains a template where nations with disputes need to resolve the same without using threats or force that in either way will increase the inflammatory potential of disputes constricting peace and stability.[12] To Beijing, India's issuing a statement justifying the UNCLOS is akin to piggyback riding with the United States. It would earn India points with China if that same statement was to call upon all countries to sign and ratify the UNCLOS—something which the United States has not ratified and considers a 'codification of international law'. When Donald Trump was in the White House, policymaking in the United States appeared pretty spasmodic (or Twitteric!) and akin to top-level positions looking like a game of revolving chairs! The Joseph Biden years are different!

Second, are the increased levels of Chinese influence in the Indian Ocean Rim. Every year sees the visible increase of China's efforts at promoting trade with the nations of the region and also providing security escorts to vulnerable shipping in waters contested by freelance pirates. China has sent more than two dozen naval expeditions to the Indian Ocean, since 2008. China's naval base in Djibouti makes that island's space more crowded with bases established by the United States and interestingly, Japan's Maritime Self Defense force, all providing tiny Djibouti with a perch much larger than its geographical renting abilities! What prevented India from recognizing Djibouti's 'free market' in offering bases? Piracy would have been an aspect that could have motivated India to think *laissez faire* in strategic matters, articulating the need for commercial shipping towards India requiring the means to prevent any interdiction by non-state actors!

Third, China's overseas expressions of participating and creating new maritime wherewithal have come at a time when the 'One Belt, One Road' is an existential expression of an economic power extending security and trade as a new political and economic ideal pretending to be an idyll. The security outreach is possible to tackle counter-piracy without any allies, but with embedded features of projecting power in the region. It helps to understand that India has never displayed any economic outreach to the region, or military bases in the region. India lays stress on its diaspora in the region who are mostly known for being individual economic agents more than anything else and reflect internal economic travails that encourage individuals to migrate outwards rather than domestic economic growth inviting them back home. Xi Jinping's 'elevation' at least for coming decades will be configured in external form with a visible presence of China in the Indian Ocean Rim matched by a contrasting inward ingress of India in the region. Watch this space!

Significantly, China has succeeded in creating an economy that is the workshop of the world and is leagues and decades ahead of India when it comes to innovation and country-wide infrastructure that is lacking sorely in India. A contestation I make is that the growing influence of China has dwarfed India's in the region not just economically but also politically, with its democratic credentials not being espoused and articulated, beyond predictable anodyne statements before national occasions. It could be argued that strategically India is now left with a huge trust deficit and trade shortfalls in the region that need to be identified as a sphere of existential stasis in the making.

In the last few years, border transgressions and deliberate occupation of land under India's control in Sikkim and Ladakh by China have led to near conflictual situations. These gross violations of international law led India to make a common cause with the United States regarding China and its bellicose behaviour. The outcome of Washington and New Delhi coming together was the Quadrilateral with Japan and Australia joining the group. Identifying Indo-Pacific as the core region of global security, the Quadrilateral is shaping itself to become the next NATO.

This makes one wonder aloud…what is the Indo-Pacific all about? Stretching from the western shore of South Asia, especially India, to the Eastern shores of the Pacific, the domain includes maritime Asia and the Pacific. Broadening the imagination would involve taking into account the Eastern rim of Africa and the Middle East. Sadly, the idea, appealing though it is, leaves out China, constricted as it is by Taiwan (the unsinkable battleship!) and access to the oceans patrolled by norm beholder (sic.)—United States—who finds it impossible to ratify UNCLOS! For India, to succeed in its economic profile requires an agenda that supports domestic political cohesion on external affairs and economic fruition with the determinant that security in its periphery remains conducive and not shouting matches between member states.[13] Taiwan thus, as an entity with an identity in the Asia-Pacific, is an example of India wanting its 'Act East Policy' to succeed fast. Political cohesion domestically in Taiwan will evolve into a force multiplier, since China is displaying 'divide and rule' attributes, which colonial England had exemplified in an earlier era.

Critically analyzing, complexities keep evolving and China is becoming the essential and central Indo-Pacific power...not India. India has never been the locus of Indo-Pacific power. It was for long on the periphery and held forth through its engagement in the region through a prism that saw it as a different voice. The NAM was an ideological pillar of India's foreign policy in the post-World War decades. This held through the Cold War but with a cost—economic stagnation. The renewed impetus India sought in the early 1990s was accompanied by a political agenda which venerated coalitions at the helm leading to a decisional stasis. Post 2014, a strong political centralization has taken over with decisional stasis remaining since current political centralism taking place has little idea of how to express India's external thrust and how to sequester domestic political shifts from an insulated and cohesive external policy that is regime neutral. That may be the price to pay for a democracy to reinvent domestic sources of expression and legitimacy by marginalizing existing political arrangements and constructing newer political expressions stitching together social alliances with social compacts but one that keeps foreign policy in a *cul-de-sac*. Beijing is the beneficiary of this stasis from New Delhi.

India has the resources to challenge China's aims towards the region in a limited manner for sure, but not the financial wherewithal or diplomatic initiatives to chart out a role of itself in the region either alone or to think of supplanting Beijing's initiatives. In other words, it galls that a lively democracy like India has failed to articulate a vision for itself and what it believes in for the region and beyond.[14] Since the time of independence, an incongruous feature of Indian foreign policy has been its oscillating temperament and lack of long-term vision regarding relations with its neighbours. Looking back, the non-aligned movement of the past until the economic reforms in India in the early 1990s appears illusory and a self-limiting exercise. India's 'China policy' if any, also suffers from this anomaly. The defeat in 1962 to China in many ways dealt a blow to India's vaunted stature of a voluble presence in the international domain in the Nehru years—personality before process! The success of China in the realm of economics in a post-Mao setting has cast its awe on India's economic potential in comparison to what China has done and doing.

In foreign policy, it appears that India has presided over a phase where India's voice is no longer the dominant voice in South Asia. Whether India resonates elsewhere can only be, if the foreign policy has a pan-Indian view and irrespective of the political party at the helm, expressions of foreign policy need to have a pan-political prism.

Significantly, China's 'India policy' too, if any, suffers from a straitjacketing with multiple institutional interests speaking the same language and creating the impression that the principal contradiction—the unsettled boundary dispute as a leftover from history—is cause for discomfort in the bilateral. The highest expression between the two countries in the form of the Special Representatives (SR) to find the contours of an eventual settlement to boundary dispute has not reached the level of the desired momentum to identify a roadmap to settle this lingering issue to the satisfaction of both sides. I argue that should the boundary dispute between China and India be settled—highly unlikely—it is not going to ease tensions nor address permanent anomalies in the bilateral. Rather, the time lag in finding a solution has led to a situation where either side appears comfortable in not initiating a radical breakthrough to end the impasse. Recent incidents of border transgressions that whipped up a lot of emotions alternately alarm and warrant further introspection from scholars since there is no well-defined, demarcated and legally instituted boundary line between Asia's two largest countries! As an aside, I mention Paul Huth who in his *Standing Your Ground* had pointed out that two democracies of long-standing in Asia—Japan and India—are circumscribed by outstanding territorial and maritime disputes reducing their bandwidth with international appeal. In economic terms, though there is no comparison between Tokyo and New Delhi.[15]

The flaw on India's part is to implement a foreign policy that resembles at most, a standard operating procedure—as exemplified by its foreign policy servitors irrespective of the government at the helm in New Delhi! There appears to be no vision, clarity of purpose or intent in New Delhi's policy of engagement with its neighbours. The vertical and horizontal ingress, New Delhi has with its neighbours cannot be replicated by any other actor, yet, it finds itself on the defensive in its own neighbourhood. For a country that loses no opportunity to highlight its growing role in global affairs and its rightful place at the high table of most international forums, New Delhi, lacks the sophistication and flexibility to articulate what it wants. The obduracy of the foreign policy establishment in New Delhi is not about holding onto a conservative view in the face of a fast-changing strategic landscape but of administrative/institutional inertia coupled with lack of political decisiveness when needed most. Can the foreign policy of a nation like India be run on a time frame that extends only up to the next round of general elections?

Within the region, a near-constant state of tensions between India and Pakistan does not pose any problems to China. Rather, this state of 'dyadic' tension makes the weaker of the dyad—Pakistan—a reliable ally that could also display 'client' behaviour suitable to China to expand its strategic influence in the region. A major force multiplier in Sino-Pak relations is that irrespective of the political temperament in Islamabad—military or civilian—relations between the two countries are politically stable. Echoes of bilateral relations depicted as 'higher than the mountains and sweeter than sugar' are but a cacophony that masks a brutal realist strand where the weaker of the two sings hosannas to a bilateral where domestic political and economic weaknesses have clouded perspectives of reaching out to the collective neighbourhood where similarities are many with historical and cultural processes very symbiotic. Finally, should China succeed in achieving long-term strategic gains in South Asia at the expense of India, the choice with the latter will be to revisit its 'strategic autonomy' posture in favour of more comprehensive 'strategic engagement' with actors awaiting such a scenario. The Quadrilateral is the answer for now.

There is no dearth of opinion in New Delhi calling upon such a strategic choice to be made and emboldened by the electoral mandate in New Delhi that brought in after three long decades, a single-party majority for the BJP in 2014 and 2019. The choice for New Delhi is to look beyond democratic centralism morphing into democratic absolutism at home not leading the country into a strategic trap in its own neighbourhood. Or worse, the retreat by India in the region is being assisted by members of the SAARC, that as a multilateral institution it has never been able to make the region even a lesser version of ASEAN. Does the future of SAARC visualize an imprimatur from Beijing? Perhaps...!

Conclusion

Any country with entrenched political culture could be witness to several deeply embedded internal owing to resource scarcities, unplanned urbanization, air and water pollution with other issues, that Homer-Dixon stated 'probably evolve along with one of two paths: the state will either fragment or it will become more authoritarian', with democracy a superficial epiphenomenon, having little to do with such long-term processes as growing population and shrinking resource base, just as 'emerging democracies' in sub-Saharan Africa are facing with established democratic frameworks not immune.[16]

Given their unresolved disputes—boundary especially, China's role as the largest arms supplier to India's neighbours, and patrols by Chinese nuclear submarines in the Indian Ocean (which New Delhi considers its strategic backyard) come at a time when domestic political machinations have forestalled a vision to enhance bilateral and multilateral relations in the external realm. This short-sightedness is perhaps 'regime neutral' and one that is worrying, as India is understandably leveraging for advantage in those spheres of influence that overlap with China. New Delhi has reached out to Asian neighbours but also faraway countries in Beijing's increasingly expansive shadow, most notably Taiwan, Vietnam, the Philippines and Japan. In today's world, New Delhi surprisingly does not speak the language of bilateral investment and enhancing bilateral trade with other countries in an innovative manner but from a perspective of a nation that is more or clueless and left behind in terms of power, pelf and ideas.

Could China and India deepen bilateral relations? Several points to put forward issues that can bear an imprint on the engagement enriching to both countries are:

First, terrorism is an aspect the two counties need to discuss at the highest possible levels. India has been the victim of terrorism and needs China to create a strong bilateral alliance that fosters cooperation in checking and eliminating terrorism fomented and sponsored by third parties. Mumbai can be the venue for an exclusive regular session on terrorism at the highest levels since China too faces violence mediated by minorities especially in Xinjiang. India has been at the receiving end of freelance terrorism sponsored in the neighbourhood and known to China. In multilateral terms what has the SCO been created for?

Second, the boundary dispute between India and China can only be resolved if there is a domestic political consensus in India on what should an eventual settlement be like. It will require political sagacity, to achieve a boundary settlement with China, one that requires more than institutional reflexes and standard operating mechanisms to settle a dispute that has morphed into becoming a continuous sore for decision-makers in India.

Third, the Indo-Pacific is the new prism of international relations much celebrated in India as being the harbinger of the country's role in the future of Asia-Pacific international relations. Taiwan plays a significant role in the Asia-Pacific despite naysayers in Beijing and New Delhi. Increasing complementarities with another democracy require multiple vectors, not circumscribed by conventional methodologies of foreign policymaking. This as a concept requires theoretical approaches explaining the portmanteau and explanations basing the ideal as a construct.

Fourth, despite current tensions, there is a need for an annual summit between the leaders of China and India, as they represent the world's two largest populations. An annual summit will generate institutional creativity diversifying policymaking and innovation with benefit accruing to both. Restricting decision-making places obstacles that prevent the bilateral from reaching its true potential. Widening the decision-making process builds trust and expedites settlement of outstanding issues. If increasing investments by Taiwan in India are frowned upon by China, perhaps, the WTO rule book on investments should be referred to as guiding principles encouraging trade.

Political ideology in India is these days partial to seeking an identity and expression predating what we have known since 1947. When a political ideology seeks sustenance from religion the fallout is going to be deeply polarizing/divisive and marked by episodes of violence in the domestic realm and confusion at the international realm. By invoking the glorious past what is deflected is the haphazard progress of the country in providing health and education to all. A few states are doing well in every aspect one can think of but the majority are lagging behind on social and economic indicators. In the current epoch, can the two countries construct newer bilateral engagements supplementing existing institutional interface by expanding vertices complementing the bilateral to move beyond restrictions imposed by events of the recent past? This is time for making 'Go South' from Taiwan and 'Act East' from India establish themselves, ensuring that technology can become a bilateral force multiplier, not be seen as a disruptor of ideas and their application benefiting millions. Despite Taiwan being a theme for this chapter, China, finds more mention. The next chapter will explain in detail China's current success in sequestering India in South Asia by cultivating and winning over Sri Lanka in its strategic-economic endeavours in the region.

Notes

1. William A. Callahan, 'Chinese Visions of World Order: Post-hegemonic or a New Hegemony?', *International Studies Review* 10, no. 4 (December 2008): 749–750.
2. Zhao Tingyang, 'The Tianxia System: An Introduction to the Philosophy of World Institution' (天下制度 : 世界制度哲學概論 Tiānxià zhìdù: Shìjiè zhìdù zhéxué gàilùn) as cited in William A. Callahan, 'Chinese Visions of World Order', 751–753.
3. Bruce Gilley, 'Legitimacy and Institutional Change: The Case of China', *Comparative Political Studies* 41, no. 3 (March 2008): p.269.
4. Yanzhong Huang and Dali L. Yang, 'Bureaucratic capacity and state-society relations in China', *Journal of Chinese Political Science* 7, no. 1&2 (March 2002): 19–46.
5. 'China head pledges continued peaceful cross-strait relations', *The China Post* (Taipei) 26 February 2013. Available at: http://www.chinapost.com.tw/taiwan/china-taiwan-relations/2013/02/26/371350/China-head.htm (Retrieved on 12 April 2019). Also see, 'China Focus: Xi Jinping says CPC has duty to promote cross-strait ties' CCTV.com-English, 26 February 2013. Available at: http://english.cntv.cn/20130225/107125.shtml (Retrieved on 12 April 2019).
6. Steve Chan, 'Unbalanced Threat or Rising Integration? Explaining Relations across the Taiwan Strait', in *New Thinking about the Taiwan Issue – Theoretical*

Insights into Its Origins, Dynamics, and Prospects, ed. Jean-Marc F. Blanchard and Dennis V. Hickey (New York, NY: Routledge, 2012).

7. 'Eight Years of Reform Create a Better Taiwan' President's Notes, Office of the President, Republic of China, January 1, 2016. Available at: http://english.president.gov.tw/Default.aspx?tabid=1124&itemid=36480&rmid=3048
8. See James N. Rosenau, *Linkage Politics: Essays on the Convergence of National and International Systems* (New York, NY: The Free Press, 1969).
9. Kripa Sridharan, 'Federalism and Foreign Relations: The Nascent Role of the Indian States', *Asian Studies Review* 27, no. 4 (2003): 463–489.
10. Vipin Narang and Paul Staniland, 'Institutions and Worldviews in Indian Foreign Security Policy', *India Review* 11, no. 2 (2012): 78.
11. See Stefan Talmon, 'The South China Sea Arbitration and the Finality of "Final" Awards', *Journal of International Dispute Settlement* 8 (January 2017): 388–401.
12. Statement on Award of Arbitral Tribunal on South China Sea Under Annexure VII of UNCLOS, Ministry of External Affairs, New Delhi, 12 July 2016. Available at: https://www.mea.gov.in/pressreleases.htm?dtl/27019/Statement+on+Award+of+Arbitral+Tribunal+on+South+China+Sea+Under+Annexure+VII+of+UNCLOS
13. Rory Medcalf, 'Why the Indo-Pacific will keep trumping the Asia-Pacific', *Channel News Asia*, November 16, 2017, https://www.channelnewsasia.com/news/commentary/commentary-why-the-indo-pacific-will-keep-trumping-the-asia-9408586
14. A look at the electoral manifestos the major parties—the BJP and Congress in 2014—reveals the non- importance of foreign policy even as an election issue. See 'Your Voice Our Pledge', Congress-I, Election manifesto 2014, Item 21 on Foreign Policy on page 47 of the 48-page document. Also see 'Ek Bharat – Shreshta Bharat', Election manifesto of BJP 2014, 'Foreign relations – Nation first, universal brotherhood' on page 39–40 of the 42-page document.
15. Paul Huth, *Standing Your Ground: Territorial Disputes and International Conflict* (Ann Arbor, MI: University of Michigan Press, 1996)
16. Robert D. Kaplan, *The Ends of the Earth – A Journey to the Frontiers of Anarchy* (New York, NY: Vintage, 1997), 476.

CHAPTER 6

Studying Risks of India Being Marginalized Within Its Own Geographical Sphere

Introduction

For scholars of IR and security studies, South Asia is perhaps the most complex geographical and geopolitical reality after the Middle East. No other region, in contemporary security, encompasses such a multiplicity of extant issues reflecting almost every conceivable security conundrum, and worryingly, no other region remains as neglected from academic scrutiny and theoretical introspection. Nuclear non-proliferation, terrorism, civil war, nationalism, ethnic separatism, religious fundamentalism, sectarianism, shoddy governance, stunted polities, the impact of climate change, etc., all make South Asia a fertile petri-dish where new problems emerge even before existing ones entirely reveal themselves. The lack of viable security frameworks knitting the region—in structural and discursive terms—and the absence of any multilateral initiatives from the region to address common economic and security issues are glaring. The Colombo Plan[1] in its early years and later never strived to stich an economic or security framework for the region—a lacuna most glaring today.

This chapter argues that a strategic paradox exists in South Asia with India remaining the central pillar and regional superpower—owing more to geography—while China is fast making inroads into the region, sidestepping India in the process and emerge as the new fulcrum. A malaise afflicting political decision-makers in India is their exclusive focus on domestic political arrangements and accommodations without any vision regarding how the country positions itself in its foreign policy in South Asia allowing other powers to encroach and reshuffle geopolitical influence dynamics.

The vacuous attempts made by countries comprising South Asia in discussing security issues of common concern commence from perhaps the very arbitrary nature of the creation of states in this region by its former colonial overlord—Great Britain. South Asian elites identify the messy and violent creation of India and Pakistan in 1947 as a 'trigger' for many problems haunting the region today. This however is a feint. It does not excuse the venality and reflexively distrustful leaderships comprising political/military/bureaucratic elites of two specific states in the region from polarizing people and scheming newer intrigues to retain power and pelf beyond any kind of democratic accountability to their people save periodic elections celebrated as rightly legitimate but very short term in nature.

Consequently, the people of South Asia have been effectively marginalized from comprehensively participating in the global processes of change and technological development. It is a sad commentary on a region which development indices reveal to be a laggard in providing basic deliverables such as education, health, access to water, roads and electricity. After seven decades of democracy, India is now going through the processes of economic progress and lack of it revealing a divide that is geographical and is sadly beyond the scope of this chapter.

Section I
Arguments and Methodological Approach

Into this heady medley of regional insecurity, with prolonged domestic strife of various hues and constantly evolving strategic concerns comes a new external factor—China. China's entry into South Asia as a potential strategic arbiter poses the inveterate question—whether the region can accommodate another 'actor' or opportunistically engage the new 'actor' to settle existing differences within the region and relegate the hitherto centrifugal force of the region—India—to a lesser perch? Whatever will be the outcome of China's increasing stakes in South Asia, the geopolitics and geo-economics of this, at times, volatile region is undergoing visible tectonic changes, the contours of which appear hazy and worryingly, inchoate for now.

The main thrust of this chapter attempts to track a shift in the centre of gravity in South Asian geopolitics—the growing importance of China to the region accompanied by a commensurate decline of India's relative significance and import within the region. The vastness of the topic makes it imperative to situate 'locales' and explain hypotheses motivating the arguments in this chapter. I have chosen Sri Lanka where China's influence has increased comprehensively in a limited time frame and one that comes at the expense of India, becoming gradually sidelined.

A critical stance running through this chapter hinges upon links that emerge from a reading of contemporary literature. This approach attempts to synthesize the empirical and the conceptual. The inherent complexities woven into any analysis on the intricacies and incidents in the region have a multi-textured and multi-layered perspective. By making an effort, not to restrict to current discourses, rather, the chapter is to be seen as an attempt at teasing out the inconsistencies that make New Delhi's foreign policy lacking gravitas and held hostage by the democratic shifts taking place within and the erstwhile centrality of the Congress and its various expressions in power yielding to newer arrangements where the 'domestic' dominates over any other objective.

There are five (falsifiable) arguments around which this chapter revolves. They are:

Argument 1
To Beijing, it must appear that India presents the frame of being hostage to the very region it is located in, with little room to maneuver. Keeping India strategically isolated and quarantined in its own

region does act as a brake to India's highly advertised geopolitical ambitions. It is difficult, yet not impossible to partially subscribe to this line of reasoning.

Argument 2
China's visible outflanking of India in South Asia has a strong geographical element to it, analogous to two latitudinal lines, with one being continental and the other, maritime. Excluding India, countries with which China shares land borders in South Asia, have witnessed an incremental rise in China's interactions and investments. A maritime component to this is evolving with China quickly usurping India's central role *vis-a-vis* island countries like Sri Lanka, Mauritius and Maldives.

Argument 3
Beijing's imprimatur in South Asia reflects its growing interest in the region as a commercial highway and potential resource base that will benefit China's 'Go West' strategy as also Xi Jinping's 'Maritime Silk Route' initiative—its next stage of internal economic development that will include its western and south-western provinces that abut South Asia.

Argument 4
India is going through a more than welcome phase of democratic renewal and depth of a polity that subscribes to values epitomizing a culture where popular mandate legitimizes the elected and empowers the electors as being the world's largest democratic country. This phase however comes as a cropper in the country's foreign policy as high-level visits do not ensure the success or progress of long-term institutional frames that are bilateral and multilateral and without ideological levers.

Argument 5
India has surprisingly shown a trait where its relations with neighbours have reached a point of institutional stasis making the region open to inducements—economic and strategic—from Beijing, motivated by the 'OBOR' as a template for the region, not accepted by India, and playing a role as 'observer' to changes taking place where its influence is being made to retreat.

Methodology Adopted

Adopting a critical tone, this chapter examines in a detailed manner China's expanding influence in South Asia and the gradual strategic/ geopolitical reverse India faces in the region. The contemporaneous nature of the chapter theme precludes an over-emphasis on the factors leading the two countries towards a path of conflict in 1962, the haemorrhaging of which influences, informs and reiterates perceptions of each other to date. Staying the course of undertaking a critical academic evaluation of the topic, this chapter strives to stimulate a debate on the subject by subscribing to a critical discourse analysis.[2]

Some of the most prominent figures of the first generation of Critical Theorists were, Max Horkheimer (1895–1973), Theodor Adorno (1903–1969), Herbert Marcuse (1898–1979), Walter Benjamin (1892–1940), Friedrich Pollock (1894–1970), Leo Lowenthal (1900–1993), and Eric Fromm (1900–1980). Since the 1970s, the second generation has been led by Jürgen Habermas who has greatly contributed to fostering the dialogue between the so-called 'continental' and 'analytical' tradition.

The discipline of IR has always been in academic ferment with methodological approaches attempting to conjecture events, trends and shifts that consistently display a single flexible constant—flux! Into this mélange, I introduce 'consistent criticality' as an inescapable part of IR with the 'complex, dynamic and constantly changing' environment making IR a critical arena for interpretive analyses.[3] Intrinsic to the running theme of criticality is the adoption of 'frame' as a conceptual structure to facilitate the perceptions and analyses of a particular issue.

If South Asia were to be seen as a 'frame' the geographical axis and dependent variable is India. Yet, if the region were to be seen in an expanded context—geographically—the 'frame' alters to become a 'meta frame' and accommodates a newer reality in the form of China as an extraneous/control variable taking into account contemporary developments at the strategic realm. Discursive processes in South Asian security are aware of the changing dynamics of the region and are part of a process that seek to engage and identify patterns, approaches, traits and symbols that go into creating an 'institutional—constructivist meta frame'[4] to identify sets of evolving social realities and juxtapose these with the inadequacies and limitations of institutional capacities to constrain or absorb newer variables.

In other words, the 'framing effects' focus 'attention on specific dimensions (explanations) for understanding issues'[5] and connections between issues begin to influence discourse. It is here that 'norm entrepreneurs' are able to 'frame' normative ideas that resonate with audiences, with 'framing' being an intrinsic part of successful persuasion.[6] A 'frame' captures the particularities of the development at a moment amplifying the characteristics embedded within. The strategic processes of action and structural reflexes to consequent developments enhance the 'framing' of the issue providing a layered narrative—an approach that best captures the inter-linkages of security issues in South Asia.

This chapter is divided into four sections beginning with a 'framing' of the geopolitical transition taking place in South Asia, followed by an analysis of Chinese and Indian interests in Sri Lanka. Inferences made on the theme are in the conclusion.

Section II
'Framing' a Geopolitical Transition

As long as India remains more concerned with consolidating national power aspirations than developing the norms and institutions of global governance, it will remain an incomplete power, limited by its own narrow ambitions, with material grasp being longer than their normative reach. India should make a deliberate effort to learn how to shift its default foreign policy mode from the universal multilateralism of the weak of yesteryear, to norm-advancing selective coalitions of the influential as the diplomacy of the future.[7]

From Ramesh Thakur's quote above it is to be inferred that the stark reality of India's strategic engagement and postures remains the need to decide what it wants...rather than waiting for events to unfold and bypass its 'tryst with destiny'.[8] The reality is we are all participants to a process where democratic centralism has clouded over initiatives that in the past had given India a profile beyond the region. A process of looking inwards has sidelined a view outwards that in very many ways gave gravitas to Indian foreign policy until the current 'inwards' has sequestered Indian politics to a very domestic orientation where foreign policy is left rudderless.

I begin by laying out the proposition that was the China–India bilateral to be seen as a frame accommodating varying scenarios, it is palpable that in the early part of their relationship, their respective foreign policies had overt characterizations shaded with an ideological lens. Intriguingly, before reaching out to each other—as newly independent neighbouring states—the two countries initially were keener to announce their new-found independence to the wider world, especially in Southeast Asia[9] and Africa.[10]

For India, freed from the yoke of colonialism, the world order presented a challenge—existential, structural and discursive—with the presence of a Western bloc led by the United States and a military alliance exemplified by the NATO[11] and an Eastern bloc led by the Soviet Union, comprising its satellite states from Eastern Europe in an alliance called the 'Warsaw Pact'.[12] Resisting the urge to join either bloc and calculating that its priorities of domestic development necessitated not participating in either, India opted for a policy of 'non-alignment'[13] which became a pulpit from which declamations could be made about the polarized world order in the post-world war setting.[14] The illusory path chosen by India to redefine realpolitik had its adherents and camp followers for a short duration, before the reality and inchoate nature of the quasi-alliance being stitched emerged. China, on the other hand, presented a contrasting study. It was firmly a member of the 'socialist camp' and invoked the 'lean to one side'[15] policy in its initial years, before highlighting the 'Bandung spirit'[16] from 1955 onwards for a couple of years and then gravitating towards a semi-isolationist and increasingly radical and violently revolutionary stance from the late 1950s until rapprochement and a beneficial strategic accommodation with the United States in the 1970s. In comparison, to China's rocky oscillation and periodic 'shifting frames of ideology' in its foreign policy, India's adoption of the Non-Aligned Movement, as a vehicle to promote its foreign policy values, seemed to be an ideology following a linear pattern, until the early 1990s.

For Beijing, there are several perceptions of India and its role in South Asia, but a clearer picture emerges in a post-1998 setting after India (and Pakistan) tested nuclear devices. To Zou Yunhua, India's nuclear capability is to be seen as a 'prerequisite for the attainment of world-power status as well as the needed VIP ticket (sic.) for admission to the UN Security Council'.[17] From a Chinese viewpoint, India's nuclear tests were to balance China's nuclear capabilities and send Beijing a message that a repeat of 1962 would not be possible. Further, Chinese scholars do not hesitate to label India's global ambitions as being reflective of a 'superpower complex'.[18] The language of 'framing' India in strategic terms does appear to gravitate in the direction of considered skepticism bordering on condescension.

Undoubtedly, for any well-informed strategic analyst in Beijing, India looms large in South Asia dwarfing the region by its sheer geographical size, centrality in historical, political, economic, sociological and cultural terms. At the policy level, however a dichotomy appears with Beijing reflexively inclined to dismiss and even degrade India as a 'regional power'—as it does often—and spare no effort in keeping India to the margins of forums like the ASEAN Regional Forum (ARF), the East Asian Community (EAC) in Asia and other multilateral groupings bringing Asian countries together.[19] Beijing is also indifferent, for instance, to India's claims to a permanent seat on the UN Security Council (UNSC) and its behaviour at the NSG that granted a waiver to India in 2008 to import enrichment and reprocessing equipment and technology (ENR).[20] It surprised India and other countries when Beijing reacted rather churlishly by issuing a démarche when India in concert with Australia, Japan, Singapore and the United States jointly held naval exercises in the Bay of Bengal in 2007. Minus Singapore, this grouping has become the Quadrilateral, annoying China to no end. These behavioural traits by Beijing reinforce policymakers in India to conclude that China will not countenance the emergence of India as a 'rising power' in its own right ... even within its own extended geographical sphere.

Independent of China's attempts to degrade India a notch by parsing it as a regional power is the recognition that India is indeed a presence in the Indian Ocean Region (IOR). China's outreach into the IOR *is not* (italics mine) going to be a smooth affair with the Indian navy rapidly taking countermeasures to ensure that Beijing does not succeed to marginalize New Delhi in its maritime domain. Apart from its publicized aim of equipping itself with three fleets and attaining second-strike capability, the Indian navy has the flexibility to partner and cooperate with other powerful actors' navies from time to time—an option that China does not have as yet.[21]

With strategic considerations described above playing an influential role in China–India relations, the narrative shifts to detailing the case study—Sri Lanka (also to be seen as a maritime latitudinal line) to compare and contrast, China's growing influence with India's relatively lessening, or marginalized one.

Section III
Sri Lanka—A 'Rising' China and a 'Waning' India?

Sri Lanka offers a classic case in understanding the depth, intensity and long-term commitment of China towards a country in South Asia other than Pakistan. China's recent success in becoming indispensable to Sri Lanka comes with a substantial price for India—its marginalization as a strategic power in Sri Lanka's worldview and priorities. Worryingly for India, this development is regime-neutral in Sri Lanka!

The victory over the Liberation Tigers of Tamil Eelam (LTTE) in May 2009 by the Sri Lankan government was a turning point in the country's violent history of internal ethnic conflict and engagement with the outside world.[22] The 'scorched earth' policy the Sri Lankan government adopted to eliminate the LTTE without fear of any recrimination from the global community was only possible due to the diplomatic and military assistance provided by countries like China and Pakistan. As a veto cardholder at the UNSC, China was assiduously cultivated by the then Sri Lankan leadership during the final and extremely violent last phase of the ethnic conflict. India's assistance to Sri Lanka during the terminal phase of the ethnic conflict in 2009 was of a covert nature with Sri Lanka's navy benefiting from intelligence provided by India to identify, intercept and destroy boats smuggling weapons to the LTTE bases in the island's northeast.[23] India's policy on supplying arms and equipment to the Sri Lankan army was constrained by two mutually reinforcing factors—strong domestic pressure from the state of Tamil Nadu where sympathies with the plight of minority Tamils in Sri Lanka was strong; and, the global embargo on selling arms to Sri Lanka adopted by western countries owing to repeated human rights violations.

Caught between these two powerful factors, New Delhi's policy towards Colombo in the last phase of the civil war (2007–2009) was one of drift and dither. China reaped the benefits of India's policy stalemate and emerged as Sri Lanka's largest investor and second-largest trading partner in less than a decade. The Strategic Cooperative Partnership signed in May 2013 between the two countries is a pointer to a changed equation in the way the island conducts its relations with external powers. The Strategic partnership follows the 'China—Sri Lanka All-round Cooperation Partnership of Sincere Mutual Support and Ever-lasting Friendship' proclaimed in 2005.[24]

The increasing influence of China in Sri Lanka is evidenced by the bilateral trade between Sri Lanka and China in less than a decade. The figures below indicate the stagnancy in bilateral trade between Sri Lanka and India coinciding with buoyancy in trade between Sri Lanka and China, with the latter emerging as a trader, conciliator and arbitrator reflecting, strangely, the lack of policy options in New Delhi *vis-a-vis* its neighbourhood.

Table 6.1 below explains the growing role of China in Sri Lanka's bilateral trade at the expense of India.

Trade apart, the list of Chinese infrastructure investments in Sri Lanka are indeed of a scale that appear to defy logic, making New Delhi envious and incandescent. It has been estimated that from 2007 to 2011, China committed USD 2.13 billion in loans to Colombo.[25] In 2016, Sri Lanka imported raw materials from China worth USD 4.2 billion in the form of machines, electronics, transport equipment, metals and chemicals revealing their glaring shortages in Sri Lanka and

Table 6.1 Sri Lanka Trade with China and India (2011–2019)

Year	China (USD billion)	India (USD billion)
2011	2.10	4.34
2012	2.68	3.48
2013	2.96	3.12
2014	3.46	3.97
2015	3.71	4.27
2016	4.60	3.82
2017	4.35	5.28
2018	4.35	4.93
2019	4.26	4.59

Source: Compiled by the author from Embassy of Sri Lanka in the People's Republic of China, and Ministry of External Affairs, India, *Major Origins of Imports, International Trade Statistics of Sri Lanka*. Colombo: Department of Commerce Ministry of Industry and Commerce, Colombo, Sri Lanka, 2016, xv.).

the failure of SAARC to knit the region as a trading bloc. In contrast to its imports from China, Sri Lanka's exports to China were worth only USD 211 million comprising textiles, footwear, rubber, tea and vegetables, revealing the very basic nature of Sri Lanka's economy.

A fresh grant of 2 billion yuan (USD 295 million) in July 2018[26] adds a new strategic veneer to the China–Sri Lanka bilateral even as allegations swirl in Colombo regarding the financial links the previous Rajapaksa government had cultivated with Beijing.

During former Sri Lankan President Mahinda Rajapaksa's visit to Beijing in May 2013—his sixth—China is stated to have 'offered a fresh USD 2.2 billion loan for infrastructure projects, especially for the northern express highway connecting the central highlands city of Kandy with the northern town of Jaffna at the cost of USD 1.8 billion'.[27] Colombo's deepwater port is now host to an International Container Terminal, built under a 35-year build- operate-agreement and to be run by China Merchants Holdings (International) with a USD 350 million loan from the China Development Bank.[28] China is also funding the construction of a 350-meter tall multi-functional telecommunication tower and entertainment centre called *Nelum Kuluna* (Lotus Tower) on the banks of the Beira lake in Colombo. Much has also been written about the port of Hambantota (initially offered to India for development!) that has been constructed by companies China Harbour Engineering Company and Sinohydro Corporation.[29]

Astride the busy commercial shipping lanes of the Indian Ocean, China's readiness to involve itself in the Hambantota project is motivated by the much-quoted 'String of Pearls' strategy and in a practical sense ensures that it has access to vital shipping lanes, from a port in a country willing to display a 'client tendency.' The first phase of this ambitious project was completed in 2010 with a cost of USD 360 million—85 per cent of which was funded by China and the rest by the Sri Lanka Ports Authority. The second phase of the project is estimated to cost around USD 750 million, and when finally completed, will become South Asia's largest port. China Harbour Engineering Company (in a first) also constructed the Mattala Rajapaksa International Airport costing USD 200 million in Hambantota.

In a move designed to invite an Indian response, Mahinda Rajapaksa in his May 2013 visit to Beijing also initiated discussions regarding the launching of a telecommunication satellite in partnership with China's Great Wall Industry Corporation at a cost of USD 320 million. Colombo cultivating Beijing is realpolitik that has come with a price. In 2006, Sri Lanka's external debt was only USD 10.6 billion despite decades of civil strife. Post-2009, with a violent ending to the civil conflict, Sri Lanka's external debt has over the last decade come to over USD 50 billion. Of this, Sri Lanka owes more than USD 5 billion to China, a figure increasing rapidly since the last decade.[30]

The amount ploughed in by China in Sri Lanka and the very scale of the endeavour have left New Delhi floundering for an answer or response. Post-conflict Sri Lanka–India relations have visibly cooled with the two capitals talking different languages on contentious issues. If India has been playing by the rule book and asking Colombo to devolve power and grant regional autonomy to the Northern Province dominated by Tamils, Sri Lanka's response has been to garrison the region and tighten control. Ironically, New Delhi does not practice at home, what it preaches to Colombo. New Delhi and Colombo have been at a different wavelength since the UN Human Rights Council adopted a resolution (which was eventually watered down) against Sri Lanka. India had voted against Sri Lanka in 2009, 2012 and 2013 when the issue of human rights abuses and civilian casualties during the final stages of the ethnic conflict came up for discussion, while China had supported Sri Lanka. A course correction of sorts by New Delhi was in evidence when it abstained from voting against Sri Lanka in March 2014 when a US-backed resolution seeking a probe into Sri Lanka's war crimes was passed by the UN Human Rights Council. India's volte-face could also be interpreted as a reflection of its domestic politics since the Dravida Munnetra Kazhagam (DMK) a Dravidian party with strong political roots in Tamil Nadu had exited the Congress party–led UPA at the centre and New Delhi was signaling to Colombo its flexibility and not the coalition constraints it had exhibited earlier to retain an ally from the southern state of Tamil Nadu that espoused the cause of minority Tamils in Sri Lanka.

The consequence of Colombo's strategic orientation towards China has reciprocity woven into it. China's support ensures that criticism of Colombo at the UNSC and other multilateral forums will always be watered down, while in return, Colombo will strongly argue for a more robust role for China in South Asia and especially in the SAARC. The SAARC, amongst regional multilateral forums, is not known to be a qualified success, and perhaps, Colombo hopes to play off China's infectious dynamism into a SAARC dominated by India.

India's policy on Sri Lanka post-2009 has been one of 'quiet diplomacy' in troubled times! It provided humanitarian assistance to the internally displaced people (IDP) in the conflict theatre and also supplied construction materiel and agricultural implements to IDPs. India has also undertaken to support a program to reconstruct 50,000 houses in northern Sri Lanka at a cost of USD 270 million. The information collated from the 'Bilateral Brief' on relations with Sri Lanka and brought out by the Ministry of External Affairs, says that '(A)ccording to Sri Lankan Customs, bilateral trade in 2016 amounted to USD 4.38 billion. Exports from India to Sri Lanka in 2016 were USD 3.83 billion, while exports from Sri Lanka to India were USD 551 million'.[32] It does make for some grim reading that in 2011, bilateral trade between the two countries was to the tune of USD 4.86 billion.[33] The India—Sri Lanka Free Trade Agreement signed in March 2000 has been responsible for this commercial engagement between the two countries.

Unlike Chinese investments in Sri Lanka which are mostly by state entities, and have to do with infrastructure and grandiose architecture, India has cumulative investments of over USD 800 million in areas as diverse as retail petroleum, telecom, hospitality & tourism, health sector, real estate, IT and food processing. Most Indian investments in Sri Lanka are by private entities and companies like Tata, Airtel, L&T, Ashok Leyland and Taj Hotels. The notable Indian state-owned enterprise (SOE) operating from Sri Lanka is the Indian Oil Corporation (IOC), which operates partly an oil tank storage farm, interestingly called the China Bay Tank Farm.[34]

Beijing's involvement in Sri Lanka coincided with an upward swing in political authoritarianism camouflaged as being necessary for democratic expediencies and closely linked to Mahinda Rajapaksa's earlier tenure. Victory by Colombo in its long-running ethnic conflict with the Tamils represented by the erstwhile LTTE, had led to the 'manufacturing of consensus' in favour of Mahinda Rajapaksa (and his brothers and extended family!) to subvert long institutionalized procedures of moderation to one where the persona of a 'leader' looms large over a nation that was known for the durability of its democratic institutions irrespective of ethnic and religious tensions. A triumphalism of the majority over the minority has manifested itself into Sri Lankan polity with a Derridian 'auto-affection' taking over and political space overwhelmingly dominated by the echoes of the 'victorious' constantly reiterating the hard-won unity of the nation.[35]

Current President Gotabaya Rajapaksa is representative not only of political family lineage but also of a majoritarian temperament where religion and democracy are intertwined to create an identity where Sinhala interests are supreme. This expression of a political difference has support, with his party Sri Lanka Podujana Peramuna (SLPP) promoting economic development to make Sri Lanka, the Singapore of South Asia with infrastructure and deep-sea harbours to facilitate trade in the Indian Ocean. These, appeal to Xi Jinping's China, making fast inroads into Sri Lanka with economic and strategic motives. India, owing to its flailing policymaking has made decision-making on Sri Lanka a visible casualty. Advantage China.

By voting against Sri Lanka at the UN Human Rights Council and also dithering in supplying arms to Colombo during the last stages of the conflict with the LTTE in 2009, Sri Lanka's current political leadership is convinced that sidelining India makes for a good strategic decision.[36] Rewarding China which had no qualms in satisfying Colombo's military requirements at short notice also ensures that at the highest levels of the UNSC there is a patron who can dilute and stymie initiatives to censure Sri Lanka. Post-Rajapaksa, while there appears to be course correction with Maithiripala Sirisena and Ranil Wickramsinghe at the helm of political affairs in Sri Lanka, opinion poll electoral results pointed to the possible return of a Rajapaksa and the politics of espousing ('family first'!) in 2020. It is moot whether New Delhi plays a central role or not in Sri Lanka's international orientation in a post-conflict scenario. When Colombo has more powerful sponsors (financial and strategic), China is where Sri Lanka is looking at a benefactor.

What motivates Beijing's strategic interests and calculations in Sri Lanka? To quote Yan Xuetong, the éminence grise in China on strategic security:

> But mutual trust is not the answer. Perhaps the best that fierce competitors like China and America should strive for is cooperation on shared interests and an open dialogue on conflicting interests. It is not even clear what mutual trust between nations means. There are countless examples throughout history of cooperation between major powers that lacked any of this so-called mutual trust. In fact, the lack of trust has been the norm in successful international relationships.[37]

Section IV
Preliminary Findings

Since the time of independence, an incongruous feature of Indian foreign policy has been its oscillating temperament and lack of long-term vision regarding relations with its neighbours. India's 'China policy' if any, also suffers from this anomaly. Significantly, China's 'India policy' too, if any, suffers from a straitjacketing with multiple institutional interests speaking the same language and creating the impression that the principal contradiction—the unsettled boundary dispute as a leftover from history—is cause for discomfort in the bilateral. I argue that should the boundary dispute between China and India be settled—a highly unlikely event in the near term—it is not going to ease tensions nor address anomalies in the bilateral. Rather, the time lag in finding a solution has led to a situation where either side appears comfortable in not initiating a radical breakthrough to end the impasse. Recent incidents of border transgressions that whipped up a lot of emotions alternately alarm and warrant further introspection from scholars since there is no well-defined, demarcated and legally instituted boundary line between Asia's two largest countries! The 'border' thus is a matter of perception and custom on the ground with one side considering the erstwhile McMahon line as the LAC and the other disagreeing with large sections of the LAC as it is to be understood in the Eastern sector.

The western sector has its share of disagreements too with India's claim over Aksai Chin not being reflected anywhere but in its own maps ever since that region was lost in the battles of 1962 making the cartographic impasse between the two sides an intractable issue. Even as Beijing settles into an expanded role in South Asia, it needs to be apprehensive of the complexities of the region and not overstretch its recently gained influence to overtly sideline India or run roughshod over local interests in the quest for protecting its commercial gains. The political minefields of South Asia are closely linked to other interests (economic, ethnic and intricate local dynamics which need not always be in conformity to what the ruling elite think) and once the euphoric gains of a new alliance, or strategic choice, start to wilt, the pressure on Beijing from entirely unexpected quarters on inherently domestic issues in respective countries will mount. Is Beijing prepared for this? In Sri Lanka, India waded into an ethnic conflict in the late 1980s, by thrusting itself as the sole arbiter and ran into a maelstrom dictated by local conditions that witnessed erstwhile enemies collaborating to throw out an invited external actor.

The flaw on India's part is to implement a foreign policy that resembles at most a standard operating procedure (SOP)—as exemplified by its foreign policy servitors irrespective of the government at the helm in New Delhi! There appears to be no vision, clarity of purpose or intent in New Delhi's policy of engagement with its neighbours. The vertical and horizontal ingress, New Delhi has with its neighbours cannot be replicated by any other actor, yet, it finds itself on the defensive in its own neighbourhood. For a country that loses no opportunity to highlight its growing role in global affairs and its rightful place at the high table of most international forums, New Delhi, lacks the sophistication and flexibility to articulate what it wants. The obduracy of the foreign policy establishment in New Delhi is not about holding onto a conservative view in the face of a fast-changing strategic landscape but of administrative/institutional inertia coupled with lack of political decisiveness when needed most. In an era of coalitional arrangements till the elections of April–May 2014, the least New Delhi could do was to generate political maturity and consensus to agree upon certain fundamental principles that guide its foreign policy that is neutral of changing governments at the centre. Can the foreign policy of a nation be run on a time frame that extends only up to the next round of general elections! Within the region, a near-constant state of tensions between India and Pakistan does not pose any problems to China. Rather, this state of 'dyadic' tension makes the weaker of the dyad—Pakistan—a reliable ally that could also display 'client' behaviour suitable to China to expand its strategic influence in the region. A major force multiplier in Sino-Pak relations is that irrespective of the political disposition in Islamabad—military or civilian—relations between the two countries are politically stable.

Finally, should China succeed in achieving long-term strategic gains in South Asia at the expense of India, the choice with the latter will be to revisit its 'strategic autonomy' posture in favour of deeper and more comprehensive 'strategic engagement' with actors awaiting such a scenario. There is no dearth of opinion in New Delhi calling upon for such a strategic choice to be made and emboldened by the electoral mandate in New Delhi that brought in after three long decades a single-party majority for the BJP in 2014. The choice for New Delhi is to look beyond democratic centralism at home not leading the country into a strategic cul-de-sac in its own neighbourhood.

Conclusion

The image of South Asian security has for long been dominated by the dyadic rivalry between India and Pakistan. Events in the subcontinent since the nuclear tests of 1998 have evolved in such a manner that India finds more flexibility in articulating a security framework that resonates more beyond the region, while the region opens up to inducements—strategic and economic—from China.

A malaise afflicting political decision-makers in India is their exclusive focus on reordering and rearranging domestic political arrangements and accommodations without any vision regarding how the country positions itself in its neighbourhood allowing other powers to encroach and reshuffle regional power dynamics. The foreign policy of the country is the casualty. China is best positioned in influencing the region and OBOR is the beginning of this shift. New Delhi does not have the strategic heft to convince the region of its strategic centrality. What existed before was the reflection of a politics and process where New Delhi's centrality to the region did intimidate and puzzle neighbours, as also the wars and episodic tensions with Pakistan giving an exaggerated self and centrality to New Delhi. New Delhi's sway in the region has perhaps come to a halt. This has receded in the last decade and accompanies the unstoppable rise of China.

Internally, New Delhi is going through a political expression where looking inwards dominates and not an expression of identity that goes beyond. From 2014 onwards it is very visible that the political expressions of the ruling BJP cannot be compared to that of the Congress-led UPA. I argue that the BJP is in the process of consolidating itself as the dominant pole in Indian politics and foreign policy is not a sphere of expression, as yet. The distinction made by the BJP is that it claims to be a majoritarian political construct and invokes pantheons from Hinduism to strike a chord with the majority and preying on fears the majority has regarding the minority (e.g. Love Jihad!). In political discourse, the word 'secular' is missing ('sickular' to the BJP!). Does it mean the beginning of the hollowing out of the term 'secular' in the Constitution? Or, is it just the political exuberance of the day sidelining a very intrinsic part of India's political ethos since 1947? Whatever, India's political ethos has changed. The years ahead will outline the shades of expression that go beyond the middle of the road adherence to norms—political and legal.

The BJP-led NDA presents a different style of FPDM. The NDA is the political coming together of political parties swearing by the leadership of the BJP. The demise of former prime minister Atal Behari Vajpayee was mourned by the entire political spectrum as he presided over a BJP more central in political temperament (and more secular!) than the divisive and vituperative politics of today, where India stares at a future where the relative success of economic reforms has regional expressions, leading to respective strong regional parties, not in sync with the party at the centre. The fissiparous tendencies in this development are just in their incipient stages.

The erstwhile UPA was led by the Congress-I and was a coalition presided over by Dr Manmohan Singh from 2004 to 2014. The tension in FPDM in India can be ascribed to a new coalition taking over the reins of an administration where a new compact sequesters itself from learning or even imbibing nuances of foreign policy from the earlier administration. I wish to argue that the overwhelming influence of the MEA has constricted other important ministries like the Ministry of Commerce, the Ministry of Science and Technology as also the Ministry of Human Resources Development from interpreting respective views on foreign policy, where their expertise is circumvented and subverted from within. A pity indeed. Bureaucratic silos are not the way forward to function, for the world's largest proclaimed democracy.

In a democracy like India, every new administration must display the willingness to learn, debate and improve established parameters of foreign policy and its security linkages anew. To be guided by an establishment that practices foreign policy with its own in-built reflexes, displaying a lack of theoretical prisms and praxis that goes beyond electoral calculations and terms is a sure way to achieve diplomatic stasis save high-level summits and the high octane speeches. There appears to be no simulation of national foreign policy interests and objectives acting as a cushion or trial balloon attracting opinions from wider audiences. The weakness of this decision-making appears as there is a transition in political power and the emergence of a new compact—contested and not absolute, relatively elitist yet not exclusivist, fragmented and not united, statist by caveats and not decree. As a democracy, Germany is known for think tanks of important political parties who debate policies—domestic and external—with an agenda to enrich debate and decision-making.[38] Not India!

The BJP is a party that has to be seen as a post-Congress centrifugal force. The Congress in power for decades—alternated between a single expression of power and as a leader of coalitions—became the political exigencies of a family. Secularism was the hallmark of the Congress but that was because the family represented an ethos considered cosmopolitan by many. The BJP innovatively claims it is a party with a difference—it is—and not a family business—it isn't! The distinction made by the BJP is that it claims to be a majoritarian political construct and invokes pantheons from Hinduism to strike a chord with the majority and preying on fears the majority has regarding the minority. In other words, a political rewriting of history post-independence has been initiated. A liberal constitution and a worryingly illiberal society interacting with a political party stemming its identity through its waxing the language of societal conservatism is rewriting the rules of and on India's democracy…and its impact beyond.

The paucity of academic discourse on foreign policy and negligible mention of foreign policy in electoral forums esp. the election manifestos [39] are indications of a political system looking inward for democratic solace, consolidation and expression. Foreign policy cannot be a point of reference when the political system is entirely geared towards domestic issues. Before concluding this draft article, I wish to point out the failure of the SAARC in economic and security terms. There is a palpable disconnect between the people of this region when it comes to simple issues of visas and education. This draft essay only explains Sri Lanka–India relations of an extremely recent period. Each country in South Asia is going through a phase where the erstwhile centrality of India in their respective foreign policies, is retreating, and

China stepping into the space created by India displaying an awkward limitation in its FPDM.

FPDM and the stasis today is revelatory through the case study of Sri Lanka looking eastwards—Act East—in this chapter.

Notes

1. The Colombo Plan for Cooperative Economic and Social Development in Asia and the Pacific was conceived at the Commonwealth Conference on Foreign Affairs held in Colombo, Sri Lanka (formerly Ceylon) in January 1950, and was launched on 1 July 1951 as a cooperative venture for the economic and social advancement of the people of South and Southeast Asia. See, The Colombo Plan, http://www.colombo-plan.org/index.php/about-cps/history/.
2. Critical discourse analysis in the words of Jürgen Habermas describes the critical discourse theory as characterized by three types of validity claims raised by communicative acts: it is only when the conditions of truth, rightness and sincerity are raised by speech-acts that social coordination is obtained. The attraction for critical theory increases as contemporary international politics anchored in statist forms do not accurately capture diverse social forces and political challenges confronting human polity. Prime Minister Narendra Modi represents a clear departure from speech polemics to the domestic audience to a strange stasis in foreign policy not an issue to the domestic audience.
3. Steven R. Mann, 'The Reaction to Chaos', Chapter 6 in *Complexity, Global Politics, and National Security*, ed. David. S. Alberts and Thomas. J. Czerwinski (Washington, DC: National Defense University, 1997), 62.
4. Ulrich Beck, *World at Risk* (Cambridge: Polity Press, 2009), 89.
5. Alex Mintz and Steven B. Redd, 'Framing Effects in International Relations', *Synthese* 135, no. 2 (May 2003): 193.
6. Rodger A. Payne, 'Persuasion, Frames and Norm Construction', *European Journal of International Relations* 7, no.1 (March 2001): 39.
7. Ramesh Thakur, 'Beyond Commonwealth, Cricket & Curry', *The Hindu* (Chennai), 25 February 2013. Available at: http://www.thehindu.com/opinion/lead/beyond-commonwealth-cricket-curry/article4449477.ece.
8. The phrase 'tryst with destiny' has been borrowed from the title of the speech delivered by Jawaharlal Nehru on the eve of independence to the Constituent Assembly of India, close to midnight on 14 August 1947.
9. See Mohammed Ayoob, 'Southeast Asia in Indian Foreign Policy: Some Preliminary Observations', *Contemporary Southeast Asia* 9, no.1 (June 1987): 1–11.
10. 'Self-determination', 'Self-reliance' and 'Asian-African unity' were the three prongs of China's early policy towards Africa. George T. Yu, 'Sino-African Relations: A Survey'. *Asian Survey* 5, no.7 (July 1965): 322.

11. Comprising 28 members from North America and Europe (including Turkey), the NATO as an inter-governmental military alliance came into being with the signing of the North Atlantic Treaty on 4 April 1949.
12. The Warsaw Pact came into being on 14 May 1955 with seven eastern European countries forming a military alliance in response to the Federal Republic of Germany (FRG) being accepted as a member of the NATO on 23 October 1954. Following the momentous political changes in Eastern Europe in the late 1980s and the collapse of the Soviet Union in 1991 the Warsaw pact was disbanded on 25 February 1991. Several erstwhile members of the Warsaw Pact are now members of the NATO.
13. The NAM represented developing countries that were not aligned to either bloc during the Cold war years. Its intellectual origins and conception involved Jawaharlal Nehru (India), Sukarno (Indonesia), Gamal Abdel Nasser (Egypt), Josip Broz Tito (Yugoslavia) and Kwame Nkrumah (Ghana). Never established as a formal organization, the NAM is today comprised of 120 members and 17 observers, one of whom is China. See, 'History and Evolution of Non-Aligned Movement' 22 August 2012, Ministry of External Affairs, Government of India. Available at: http://www.mea.gov.in/in-focus-article.htm?20349/History+and+Evolution+of+NonAligned+Movement (accessed on 21 May 2019), and; Rajen Harshe, 'India's Non-Alignment: An attempt at Conceptual Reconstruction', *Economic & Political Weekly* (Mumbai), Vol. 25, no. 7/8, February 17-24, 1990, pp. 399–405.
14. See Vijaya Lakshmi Pandit, 'India's Foreign Policy', *Foreign Affairs* 34, no. 3 (April 1956).
15. In the *weltanschauung* of Mao Zedong, the 'lean to one side' meant that 'whoever is not with us'—the socialist communist camp—'is against us'. See June Teufel Dreyer, 'Chinese Foreign Policy' *Footnotes - Foreign Policy Research Institute Newsletter* 12, no. 5 (February 2007). Available at: http://www.fpri.org/footnotes/125.200702.dreyer.chineseforeignpolicy.html and Leo Suryadinata, 'Overseas Chinese' in *Southeast Asia and China's Foreign Policy – An Interpretative Essay*, Research Notes and Discussions Paper No. 11, 1978, Institute of Southeast Asian Studies, Singapore.
16. Echoes of the 'Bandung Spirit'—forging unity, equality and cooperation amongst developing countries—are to be seen in China's assiduous courting of Africa and Latin America in its pursuit of economic diplomacy. See, Cao Desheng, 'Bandung spirit' lives on after 50 years', *China Daily* 19 April 2005. Available at: http://www.chinadaily.com.cn/english/doc/2005-04/19/content_435352.htm (Retrieved on 23 April 2019).
17. Zou Yunhua, 'Chinese Perspectives on the South Asian Nuclear Tests', *CIAO Working Papers* (January 1999) 3.
18. Li Li, 'India's Security Concept and Its China Policy in the Post-Cold War Era', *Chinese Journal of International Politics* (Tsinghua/Oxford) 2, no. 2 (2008): 251.

19. J. Mohan Malik, 'India's response to China's rise' in *The Rise of China and International Security – America and Asia Respond*, eds. Kevin J. Cooney and Yoichiro Sato (New York, NY: Routledge, 2009), 186–187.
20. The 'clean' waiver India got in 2008 was nullified in 2011 when the NSG adopted newer guidelines that forbid cartel members of the NSG from conducting ENR with non- signatories to the Nuclear Non-proliferation Treaty (NPT). See, Siddharth Varadarajan, 'NSG ends India's "clean" waiver' *The Hindu*, 24 June 2011. Available at: http://www.thehindu.com/news/national/nsg-ends-indias-clean-waiver/article2132457.ece
21. The Indian Ocean Naval Symposium (IONS) is perhaps the best announcement of the Indian Navy's international interactions with the Indian Ocean littoral. The Indian Navy also conducts annual exercises with France, United Kingdom, United States, Russia, Brazil, South Africa, Singapore and Japan.
22. See Rohini Mohan, *The Seasons of Trouble – Life Amid the Ruins of Sri Lanka's Civil War* (Noida: Harper Collins, 2014), 353; Sharika Thiranagama, *In My Mother's House – Civil War in Sri Lanka* (New Delhi: Zubaan, 2011), 296; and Gordon Weiss, *The Cage – The Fight for Sri Lanka and the Last Days of the Tamil Tigers* (London: Vintage, 2012), 352 as part of the growing literature on the civil conflict on the island ended most violently by the Rajapaksa regime and an indicator of a new order in Sri Lanka looking beyond New Delhi.
23. 'Kill Switches and Safety Catches' *The Economist, Technology Quarterly*, 30 November December 6, 2013, 15.
24. See 'Joint Press Communique of the People's Republic of China and the Democratic Socialist Republic of Sri Lanka' 4 March 2007. Available at: http://www.mfa.gov.lk/index.php/en/divisions/internal-audit-and-o-a-m-division/314-independence-day.
25. Panini Wijesiriwardane, 'Sri Lankan president signs "strategic cooperative partnership" with China', World Socialist Website, June 11, 2013. Available at: http://www.wsws.org/en/articles/2013/06/11/sril-j11.html
26. China's Xi offers fresh USD 295 million grant to Sri Lanka, Reuters (Colombo), 22 July 2018. Available at https://www.reuters.com/article/us-sri-lanka-china-grant/chinas-xi-offers-fresh-295-million-grant-to-sri-lanka-idUSKBN1KC0D8
27. Wijesiriwardane, 'Sri Lankan President Signs'.
28. Wang Zhaokun, 'China-built port terminal opens in Sri Lanka capital', *Global Times* (Beijing), 6 August 2013. Available at http://www.globaltimes.cn/content/801743.shtml.
29. For China's economic ingress made into Sri Lanka read Saman Kelegama, 'China–Sri Lanka Economic Relations: An Overview' *China Report* 50, no. 2 (2014): 131–149.
30. Nimal Sanderatne, 'Sri Lanka's massive foreign debt generates a debt trap', The Sunday Times (Colombo) April 23, 2017. Available at: http://www.sundaytimes.lk/170423/columns/sri-lankas-massive-foreign-debt-generates-a-debt-trap-238010.html

31. Umesh Moramudali, 'Sri Lanka's debt and China's Money' The Diplomat, 16 August 2017. Available at https://thediplomat.com/2017/08/sri-lankas-debt-and-chinas-money/
32. 'India–Sri Lanka Relations, Bilateral Brief', Ministry of External Affairs (November 2017) http://www.mea.gov.in/Portal/ForeignRelation/Sri_Lanka_November_2017_NEW.pdf
33. 'India-Sri Lanka Relations', Ministry of External Affairs, Government of India (February 2013). Available at http://mea.gov.in/Portal/ForeignRelation/India_-_Sri_Lanka_Relations.pdf
34. An extract from an article by R. K. Radhakrishnan in *The Hindu* makes for interesting reading. See next page.

> The China Bay Tank farm is the largest one located between West Asia and Singapore. The tank farm connects to Trincomalee harbour, which is the fifth largest all-weather, non-tidal natural harbour in the world, with a 56-km shoreline, making this tank farm most effective for fuel receipt, storage and supply. During the Second World War, Trincomalee was an important port and played host to the biggest oil tank farm in the British Empire. When the war raged, a desperate Japan tried to strike at the oil farm in a bid to cripple the war effort. In 1942, a Japanese fighter plane with its armament intact, tried to crash-land in a bid to blow up the tank farm. But the design of each of the 99 tanks was so unique that there was no conflagration. Just the one tank that the fighter landed into was destroyed. There was no damage in any of the other 98 tanks! The tank farm, formerly operated by Ceylon Petroleum Corporation is now being maintained by the Lanka Indian Oil Corporation, a fully-owned subsidiary of IOC. Currently, only 15 of these tanks are operational.

See, 'Hidden in history' *The Hindu*, 1 January 2012. Available at http://www.thehindu.com/todays-paper/tp-features/tp-sundaymagazine/hidden-in-history/article2764986.ece (accessed on 23 June 2019)
35. Mangalika de Silva, 'Bunkers of Sovereignty and Sound: Logos, Void and the Untranslatability of Buddhist recession in Sri Lanka', *Cultural Studies* 28, no. 3 (May 2014), 487.
36. A post-script to be added is that in January 2015, Sri Lanka went to the polls to elect a new president two years ahead of schedule and reflecting the confidence of incumbent Mahinda Rajapaksa of getting re-elected. In a shock defeat, Rajapaksa's former Minister of Health, Maithripala Sirisena who had defected to the opposition, emerged as a common consensus candidate of the opposition, won the elections and became president. It is believed (italics mine) he wants to correct the 'drift' in Sri Lanka's foreign policy towards China of late at the expense of India. Evidence today suggests that Mr Sirisena will be replaced (electorally) by his predecessor—Mahinda Rajapaksa—in 2020.

37. Yan Xuetong, 'The Problem of "Mutual Trust"', *The New York Times*, November 15, 2012. Available at: http://www.nytimes.com/2012/11/16/opinion/the-problem-of-china-and-u-s-mutual-trust.html?_r=0
38. The Konrad-Adenauer Stiftung is associated with the Christian Democratic Union (CDU). Angela Merkel, Chancellor of Germany is the leader of the CDU. Frederick Ebert Stiftung is associated with the Social Democratic Party (SDP) and the Heinrich Boll Foundation is affiliated with the German Green Party, making the three important political parties in Germany possessing intellectual heft to debate and lobby issues of domestic and global import.
39. See the 'Ek Bharat, Shreshtha Bharat' – Sabka Saath, Sabka Vikaas, Election Manifesto of BJP 2014, pp. 39–40 on India's foreign policy in a 42-page document. Also see 'Your Voice, Our Pledge', Election Manifesto of the UPA led by the Congress-I, a 48-page document where foreign policy appears on page 47. A common denominator appears to be the expression and articulation of foreign policy at the end of both political election manifestos.

CHAPTER 7

Conclusion

FPDM is a fecund field for research enquiries of *problematique* in national foreign policies. Theoretical and practical rationale are foundational elements making FPDM a discipline within an overarching sphere where IR, area studies, geographies, histories, economies, societies, philosophies, cultures and politics intertwine creating a necessity for identifying causal variables and determinants.

China and India, with civilizational expressions known since history began to be recorded, are considered exemplary nations with unlimited potential for economic growth. It is this aspect needing deciphering and much contemplating that motivates the book where FPDM is consistently inconsistent! As nations with exemplary histories, China and India need to be looked at not in a quarantined Westphalian manner but as a civilizational continuum. Hu Shih, a philosopher and political aesthete, heading *Academia Sinica*, based in Taipei, had said that India had culturally dominated China for 2,000 years without sending a soldier over the high Himalayas. He was not wrong, as Buddhism had reached China through Tibet and was practised as a way of life until political tremors changed China in 1949. Hu Shih's remarks were made after the China–India war of 1962, where a defeat forced India to take stock of FPDM.

Since Independence in August 1947, India became template initiating a global process of freedom from colonial fetters which had reverberatory effects in Asia and Africa. Political attributes of being a democracy made India an example for other countries to emulate. Post-Independence, India's foreign policy encountered bloc rivalries with the United States and the Soviet Union forcefully articulating a geopolitical vision for the world adapting to a world where world wars were to be interpreted as historical anomalies, requiring correction, forever.

Two competing ideologies were not a blessing to a country like India, but a dilemma of opting for the US-led world order as exemplified by structural expressions like UN as an umbrella accommodative of all nations, irrespective of political ideologies, or, whether becoming closer to Soviet bloc that would ensure security and economic support. A way out of this dilemma was Jawaharlal Nehru with other leaders of nations stitching together an alternative called the NAM. Other leaders encouraging and creating NAM were Sukarno (Kusno Sosrodihardjo) of Indonesia, Josip Broz Tito of Yugoslavia, Gamal Abdel Nasser of Egypt and Kwame Nkrumah of Ghana.

After a period of international resonance, the NAM became a vehicle for opportunistic leaders—civilian and military—of newly independent countries. In India's case, the country's FPDM was personality-based where the political predilection of a single personality prevailed over other opinions if any! The NAM phase witnessed India getting closer to the Soviet bloc, with resistance to what was termed as 'western' influences. This FPDM, continued until, economic reforms of 1991, ushered fresh thinking, requiring valued inputs from economically successful countries who had adopted the western way of private capital in deciding commercial aspects with a limited role for the state. The collapse of the Soviet Union was owing to economic and political laggardness, which forced India to shift gears. The country did relatively well in its economy being identified as an 'economic power' with statistics attesting to moderate growth rates for close to three decades, making India move from the least developed country (LDC) categorization to Developing Country.

While India's economy has largely revealed its transformation in economic terms, where things go in another direction is FPDM! While Nehruvian decades revealed a foreign policy process where 'personality' prevailed after a brief interregnum was his daughter Indira Gandhi, who in several stints as Prime Minister personalized FPDM to unbelievable levels. Adhering to NAM, what was on display was India's 'Nehruvianism'. After her assassination in 1984, her son Rajiv Gandhi became Prime Minister after general elections where 'sympathy wave' brought 'Nehruvianism' in domestic policies and FPDM as a constant. In effect, the first four decades of India, circumscribed FPDM in India, to levels where the 'person' prevailed over cabinet opinions and wider discussions. The NAM, Commonwealth Heads of Government Meeting (CHOGM) and SAARC evolved into becoming 'talk shops' and little else.

A change that happened was in 1991, when, then Prime Minister, Narasimha Rao, practiced realism. He cognized the necessity of the country becoming an economy where 'white elephants' exemplified by hundreds of public sector units (PSUs) were to be made more competitive and private enterprise encouraged. Seeking annual loans from International Monetary Fund (IMF) and World Bank was turning out to be a regular rigmarole with outstretched hands for the economy. In foreign policy, FPDM was facing a huge problem as 'economic diplomacy' was *terra incognita* to most in the MEA. Over decades since, while India's economy has grown with statistics revealing a drop in overall poverty levels from 'absolute' to 'relative', confusion remains regarding what are national interests, and, is national security the architecture where domestic economy and its 'relative' success are frowned upon by others, especially neighbours to the west and north?

Extrapolating China's FPDM in early chapters, where the dense interlinkages of various CPC bureau's/departments/committees, an undercurrent being woven was, what about India? To India, regarding FPDM, the inescapable realities, are as follows:

1. India's process of economic reforms since 1991 has transformed its political culture at the centre with coalition governments/arrangements becoming the mainstay. In Beijing, 'Open Door' policy of China, over four decades has comprehensively transformed its FPDM.

2. Coalition governments in India, at the centre are dependent on powerful regional political parties for 'term continuity' and hence have to acquiesce their partners on domestic policy issues. FPDM comes as a restricted sphere where the only voice is that of the centre.
3. Regional parties are enlarging their political brief by engaging the centre on policy issues that involve relations with neighbours. As a democracy, Parliament has to be a forum where FPDM is discussed and opinions sought on issues escaping the attention of centre.
4. Regional parties make full use of every opportunity they have to embarrass the centre on contentious issues involving neighbouring countries. FPDM has to accommodate regional opinions, if meritorious, and reveal in the policy adopted.

Every state in India which has a territorial border with Bangladesh, Myanmar, Pakistan and China, has no voice in articulating or expressing views as foreign policy is an exclusively central domain.[1] Will the MEA cognize the salience of states, especially those bordering Bangladesh and Myanmar, to establish commercial relations which are not going to be a security risk, when proper procedures are in place? The central government's dominance in deciding the course as regards foreign policy with neighbours giving short shrift to domestic concerns expressed by states like West Bengal is an aspect not to be ignored. For provincial-level leaders, being part of an agreement that may affect local interests and 'rent-seeking' lobbies, could reflect in a negative outcome at the next round of an electoral mandate and hence a 'political risk' which is considered as 'security challenge' by inchoate policymakers at the centre. In the maritime realm, India's policy towards Sri Lanka will always be critically scrutinized by the southern Indian state of Tamil Nadu, since a linguo-ethnic aspect is involved. China's growing influence in Sri Lanka is an instance of the centre in New Delhi not in consonance with a state apprehensive of Chinese fishing trawlers in the Palk Straits, not distinguishing between the Bay of Bengal and the Arabian Sea waves swells coinciding with fishing catch being made. Livelihoods are at stake here. The province of Punjab in northern India would have an opinion on conducting relations with Pakistan since many important religious places for the Sikh community are in Pakistan owing to the arbitrariness of the Partition in 1947. FPDM in India is perhaps in limbo owing to an assumed 'exclusivity' that values 'generalists' over 'specialists'.

The China–India FPDM has several spectral aspects. First, the economic growth of the two countries has been commendable, more in the case of China, while India has performed well and the best is yet to come. In 2017 bilateral trade was more than USD 84 billion, with India's trade deficit being over USD 50 billion. In 2019, bilateral trade was USD 92.9 billion with India's trade deficit being more than USD 56 billion. Despite events leading to Doklam, bilateral trade has not decreased and India needs to welcome Chinese investment as it creates jobs and infuses technology in sectors where China's core competencies are known. Will our MEA accept this and separate commerce from security? When cross-strait relations between China and Taiwan have the trade of USD 91.9 billion in 2019 despite security issues and mutual non-recognition, what ails FPDM in India?

Second, beyond 'security' are there spheres where the two countries could coordinate? Education is an important sphere where civil society has to take an active interest. A mutual vector of convergence emerges if universities in both countries were to acknowledge and recognize each other's higher education degrees and coordinate by offering joint courses and exchange of credits plus offering student fellowships. This is a sphere where only respective ministries of education need to evolve a methodology not infringed upon by other competing bureaucratic interests. Education is where China and India can build a bridge that will consecrate a much-needed dynamism with the potential to break through the shibboleths of the past. India's expertise in medical technologies and software are two instances where the bilateral will be enriched with newer stakeholders defining the Asia-Pacific through societal connectivity. This aspect will not fructify owing to 'security' concerns.

Third, as explained in a chapter, climate change is an issue of urgent importance as the economies of both countries could face prolonged economic downturn if global warming induces 'climate shock' hobbling stock markets and influencing events with strong domestic overtones leading to job losses and economic capacity rendered idle. Climate change is an issue where the two countries need to implement technologies without significant carbon imprint and beneficial to respective domestic economies. A high-level bilateral Climate Change Commission represented by technologists and professionals from trade and industry focusing on alternative energies needs to be established where successful programmes in either country are studied and expertise lent on a bilateral basis. Such an initiative will lead to a common negotiating position at the UNFCCC where the two countries face hostility from an organized plethora of interests masquerading largely as civil society interests. This will also inspire other countries in the Asia-Pacific to learn from the two exemplars. When the two countries could coordinate positions at UNFCCC, does this reflect possibilities of cooperation in contentious aspects bedeviling bilateral?

Fourth, the continuity of domestic reform and structural changes along with compliance to existing principles will determine China's FPDM in the coming years.

The analyses and policy options made by think tanks in China for consideration by the leadership owe their origin to the 'academic vacuum' in governance that existed for close to two decades after the Cultural Revolution.

Fifth, terrorism is an aspect China and India need to discuss and collaborate institutionally, at the highest possible levels. The SCO could have become the first multilateral forum defining 'terrorism' and creating cooperative security structures sharing information. A particular member of SCO may have reservations on information sharing and has to be labelled as being 'obstructionist' to a shared commitment to check and eliminate terrorism. India has been the victim of terrorism and needs China to create a strong bilateral alliance that fosters cooperation in checking and eliminating terrorism fomented and sponsored by third parties. Mumbai can be the venue for an exclusive regular session on terrorism at the highest levels since China too faces violence mediated by minorities especially in Xinjiang. India has been at the receiving end of freelance terrorism sponsored in the neighbourhood and known to China. The SCO, owing to its

China-centric template, could be considered as having joined the exclusive club of talking shops like the few mentioned earlier!

Fifth, the boundary dispute between India and China can only be resolved if there is a domestic political consensus in India on what should the eventual settlement be like. It will require political sagacity, to achieve a boundary settlement with China, one that requires more than institutional reflexes and standard operating mechanisms on both sides—delay, prevaricate, obfuscate, complicate—the settling of a dispute that has morphed into becoming a continuous sore for decision-makers in India. For starters, as the world's largest democracy, could the Lt. Gen. Henderson Brooks—Brig. Premindra Singh Bhagat Report on the 1962 war be made accessible to researchers and scholars working on China–India relations? After six decades, if this report is officially classified as top secret, it could be construed as truth being buried for embedded revelations of official chaos and bureaucratic turf battles while a war was on! FPDM is the casualty here.

Finally, there is a need for an annual summit between the leaders of both the countries despite intermittent tensions, as they represent the world's two largest populations. An annual summit will generate institutional creativity diversifying policymaking and innovation with benefit accruing to both. Restricting decision-making places obstacles that prevent the bilateral from reaching its true potential. Widening the decision-making process builds trust and expedites the settlement of outstanding issues. Professionalism in matters relating to FPDM could be more accommodating of epistemic communities working in China, with perspectives based on research, lest academic thoughts, theories and guidance be like in China—only official okay!

In sum, regarding FPDM in India, the centre holds the upper hand while conducting foreign policy but with political arrangements being coalitional, there is greater leeway for regional parties to express their opinions and dissent on external relations especially with neighbours. An aspect of importance relating to Bangladesh–India relations is that while the conduct of foreign affairs has been dealt with by the Union List of the Seventh Schedule of the Indian Constitution aspects related to water (supplies, irrigation, canals, drainage, embankments and storage) are the domain of the province. Giving more space to states and allowing articulation, assuages concerns about an uncaring centre and attracts more flak with MEA being a magnet for its ossified processes of FPDM without wanting to adapt structurally and institutionally.

This is the time when FPDM requires more inputs from various domestic actors in both countries. Are they game, or is the game over?

Note

1. A reading of Articles 51 and 253 of the Indian Constitution make it clear that the Union (Centre) holds wide powers in arriving at the conclusion of international treaties and obligations. See P. M. Bakshi, *The Constitution of India* (New Delhi: Universal Book Traders, 2000).

Bibliography

Books

Adler, Emanuel. *Communitarian International Relations: The Epistemic Foundations of International Relations*. London and New York: Routledge, 2005.
Alberts, David. S., and Thomas J. Czerwinski, eds. *Complexity, Global Politics, and National Security*. Washington, DC: National Defense University, 1997.
Allison, Graham. *Essence of Decision: Explaining the Cuban Missile Crisis*. Boston: Little Brown, 1971.
Armstrong, J.D. *Revolutionary Diplomacy: Chinese Foreign Policy and the United Front Doctrine*. Berkeley: University of California Press, 1977.
Bakshi, P. M. *The Constitution of India*. New Delhi: Universal Book Traders, 2000.
Bardhan, Pranab. *Awakening Giants, Feet of Clay—Assessing the Economic Rise of China and India*. Princeton: Princeton University Press, 2010.
Barnett, Doak A. *The Making of Foreign Policy in China: Structure and Process*. Boulder: Westview Press, 1985.
Baumgartner, R., and Bryan D Jones. *Agenda's and Instability in American Politics*. Chicago: University of Chicago Press, 1993.
Beck, Ulrich. *World at Risk*. Cambridge: Polity Press, 2009.
Blanchard, Jean-Marc F., and Dennis V. Hickey, eds. *New Thinking about the Taiwan Issue – Theoretical Insights into Its Origins, Dynamics, and Prospects*. New York, NY: Routledge, 2012.
Bobrow, Davis B., Steve Chan, and John A Kringen. *Understanding Foreign Policy Decisions: The Chinese Case*. New York: Macmillan – The Free Press, 1979.
Bueno de Mesquita, Bruce and David Lalman. *War and Reason: Domestic and International Imperatives*. New Haven: Yale University Press, 1992.
Buzan, Barry, Ole Waever, and Jaap de Wilde. *Security – A New Framework for Analysis*. Boulder: Lynne Rienner, 1998.
Carlsnaes, Walter. *Ideology and Foreign Policy: Problems of Comparative Conceptualisation*. New York: Basil Blackwell, 1987.
Carlson, Allen. *Unifying China, Integrating with the World – Securing Chinese Sovereignty in the Reform Era*. Stanford: Stanford University Press, 2005.
Cashman, Greg, and Leonard C. Robinson. *An Introduction to the Causes of War – Patterns of Inter-State Conflict from World War I to Iraq*. Lanham: Rowman & Littlefield, 2007.
Chang, Parris H. *Power and Policy in China*. University Park: The Pennsylvania State University Press, 1975.

Chasek, Pamela S., David L. Downie, and Janet Welsh Brown. *Global Environmental Politics*, 5th ed. Boulder: Westview Press, 2010.
Chen, Gang. *Politics of China's Environmental Protection: Problems and Progress*. Singapore: World Scientific, 2009.
Chen, King C., ed. *China and The Three Worlds: A Foreign Policy Reader*. While Plains: M.E. Sharpe, 1979.
CiHai. Shanghai: Shanghai Dictionary Publishing House, 1979.
Cooney, Kevin J., and Yoichiro Sato, eds. *The Rise of China and International Security – America and Asia Respond*. New York: Routledge, 2009.
Dalvi, John P. *Himalayan Blunder*. Delhi: Pocket Books, 1969.
Xiaoping, Deng. *Selected Works of Deng Xiaoping (1975-1982)*.Beijing: Foreign Languages Press, 1984.
Deng, Yong, and Fei-ling Wang, eds. *China Rising: Power and Motivation in Chinese Foreign Policy*. Lanham: Rowman and Littlefield, 2005.
Deutsch, Karl. *The Nerves of Government: Models of Political Communication and Control*. New York: The Free Press of Glencoe, 1963.
Ding, Xueliang. *The Decline of Communism in China's Legitimacy Crisis, 1977-1989*. New York: Cambridge University Press, 1994.
Dittmer, Lowell, ed. *South Asia's Nuclear Security Dilemma – India, Pakistan, and China*. New York: M.E. Sharpe, 2005.
Dittmer, Lowell, and Guoli Liu, eds. *China's Deep Reform – Domestic Politics in Transition*. Lanham: Rowman & Littlefield, 2006.
Ellison, Graham T. *Essence of Decision*. Boston: Little Brown and Company, 1971.
Esherick, Joseph, Paul G. Pickowicz, and Andrew G. Walder, eds. *The Chinese Cultural Revolution as History*. Stanford: Stanford University Press, 2006.
Evans, Peter B., Harold K. Jacobson, and Robert D. Putnam, eds. *International Bargaining and Domestic Politics – Double Edged Diplomacy*. Berkeley: University of California Press, 1993.
Fairbank, J. K., ed. *The Chinese World Order*. Cambridge, MA: Harvard University Press, 1968.
Farrell, R. Barry, ed. *Approaches to Comparative and International Politics*. Evanston: Northwestern University Press, 1966.
Fewsmith, Joseph. *Dilemmas of Reform in China: Political Conflict and Economic Debate*. NY: M.E. Sharpe, 1994.
———. *China Since Tiananmen – The Politics of Transition*. New York: Cambridge University Press, 2001.
Finkelstein, David M., and Maryanne Kivlehan, eds. *China's Leadership in the 21st Century: The Rise of the Fourth Generation*. Armonk: M. E. Sharpe, 2003.
Fitzgerald, C. P. *The Chinese View of Their Place in the World*. London: Oxford University Press & Faber and Faber, 1964 & 1967.
Gao, Shanquan, and Fulin Chi. *Theory and Reality of Transition to a Market Economy*. Beijing: Foreign Languages Press, 1995.
Garver, John. *China's Decision for Rapprochement with the United States*. Boulder: Westview Press, 1982.

Geva, Nehemia, and Alex Minz, eds. *Decisionmaking on War and Peace: The Cognitive Rational Debate*s. Boulder: Lynne Reiner, 1997.
Gill, Stephen. *American Hegemony and the Trilateral Commission*. Cambridge: Cambridge University Press, 1995.
Gittings, John. *The World and China, 1922-1972*. New York: Harper and Row, 1974.
Goldman, Merle. *China's Intellectuals: Advise and Dissent*. Cambridge: Harvard University Press, 1981.
Goldman, Merle, and Roderick MacFarquhar, eds. *The Paradox of China's Post-Mao Reforms*. Cambridge: Harvard University Press, 1999.
Goldman, Merle, Timothy Cheek, and Carol Lee Hamrin, eds. *China's Intellectuals and the State: In Search of a New Relationship*. London: Harvard University Press, 1987.
Goldstein, Judith, and Keohane, Robert, eds. *Ideas and Foreign Policy: Beliefs, Institutions and Political Change*. Ithaca: Cornell University Press, 1993.
Grubb, Michael, Christiaan Vrolijk, and Duncan Brack. *The Kyoto Protocol – A Guide and Assessment*. London: Royal Institute of International Affairs, 1999.
Guo, Sujian, and Shiping Hua, eds. *New Dimensions of Chinese Foreign Policy*. Lanham: Lexington Books, 2007.
Gurtov, Mel, and Byong-moo Hwang. *China Under Threat: The Politics of Strategy and Diplomacy*. Baltimore: John Hopkins University Press, 1980.
Hao, Zhidong. *Chinese Intellectuals at a Crossroads: The Changing Politics of the Chinese Knowledge Workers*. Albany: State University of New York Press, 2003.
Harding, Harry, ed. *China's Foreign Relations in1980s*. New Haven: Yale University Press, 1984.
Harris, Paul G., ed. *Confronting Environmental Change in East and Southeast Asia: Eco-Politics, Foreign Policy, and Sustainable Development*. London and Stirling: Earthscan, 2005.
Hasan, Zoya. *Quest for Power: Oppositional movements and Post-Congress Politics in Uttar Pradesh*. New Delhi: Oxford University Press, 1998.
Hinton, Harold C. *China's Turbulent Quest*. Bloomington: Indiana University Press, 1972.
———. *The People's Republic of China 1979-1984: A Documentary Survey*. Wilmington: Scholarly Resources Inc, 1986.
Ho, Ping-Ti, and Tang Tsou, eds. *China in Crisis, Vol. 1*. Chicago: Chicago University Press, 1968.
Holsti, K. J. *Why Nations Realign: Foreign Policy Restructuring in the Post war World*. London: George Allen & Unwin Ltd, 1982.
Hua, Shiping. *Scientism and Humanism – Two Cultures in Post-Mao China (1978-1989)*. Albany: State University of New York, 1995.
Huang Shuofeng. *On Comprehensive National Power*. Beijing: Chinese Academy of Social Science Press, 1992.
Huth, Paul. *Standing Your Ground*. Ann Arbor: University of Michigan Press, 1996.

Ip, Hung-yok. *Intellectuals in Revolutionary China, 1921-1949 – Leaders, Heroes and Sophisticates*. Abingdon: Routledge, 2005.

Jacobson, Harold K., and Michael Oksenberg. *China's Participation in the IMF, the World Bank and GATT – Towards a Global Economic Order*. Chicago: University of Michigan Press, 1990.

Johnston, Alastair Iain. *Cultural Realism: Strategic Culture and Grand Strategy in Chinese History*. Princeton: Princeton University Press, 1995.

Jørgensen, Marianne, and Louise J. Philips. *Discourse Analysis as Theory and Method*. London: Sage Publication, 2002.

Kameyama Yasuko, Agus P. Sari, Moekti H. Soejachmoen, Norichika Kanie, eds. *Climate Change in Asia: Perspectives on the Future Climate Regime*. Tokyo: United Nations University Press, 2008.

Kaplan, Robert D. *The Ends of the Earth – A Journey to the Frontiers of Anarchy*. New York: Vintage, 1997.

Kasa, Sjur, Anne T. Gullberg, and Gorild Heggelund. 'The Group of 77 in the International Climate Negotiation: Recent Developments and Future Directions', *International Environmental Agreements* 8, no. 2 (2008): 113–27.

Keck, Margaret, and Kathryn Sikkink. *Activists Beyond Borders: Advocacy Networks in International Politics*. Ithaca: Cornell University Press, 1998.

Kelstrup, Morten, and Michael C. Williams, eds. *International Relations Theory and the Politics of European Integration – Power, Security and Community*. London and New York: Routledge, 2000.

Keohane, Robert, and Helen Milner, eds. *Internationalization and Domestic Politics*. New York: Cambridge University Press, 1996.

Kim, Samuel S. *China and the World: New Directions in Chinese Foreign Relations*, 2nd ed. Boulder: Westview Press, 1989.

———. (ed.) *China and the World: Chinese Foreign Relations in the Post-Cold War Era*. Boulder: Westview Press, 1994.

———. *China and the World*. New York: Routledge, 1998.

Kingdon, John W. *Agenda's Alternatives and Public Policies*, 2nd ed. New York: Harper Collins, 1995.

Krasner, Stephen, ed. *International Regimes*. Ithaca: Cornell University Press, 1983.

Lamb, Alastair. *The China-India Border: The Origins of the Disputed Boundaries*. London: Oxford University Press, 1964a.

———. *The McMahon Line: A Study in the Relations between India, China and Tibet, 1904-1914*. London: Routledge & Kegan Paul, 1964b.

Lampton, David M. *Policy Implementation in Post-Mao China*. Berkeley and Los Angeles: University of California Press, 1987.

———. *The Making of Chinese Foreign and Security Policy in the Era of Reform, 1978-2000*. Stanford: Stanford University Press, 2001.

Lane, Jan-Erik. *Comparative Politics – The Principal-Agent Perspective*. Abingdon: Routledge, 2008.

Liao, Xuanli. *Chinese Foreign Policy Think Tanks and China's Policy Towards Japan*. Hong Kong: The Chinese University Press, 2006.

Lieberthal, Kenneth and Michel Oksenberg. *Policy Making in China: Leaders, Structures and Processes*. Princeton, NJ: Princeton University Press, 1988.
Lieberthal, Kenneth, and David M. Lampton, eds. *Bureaucracy, Politics and Decision-Making in Post-Mao China*. Berkeley: University of California Press, 1996.
Linnerooth–Bayer, Joanne, Ragnar E. Lofstedt, and Gunnar Sjostedt, eds. *Transboundary Risk Management*. London: Earthscan Publications, 2001.
Litfin, Karen T. *The Greening of Sovereignty in World Politics*. Cambridge, MA: MIT Press, 1998.
Liu, Ta Jen. *A History of Sino-American Diplomatic Relations, 1840-1974*, Chinese Culture Series 2-2. Taipei: China Culture Academy, 1978.
Lu, Ning. *The Dynamics of Foreign Policy Decisionmaking in China*. Boulder: Westview Press, 1997.
Lu, Yi, Guanfu Gu, Yu Zhenglian, and Fu Yaozu, eds. *Xin Shiqi Zhongguo Guoji Guanxi Lilun Yanjiu (Research on International Relations Theories in China's New Era)*. Beijing: Shishi Chubanshe, 1999.
Lynch, Daniel C. *After the Propaganda State – Media, Politics, and "Thought Work" in Reformed China*. Stanford: Stanford University Press, 1999.
———. *Political Transformations of Thailand, China and Taiwan*. Stanford: Stanford University Press, 2006.
MacFarquhar, Roderick. *Origins of the Cultural Revolution – Vol.1*. New York: Columbia University Press, 1974.
MacFarquhar, Roderick, and Michel Schoenhals. *Mao's Last Revolution*. Cambridge and London: The Belknap Press of Harvard University Press, 2006.
Macridis, Ray C., ed. *Foreign Policy in World Politics*. Englewood Cliffs: Prentice Hall, 1985.
Mancall, Mark. *China at the Centre: 300 Years of Foreign Policy*. New York: Free Press, 1984.
Mao Zedong. *Four Essays on Philosophy*. Beijing: Foreign Languages Press, 1966.
Mearsheimer, John J. *The Tragedy of Great Power Politics*. New York: Norton, 2001.
Mehra, Parshotam. *The North-eastern Frontier: A Documentary Study of the Internecine Rivalry between India, Tibet, and China*. Delhi: Oxford University Press, 1979.
———. *Negotiating with the Chinese, 1846-1987: Problems and Perspectives*. New Delhi: Reliance Publishing House, 1989.
———. *An 'Agreed' Frontier: Ladakh and India's Northernmost Borders, 1846-1947*. Delhi: Oxford University Press, 1992.
———. *Essays in Frontier History: India, China, and the Disputed Border*. Delhi; Oxford: Oxford University Press, 2007.
Milner, Helen. V. *Interests, Institutions, and Information: Domestic Politics and International Relations*. Princeton: Princeton University Press, 1997.
Ming, Ruan. *Hu Yaobang on the Turning Point of History*. Hong Kong: Global Publishing, 1991.

Mintzer, Irving M., and J. Amber Leonard, eds. *Negotiating Climate Change – The Inside Story of the Rio Convention.* Cambridge: Cambridge University Press, 1994.
Mitchell, Ronald B., William C. Clark, David W. Cash, and Nancy M. Dickson, eds. *Global Environmental Assessments: Information and Influence.* Cambridge: MIT Press, 2006.
Mohan, Rohini. *The Seasons of Trouble – Life Amid the Ruins of Sri Lanka's Civil War.* Noida: Harper Collins, 2014.
Mok, Ka-ho. *Intellectuals and the State in Post-Mao China.* London: Macmillan, 1998.
Moody, Peter. *Opposition and Dissent in Contemporary China.* Stanford: Hoover Institute, 1977.
Moore, Barrington. *Soviet Politics– The Dilemma of Power, the Role of Ideas in Social Change.* Cambridge: Harvard University Press, 1950.
Myers, Ramon H., Michel C. Oksenberg, and David Shambaugh, eds. *Making China Policy – Lessons from the Bush and Clinton Administrations.* Lanham: Rowman & Littlefield, 2001.
Nye, Joseph S. *Soft Power – the Means to Success in World Politics.* New York: Public Affairs, 2004.
O'Leary, Greg. *The Shaping of Chinese Foreign Policy.* Berkeley: University of California Press, 1970.
O'Neill, Kate. *The Environment and International Relations.* Cambridge, UK and New York: Cambridge University Press, 2009.
Patterson, George N. *Peking versus Delhi.* New York: Praeger, 1964.
Perkovich, George. *India's Nuclear Bomb - The Impact on Global Proliferation.* Berkeley: University of California Press, 1999.
Pollack, Jonathan D. *The Sino-Soviet Rivalry and Chinese Security Debate.* Santa Monica: Rand Corporation, 1982.
Pye, Lucian W. *The Dynamics of Chinese Politics.* Cambridge: Oelgeschlager, Gunn & Hain, 1981.
Rhee, San-Woo, ed. *China's Reform Politics.* Seoul: Sogang University Press, 1986.
Robinson, T. W., and D. Shambaugh, eds. *Chinese Foreign Policy: Theory and Practice.* New York: Oxford University Press, 1993.
Rosenau, James N. *Linkage Politics: Essays on the Convergence of National and International Systems.* New York: The Free Press, 1969.
Rosenau, James N., ed. *International Politics and Foreign Policy.* New York: The Free Press, 1969.
Rossabi, Morris. *China Among Equals: The Middle Kingdom and its Neighbours.* Berkeley: University of California Press, 1983.
Rowland, John. *A History of Sino-Indian Relations: Hostile Coexistence.* Princeton: D. Van Nostrand Company Inc, 1967.
Rudolph, Susanne Hoeber, and Lloyd I Rudolph. *Explaining Indian Democracy: A Fifty Year Perspective, 1956-2006 The Realm of Ideas – Enquiry and Theory, Vol. I.* New Delhi: Oxford University Press, 2008.

Schattschneider, E. E. *The Semi-Sovereign People*. New York: Holt, Rinehart & Winston, 1960.

Schurmann, Franz. *Ideology and Organisation in Communist China*. Berkeley: University of California Press, 1966.

Schwab, George, ed. *Ideology and Foreign Policy*. New York: Cycro Press, 1978.

Schwartz, Benjamin I. *Communism and China: Ideology in Flux*. Cambridge: Harvard University Press, 1968.

Seliger, Martin. *Ideology and Politics*. New York: The Free Press, 1976.

Sen, Amartya. *The Argumentative Indian – Writings on Indian History, Culture and Identity*. New York: Farrar, Strauss & Giroux, 2005.

Shafritz, Jay M., Karen S. Layne, and Christopher P. Borick, eds. *Classics of Public Policy*. New York: Pearson/Longman, 2005.

Shambaugh, David, ed. *Deng Xiaoping: Portrait of a Chinese statesman*. Oxford: Clarendon Press, 1995.

Shih, Chih Yu. *The Spirit of Chinese Foreign Policy – A Psychocultural View*. New York: Palgrave Macmillan, 1990.

———. *China's Just World: The Morality of Chinese Foreign Policy*. Boulder: Lynne Rienner, 1992.

———. *China's Just World – The Morality of Chinese Foreign Policy*. Boulder: Lynne Reiner, 1993a.

———. *China's Just World – The Morality of Chinese Foreign Policy*. Boulder, CO: Lynne Reiner, 1993b.

Sjostedt, Gunnar, ed. *International Environmental Negotiation*. Newbury Park: Sage Publication, 1993.

Smil, Vaclav. *China's Environmental Crisis: An Inquiry into the Limits of National Development*. New York: M.E. Sharpe, 1993.

Snyder, Richard C., H.W. Bruck, and Sapin Burton, eds. *Foreign Policy Decision-Making: An Approach to the Study of International Politics*. New York: Free Press of Glencoe, 1962, 1963.

Steil, Benn. *The Marshall Plan – Dawn of the Cold War*. New York: Simon & Schuster, 2018.

Stine, Deborah D. *International Environmental Decision Making*. Ann Arbor: University of Michigan, 1994.

Suisheng, Zhao, ed. *Debating Political Reform in China – Rule of Law vs. Democratization*. New York: M.E. Sharpe, 2006.

Sujian, Guo, and Shiping Hua, eds. *New Dimensions of Chinese Foreign Policy*. Lanham: Lexington Books, 2007.

Tang, Jiaxuan. *Heavy Storm and Gentle Breeze – A Memoir of China's Diplomacy*, 1st ed. Beijing: Foreign Languages Press, 2011.

Thiranagama, Sharika. *In My Mother's House – Civil War in Sri Lanka*. New Delhi: Zubaan, 2011.

Tideman, Nicolaus. *Collective Decisions and Voting – The Potential for Public Choice*. Aldershot: Ashgate, 2006.

Dunne, Tim, Milja Kurki, and Steve Smith, eds. *International Relations Theories – Discipline and Diversity, 3rd ed.* Oxford: Oxford University Press, 2013.

Twitchett, D. C., Fairbank, J. K., and Feuerwerker, A. *The Cambridge History of China*, Vol. 10–15. New York: Cambridge University Press, 1978.
Viotti, Paul R., and Mark V Kauppi. *International Relations and World Politics – Security, Economy, Identity*, 3rd ed. New Jersey: Pearson Education, 2007.
Vogler, John, and Mark F. Imber, eds. *The Environment and International Relations.* London: Routledge, 1996.
Walt, Stephen M. *The Origin of Alliances.* Ithaca: Cornell University Press, 1987.
Waltz, Kenneth N. *Theory of International Politics.* Reading: Addison-Wesley, 1979.
Wang, Chaohua, ed. *One China, Many Paths.* London: Verso, 2003.
Wang, Dong. *China's Unequal Treaties – Narrating National History.* Lanham: Lexington, 2005.
Wang, Yizhou. *Xifang Guoji Zhengxixue: Lishi Yu Lilun* (The Discipline of International Politics in the West: History and Theory). Shanghai: Shanghai Renmin Chubanshe, 1998.
Wasserstrom, Jeffrey N., and Elizabeth J. Perry, eds. *Popular Protest and Political Culture in Modern China*, 2nd ed. Boulder: Westview Press, 1994.
Weiss, Gordon. *The Cage – The Fight for Sri Lanka and the Last Days of the Tamil Tigers.* London: Vintage, 2012.
Whiting, Allen S. *China Crosses the Yalu: The Decision to Enter the Korean War.* Stanford: Stanford University Press, 1960.
———. *The Chinese Calculus of Deterrence.* Ann Arbor: University of Michigan Press, 1975.
———. *Chinese Domestic Politics and Foreign Policy in the 1970s.* University of Michigan, Ann Arbor, 1979.
Womack, Brantly, ed. *Contemporary Chinese Politics in Historical Perspective.* Cambridge: Cambridge University Press, 1991.
———. *China's Rise in the Historical Perspective.* London, Boulder, New York, Toronto and Plymouth, UK: Rowman & Littlefield, 2010.
Wong, Gerrit W., and Bih- Jaw Lin. *Sino-American Relations at a Time of Change.* CSIS-Washington and IIR-Taipei, 1994.
Xiaoping, Deng. *Fundamental Issues in Present-Day China.* Oxford: Pergamon Press, 1987.
Yahuda, Michael. *China's Role in World Affairs.* New York: St. Martin's Press, 1978.
———. *Towards the End of Isolationism: China's Foreign Policy After Mao.* London: Macmillan, 1983.
———. *China in and Out of the Changing World Order.* Occasional Paper, No. 21, Princeton: Princeton University Center of International Studies, World Order Studies Program, 1991.
Yan Jiaqi. *Towards a Democratic China.* Honolulu: University of Hawaii Press, 1992.
Yergin, Daniel. *The Quest: Energy, Security, and the Remaking of the Modern World.* New York: Penguin, 2011.
Young, Whan Kihl, and Laurence E. Grinter, eds. *Asian Pacific Security: Emerging Challenges and Responses.* Boulder: Lynne Rienner Publishers, 1986.

Yu, Hongyuan. *Global Warming and China's Environmental Diplomacy*. New York: Nova Science Publishers, 2008.
Yufan, Hao, and Su Lin, eds. *China's Foreign Policy Making: Societal Force and Chinese American Policy*. Aldershot: Ashgate, 2005.
Zhang, Xudong, ed. *Whither China? Intellectual Politics in Contemporary China*. Durham: Duke University Press, 2001.
Zhao, Suisheng, ed. *Chinese Foreign Policy – Pragmatism and Strategic Behaviour*. Armonk: M.E. Sharpe, 2004.
Zhi, Zhongyun, ed. *Guoji Zhengzhi Lilun Tansuo Lai Zhongguo* (Explorations of Theories of International Politics in China). Shanghai: Shanghai Renmin Chubanshe, 1998.

Articles

Ayoob, Mohammed. 'Southeast Asia in Indian Foreign Policy: Some Preliminary Observations'. *Contemporary Southeast Asia* 9, no. 1 (1987): 1–11.
Bates, Gill, and Mulvenon James. 'Chinese Military-Related Think Tanks and Research Institutions'. *The China Quarterly* 171 (2002): 617–24.
Bawa, Kamaljit S., Lian Pin Koh, Tien Ming Lee, Jianguo Liu, P. S. Ramakrishnan, Douglas W. Yu, and Ya-ping Zhang. 'China, India and the Environment'. *Science* 327 (2010): 1457–1459.
Beyer, Stephanie. 'Environmental law and Policy in the People's Republic of China'. *Chinese Journal of International Law* 5, no. 1 (2006): 185–211.
Blakie, Piers M., and Joshua S.S. Muldavin. 'Upstream, Downstream, China, India: The Politics of Environment in the Himalayan Region'. *Annals of the Association of American Geographers* 94, no. 3 (2004): 520–48.
Brands, H. W. 'India and Pakistan in American strategic planning, 1947–54: The Commonwealth as Collaborator'. *The Journal of Imperial and Commonwealth History* 15, no. 1 (1986.): 41–54.
Bureau of South and Central Asian Affairs, U.S. Department of State. U.S. Relations With India – Bilateral Relations Fact Sheet. Washington, Bureau of South and Central Asian Affairs, U.S. Department of State 2019.
Buzan, Barry, and Ole Waever. 'Macrosecuritisation and Security Constellations: Reconsidering Scale in Securitisation Theory'. *Review of International Studies* 35, no. 2 (2009): 171–201.
Byng, J. Crammer. 'The Chinese View of Their Place in the World: A Historical Perspective'. *The China Quarterly* 53 (1973): 67–79.
Cai, Shouqiu, and Mark Voigts. 'The Development of China's Environmental Diplomacy'. *Pacific Rim Law & Policy Journal* 3 (1993): 17–42.
Callahan, William A. 'Chinese Visions of World Order: Post-hegemonic or a New Hegemony?' *International Studies Review* 10, no. 4 (2008): 749–61.
Cheek, Timothy. 'Xu Jilin and the Thought Work of China's Public Intellectuals'. *The China Quarterly* 186 (2006): 401–20.

Das, Narnarayan. 'A Fresh Look at China's Hundred Flowers Period'. *China Report* 12, no. 5–6 (1976): 45–53.

de Silva, Mangalika. 'Bunkers of Sovereignty and Sound: Logos, Void and the Untranslatability of Buddhist recession in Sri Lanka'. *Cultural Studies* 28, no. 3 (2014): 463–93.

Dittmer, Lowell and Yu-Shan Wu. 'The Modernization of Factionalism in Chinese Politics'. *World Politics* 47 (1995): 467–94.

Gu, Edward X. 'Cultural Intellectuals and the Politics of the Cultural Public Space in Communist China (1979-1989): A Case Study of Three Intellectual Groups'. *The Journal of Asian Studies* 58, no. 2 (1999): 389–431.

'Ek Bharat – Shreshta Bharat', Election manifesto of BJP 2014, 'Foreign Relations – Nation First, Universal Brotherhood', 39–40.

Fairbank, J. K. 'Chinese Foreign Policy in Historical Perspective'. *Foreign Affairs* 47, no. 3 (1969): 449–63.

Feuerwerker, Albert. 'Chinese History and the Foreign Relations of Contemporary China'. *The Annals*, 402 (1972): 1–14.

Garrisson, Jean. 'Constructing the "National Interest" in U.S.-China Policy Making: How Foreign Policy Decision Groups Define and Signal Policy Choices'. *Foreign Policy Analysis* 3, no. 2 (2007): 105–126.

Gautam, P. K. 'Sino-Indian Water Issues'. *Strategic Analysis* 32, no. 6 (2008): 969–74.

———. 'Climate Change and Environmental Degradation in Tibet: Implications for Environmental Security in South Asia'. *Strategic Analysis* 34, no. 5 (2010): 744–755.

George, Alexander. 'The Operational Code: A Neglected Approach to the Study of Political leaders and Decision- Making'. *International Studies Quarterly* 13, no. 2 (1969): 190–222.

Gilley, Bruce. Legitimacy and Institutional Change: The Case of China, *Comparative Political Studies*. 41, no. 3 (2008): 259–284.

Goldman, Merle. 'Politically–Engaged Intellectuals in the Deng-Jiang Era: A Changing Relationship with the party-State'. *The China Quarterly* 145 (1996): 35–53.

Guang, Lei. 'From National Identity to National Security: China's Changing Responses Toward India in 1962 and 1998'. *The Pacific Review* 17, no. 3 (2004): 399–422.

Haas, Peter M. 'Introduction: Epistemic Communities and International Policy Coordination'. *International Organization* 46 (1992): 1–35.

Hamilton, Malcolm B. 'The Elements of the Concept of Ideology'. *Political Studies* 35, no. 1 (1987): 18–38.

Harris, Paul G. 'Peace, Security and Global Climate Change: The Vital Role of China'. *Global Change, Peace & Security: Formerly Pacifica Review: Peace, Security & Global Change* 23, no. 2 (2011): 141–145.

Harshe, Rajen. 'India's Non-Alignment: An Attempt at Conceptual Reconstruction'. *Economic and Political Weekly* 25, no.7/8 (1990): 399–405.

He, Lichao. 'China's Climate-Change Policy From Kyoto to Copenhagen: Domestic Needs and International Aspirations'. *Asian Perspective* 34, no. 3 (2010): 5–33.
He, Qinglian. 'China's Changing of the Guard: A Volcanic Stability'. *Journal of Democracy* 14, no. 1 (2003): 66–72.
Houghton, David Patrick. 'Reinvigorating the Study of Foreign Policy Decision Making: Toward a Constructivist Approach'. *Foreign Policy Analysis* 3, no. 1 (2007): 24–45.
Hu, Yaobang. 1982. 'Report to the Twelfth CCP National Congress – Create a New Situation in All Fields of Socialist Modernisation'. *Xinhua* (1982): K11–12.
Huang, Yanzhong and Dali L. Yang. 'Bureaucratic capacity and state-society relations in China'. *Journal of Chinese Political Science* 7, no. 1&2 (2002): 19–46.
Huang, Yusong and Min Huang. 'Qianxi Yindu yingdui qihou bianhua de zhengce'. (India's Policy to Address Climate Change). *Nanya yanjiu* (South Asian Studies) 1 (2010): 68–69.
Indian National Congress. 'Your Voice Our Pledge' (Election manifesto 2014, Item 21 on foreign policy). New Delhi: Indian National Congress, 2014, 47.
Information Office of the State Council, PRC. White Paper on China's Policies and Actions for Addressing Climate Change. Beijing: Information Office of the State Council, PRC, 2011.
Intergovernmental Panel on Climate Change (IPCC). *Fourth Assessment Report: Climate Change 2007*. Geneva: Intergovernmental Panel on Climate Change, 2007.
Kaarbo, Juliet. 'A Foreign Policy Analysis Perspective on the Domestic Politics Turn in IR Theory'. *International Studies Review* 17, no. 2 (2015): 189–216.
Kelegama, Saman. 'China-Sri Lanka Economic Relations: An Overview'. *China Report* 50, no. 2 (2014): 131–149.
Kennedy, Andrew B. 'India's Nuclear Odyssey – Implicit Umbrellas, Diplomatic Disappointments, and the Bomb'. *International Security* 36, no. 2 (2011): 120–153.
Kong, Fanwei. 'Qianxi zhongguo qihou waijiao de zhengce yu xingdong' (The Policies and Actions of China's Climate Diplomacy). *Xin shi ye*. (*Expanding Horizons*) 4 (2008).
Kraska, James. 'Sharing Water, Preventing War—Hydrodiplomacy in South Asia'. *Diplomacy & Statecraft*. 20, no. 3 (2009): 515–530.
Lai, Hongyi. 'External Policymaking under Hu Jintao – Multiple Players and Emerging Leadership in China'. *Issues and Studies*. 41, no. 3 (2005): 209–244.
Lan, Jiansyue. 'Shueizihyuan anchuan hezuo yu jhong yin guansi de hudong'. (The Cooperation on Water Resource Security and The Interaction of Sino-Indian Relations)'. *Guoji wunti yanjiou* (*International Studies*) 6 (2009): 37–43.
Lewis, Joanna I. 'China's Strategic Priorities in International Climate Change Negotiations'. *The Washington Quarterly* 31, no. 1 (2009): 155–174.
Li, He. 'Emergence of the Chinese Middle Class and Its Implications'. *Asian Affairs–An American Review* 33, no. 2 (2006): 67–83.

Li, Li. 'India's Security Concept and Its China Policy in the Post-Cold War Era'. *Chinese Journal of International Politics* 2, no.2 (2008): 230–62.

Li, Xiangyun, 'Cong yindu shuizhengce kan zhong yin bianjiexian zhong de shui wenti (Analysis on the Water Issues Along the Sino-Indian Border: From the Perspective of India's Water Policy)' *Shuili fazhan yanjiu (Water Resources Development Research)* 10, no. 3 (2010): 68–70.

Lin, Biao. 'Long Live the Victory of People's War'. *Peking Review* 8, no. 36 (1965): 26–29.

Lo, Ming-Cheng M. and Eileen M. Otis. 'Guangxi Civility: Processes, Potentials, and Contingencies'. *Politics & Society* 31, no. 1 (2003): 131–162.

Lynch, Daniel C. 'Envisioning China's Political Future: Elite Responses to Democracy as a Global Consultative Norm'. *International Studies Quarterly* 51, no. 3 (2007): 701–722.

Mancall, Mark. 'The Persistence Of Tradition in Chinese Foreign Policy'. *Annals of the American Academy of Political and Social Sciences* 349 (1963): 14–26.

Mccaffrey, Stephen C. 'The Harmon Doctrine One Hundred Years Later: Buried, Not Praised'. *Natural Resources Journal* 36, no. 3(2) (1996).

Mertha, Andrew C. and William R. Lowry. 'Unbuilt Dams – Seminal Events and Policy Change in China, Australia, and the United States'. *Comparative Politics* 39, no. 1 (2006): 1–20.

Miller, Alice. 'The CCP Central Committee's Leading Small Groups'. *China Leadership Monitor* 26 (2008): 1–26.

Mintz, Alex and Steven B. Redd. 'Framing Effects in International Relations'. *Synthese* 135, no. 2 (2003): 192–213.

Mohan, C. Raja. 'India: Between "Strategic Autonomy" and "Geopolitical Opportunity"'. *Asia Policy* 15 (2013): 21–5.

Narang, Vipin and Paul Staniland. 'Institutions and Worldviews in Indian Foreign Security Policy'. *India Review* 11, no. 2: 76–94.

Nathan, Andrew. 'A Factionalism Model for CCP Politics'. *China Quarterly* 53 (1973): 34–66.

Nelson, Daniel N. 'Charisma, Control, and Coercion: The Dilemma of Communist Leadership'. *Comparative Politics* 17, no. 1 (1984): 1–15.

New York Times. 'India's letter to Clinton on the Nuclear testing'. 13 May 1998: A12.

Nuechterlein, Donald E. 'The Concept of National Interest: A Time for New Approaches'. *Orbis* 23 (1979): 171–2.

Oksenberg, Michel. 'China's Political System: Challenges of the Twenty-First Century'. *China Journal* 45 (2001): 21–35.

Pandit, Vijaya Lakshmi. 'India's Foreign Policy'. *Foreign Affairs* 34, no. 3 (1956): 432–440.

Payne, Rodger A. 'Persuasion, Frames and Norm Construction'. *European Journal of International Relations* 7, no.1 (2001): 37–61.

Permanent Mission of the People's Republic of China to the United Nations Office at Geneva and Other International Organizations in Switzerland.

Implementation of the Bali Roadmap – China's Position on the Copenhagen Climate Change Conference, 2009.

Pollack, Jonathan D. 'Chinese Military Power: What Vexes the United States and Why?'. *Orbis* 51, no. 4 (2007): 635–650.

Putnam, Robert D. 'Diplomacy and Domestic Politics: The Logic of Two-Level Games'. *International Organization* 42 (1988): 427–460.

Pye, Lucien. 'On Chinese Pragmatism'. *The China Quarterly* 106 (1986): 207–234.

Rose, Nikolas and Peter Miller. 'Political Power Beyond the State: Problematics of Government'. *British Journal of Sociology* 43, no. 2 (1992): 173–205.

Rosenau, James. *'Toward the Study of National – International Linkages in Linkage Politics: Essays on the Convergence of National-International Systems* (1969): 44–66.

Rubin, Alfred P. 'The Sino-Indian Border Disputes'. *The International and Comparative Law Quarterly* 9 (1960): 96–125.

Ruggie, John Gerrard. 'Territoriality and Beyond: Problematizing Modernity in International Relations'. *International Organization.* 47, no. 1 (1993): 139–174.

Shambaugh, David. 'China's International Relations Think Tanks: Evolving Structure and Process'. *The China Quarterly* 171 (2002): 575–596.

Phillips, Steven and Keefer, Edward. 'Foreign Relations of the United States, 1969–1976'. *Office of The Historian* Vol VIII, Documents on China, 1969–1972 (Washington: Government Printing Office, 2006): 376–379.

Shelton, Samuel T. 'Jury Decision Making: Using Group Theory to Improve Deliberation'. *Politics & Society* 34, no. 4 (2006): 706–725.

Sims, Holly 'The Unsheltering Sky: China, India and the Montreal Protocol'. *Policy Studies Journal* 24, no. 2 (1996): 201–214.

Singh, Manmohan. Speech at the Plenary of Head of States/Governments, 15th Conference of Parties (COP), Copenhagen, 18 December 2009, *India Review* 6, no. 1, (1 January 2010), Embassy of India, Washington.

Slaughter, Anne-Marie. 'The Real New World Order'. *Foreign Affairs* 76, no. 5 (1997): 183–197.

Sleeboom-Faulkner, Margaret. 'Regulating Intellectual Life in China: The Case of the Chinese Academy of Social Sciences'. *The China Quarterly* 189 (2007): 83–99.

Sohn, Injoo. 'Learning to Cooperate: China's Multilateral Approach to Asian Financial Cooperation'. *The China Quarterly* 194 (2008): 309–26.

Sprinz, Detlef and Tapani Vaahtoranta. 'The Interest – Based Explanation of International Environmental Policy'. *International Organisation* 48, no. 1 (1994): 77–105.

Sridharan, Kripa. 'Federalism and Foreign relations: The Nascent Role of the Indian States'. *Asian Studies Review* 27, no. 4 (2003): 463–89.

Stahnke, Arthur A. 'The Place of International Law in Chinese Strategy and Tactics: The Case of the Sino-Indian Boundary Dispute'. *The Journal of Asian Studies* 30, no. 1 (1970): 95–119.

State Department Bureau of Intelligence and Research Intelligence Note, 'India to Go Nuclear?', 14 January 1972, History and Public Policy Program Digital Archive, National Archives, Record Group 59, 'SN 70-73, Def 18-8 India. Obtained and contributed by William Burr and included in NPIHP Research Update #4. Wilson Center Digital Archive, International History Declassified.

Strong, Maurice F. 'One Year after Stockholm: An Ecological Approach to Management'. *Foreign Affairs* 51 (1973): 690–707.

Sukumar, Ganapati and Liguang Liu. 'The Clean Development Mechanism in China and India: A Comparative Institutional Analysis'. *Public Administration and Development* 28, no.5 (2008): 351–362.

Suryadinata, Leo. 'Overseas Chinese' in *Southeast Asia and China's Foreign Policy – An Interpretative Essay*, Research Notes and Discussions, Paper No.11. Institute of Southeast Asian Studies, Singapore, 1978: 45.

Talmon, Stefan. 'The South China Sea Arbitration and the Finality of "Final" Awards'. *Journal of International Dispute Settlement* 8 (2017): 388–401.

Tang, Tsou. 'Prolegomenon to the Study of Informal Groups in Chinese Communist Party Politics'. The China Quarterly. 65 (1976): 98–114.

Tanner, Murray Scott. 'Changing Windows on a Changing China: The Evolving "Think Tank". System and the Case of the Public Security Sector'. *The China Quarterly* 171 (2002): 559–574.

Teng, Hsiao-ping. 'Speech at Special Session of the UN General Assembly'. *Peking Review* 16 (1974).

United Nations. United Nations Framework Convention on Climate Change (UNFCCC), Article 1, *Full Text of Convention*. New York: United Nations, 1992.

Walsh, Sean, Huifang Tang, John Whalley, and Manmohan Agarwal. 'China and India's participation in global climate negotiations'. *International Environment Agreements: Politics, Law and Economics* 7, no.1 (2007). (E- Journal without pagination)

Wang, Bin. 'Shilun zhong yin huanjing hezuo wenti (The Issues on Sino-Indian Environmental Cooperation)'. *Shangqiu shifan xuebao (Journal of Shangqiu Teachers College*, Henan: Shangqui) 24, no. 4 (2008): 65–66.

Wang, Hongying. 'Multilateralism in Chinese Foreign Policy: The Limits of Socialization'. *Asian Survey* 40, no. 3 (2000): 475–491.

Wang, Shaoguang. 'Changing Models of China's Policy Agenda Setting'. *Modern China* 34, no. 1 (2008): 56–87.

Weigelin-Schwiedrzik, Susanne. 'In Search of a Master narrative for 20th Century Chinese History'. *The China Quarterly*, 188 (2006): 1070–1091.

Wen, Jiabao. *Working Together for New Glories of the Oriental Civilization.* Special Address delivered to the Indian Council of World Affairs (ICWA), 2010.

Wendt, Alexander. 'Anarchy is what States Make of it: The Social Construction of Power Politics'. International Organization 46, no. 2 (1992).

Whiting, Allen S. 'The Use of Force in Foreign Policy by the People's Republic of China'. *Annals of The American Academy of Political and Social Sciences* 402 (1972): 55–66.

Xiaoguang, Kang, and Han Heng. 'Graduated Controls: The State-Society Relationship in Contemporary China'. *Modern China.* 34, no. 1 (2008): 36–55.

Yohei, Harashima. 'Environmental Governance in Selected Asian Developing Countries'. *International Review for Environmental Strategies* 1, no. 1 (2000): 193–207.

Yong, Deng. 'The Chinese Conception of National Interests in International Relations'. *China Quarterly* 154 (1998): 308–329.

Yongjin, Zhang. 'Review: International Relations Theory in China Today: The State of the Field'. *The China Journal* 47 (2002): 101–108.

Yu Hai. 'Global Environment Change and China's International Environmental Cooperation'. *International Review* 2, (2008): 16–30.

Yu, Bin, 'Containment by Stealth: Chinese Views of and Policies toward America's Alliances with Japan and Korea after the Cold War'. Institutional Paper, Asia Pacific Research Center, 1999.

Yu, George T. 'Sino-African Relations: A Survey'. *Asian Survey* 5, no. 7 (1965): 321–332.

Zhao, Quanshang. 'Achieving Maximum Advantage, Rigidity and Flexibility in Chinese Foreign Policy'. *American Asian Review* (1995): 61-93.

Zhao, Ziyang. 'Report on the Work of the Government'. *Beijing Review* (1983): 26–27.

Zhu, Xufeng. 'China's National Leading Group to Address Climate Change: Mechanism and Structure'. *East Asia Institute.* Background Brief No. 572, 2010.

Zou, Yunhua. Chinese Perspectives on the South Asian Nuclear Tests. *CIAO Working Papers,* 1999.

Websites

American Institute in Taiwan. Joint Communique on the Establishment of Diplomatic Relations between the United States of America and the People's Republic of China. Taipei: American Institute in Taiwan, 1979. Available at https://www.ait.org.tw/our-relationship/policy-history/key-u-s-foreign-policy-documents- region/u-s-prc-joint- communique-1979/ (accessed on 26 August 2021).

Becker, Markus. 'Climate Negotiations in Durban – Usual Suspects Continue to Block Emissions Deal'. *Spiegel Online International*, 2011. Available at http://www.spiegel.de/international/world/climate-negotiations-in-durban-usual-suspects-continue-to-block- emissions-deal-a-802828.html (accessed on 26 August 2021).

Cameron, Fraser, Stanley Crossick, Axel Berkofsky, and Cathryn Clüver, 'EU-China Think Tank Roundtable', *EPC Issue Paper No.21*, 6–7 December

2004, The Hague (Clingendael). Available at http://www.epc.eu/TEWN/pdf/606913435_EPC%20Issue%20Paper%2021%20EU-China%20Roundtable.pdf (accessed on 16 June 2018).)

CCTV. 'China Focus: Xi Jinping Says CPC Has Duty to Promote Cross-strait Ties'. *CCTV.com-English*, 2013. Available athttp://english.cntv.cn/20130225/107125.shtml (accessed on 26 August 2021).

China Post. 'China Head Pledges Continued Peaceful Cross-strait Relations'. 2013. Available athttp://www.chinapost.com.tw/taiwan/china-taiwan-relations/2013/02/26/371350/China-head.htm (accessed on 12 December 2020).

Colombo Plan Secretariat. The Colombo Plan. Sri Lanka: Colombo Plan Secretariat. Available at http://www.colombo- plan.org/index.php/about-cps/history/ (accessed on 10 July 2020).

Conachy, James. 'Chinese Think-tank Warns of Growing Unrest over Social Inequality'. Oak Park: World Socialist, 2001. Available at http://www.wsws.org/articles/2001/jun2001/chin-j15.shtml (accessed on 8 July 2021).

Department of Climate Change, National Development and Reform Commission. Clean Development Mechanism in China. Beijing: Department of Climate Change, National Development and Reform Commission, 2012. Available at http://cdm.ccchina.gov.cn/WebSite/CDM/UpFile/File2854.pdf (accessed on 11 June 2018).

Desheng, Cao. 'Bandung Spirit' Lives on after 50 Years'. *China Daily*, 2005. Available at http://www.chinadaily.com.cn/english/doc/2005-04/19/content_435352.htm (accessed on 26 August 2021).

Dreyer, June Teufel. 'Chinese Foreign Policy' in *Footnotes - Foreign Policy Research Institute Newsletter* 12, no. 5 (February 2007). Available at http://www.fpri.org/footnotes/125.200702.dreyer.chineseforeignpolicy.html

Du Juan. 'China to Establish Climate Change Think Tank'. *China Daily*, 2011. Available at http://www.chinadaily.com.cn/cndy/2011-11/22/content_14137549.htm (accessed on 26 August 2021).

Europa Commission. *EU and China Partnership on Climate Change* (Memo/05/298). Brussels: Europa Commission, 2005. Available at http://europa.eu/rapid/pressReleasesAction.do?reference=MEMO/05/298 (accessed on 17 June 2018).

Foreign Ministry, Sri Lanka. Joint Press Communique of the People's Republic of China and the Democratic Socialist Republic of Sri Lanka. Colombo: Foreign Ministry, Sri Lanka, 2007. Available at http://www.mfa.gov.lk/index.php/en/divisions/internal-audit-and-o-a-m- division/314-independence-day (accessed on 26 August 2021).

Indo-Asian News Service. 'India Gets Its Way as Climate Conference in Durban Closes'. Hindustan News, 2011. Available at http://www.hindustantimes.com/world-news/Africa/India-gets-its-way-as-climate-summit-in-Durban-closes/Article1-780872.aspx (accessed on 26 August 2021).

Government of Australia. *Australia-China Partnership on Climate Change*. Canberra: Government of Australia, n.d. Available at http://www.climatechange.gov.au/

government/initiatives/bilateral-cc-partnership-program.aspx (accessed on 26 August 2021).

Li Jijun, *Traditional Military Thinking and the Defensive Strategy of China*. Carlisle Barracks: Strategic Studies Institute, 1997. Available at http://www.fas.org/nuke/guide/china/doctrine/china-li.pdf (accessed on 14 June 2018).

Malik, Mohan. 'India-China Competition Revealed in Ongoing Border Disputes'. Power and Interest News Report (PINR), 2007. Available at http://www.worldsecuritynetwork.com/showArticle3.cfm?article_id=14981 (accessed on 26 August 2021).

Medcalf, Rory. 'Why the Indo-Pacific will keep trumping the Asia-Pacific'. *Channel News Asia*, 2017. Available at https://www.channelnewsasia.com/news/commentary/commentary-why-the-indo-pacific-will-keep-trumping-the-asia-9408586 (accessed on 12 July 2021).

Ministry of External Affairs. 'Declaration on Principles for Relations and Comprehensive Cooperation between the Republic of India and the People's Republic of China'. New Delhi: Ministry of External Affairs, 2003. Available at http://www.meaindia.nic.in/declarestatement/2003/06/23jd01.htm (accessed on 12 July 2021).

———. Agreement between the Government of the Republic of India and the Government of the People's Republic of China on the Political Parameters and Guiding Principles for the Settlement of the India-China Boundary Question. New Delhi: Ministry of External Affairs, 2005. Available at https://mea.gov.in/bilateral-documents.htm?dtl/6534/Agreement+between+the+Government+of+the+Republic+of+India+and+the+Government+of+the+Peoples+Republic+of+China+on+the+Political+Parameters+and+Guiding+Principles+for+the+Settlement+of+the+IndiaChina+Boundary+Question (accessed on 12 July 2021).

———. 'Water Sharing Relations with China' (Rajya Sabha Unstarred Question No. 3910 by Kumar Deepak Das). New Delhi: 2011, Ministry of External Affairs, Government of India. Available at http://mea.gov.in/mystart.php?id=220118234 (accessed on 26 August 2021).

———. 'History and Evolution of Non-Aligned Movement'. New Delhi: Ministry of External Affairs, Government of India, 2012. Available at http://www.mea.gov.in/in-focus-article.htm?20349/History+and+Evolution+of+NonAligned+Movement (accessed on 26 August 2021).

———. 'India-Sri Lanka Relations'. New Delhi: Ministry of External Affairs, Government of India, 2013. Available at http://mea.gov.in/Portal/ForeignRelation/India_-_Sri_Lanka_Relations.pdf (accessed on 26 August 2021).

———. Statement on Award of Arbitral Tribunal on South China Sea Under Annexure VII of UNCLOS. New Delhi: Ministry of External Affairs, 2016. Available at https://www.mea.gov.in/pressreleases.htm?dtl/27019/Statement+on+Award+of+Arbitral+Tribunal+on+South+China+Sea+Under+Annexure+VII+of+UNCLOS (accessed on 26 August 2021).

Ministry of External Affairs. 'India – Sri Lanka Relations, Bilateral Brief'. New Delhi: Ministry of External Affairs, 2017. Available at http://www.mea.gov.in/Portal/ForeignRelation/Sri_Lanka_November_2017_NEW.pdf (accessed on 26 August 2021).

Ministry of Foreign Affairs, PRC. 'Independent Foreign Policy of Peace'. Beijing: Ministry of Foreign Affairs, PRC. Available at http://www.fmprc.gov.cn/eng/wjdt/wjzc/t24881.htm (accessed on 13 June 2018).

Ministry of Foreign Affairs, PRC. 'China's Position Paper on the New Security Concept'. Beijing: Ministry of Foreign Affairs, PRC, 2002. Available at http://www.fmprc.gov.cn/eng/wjb/zzjg/gjs/gjzzyhy/2612/2614/t15319.htm (accessed on 18 June 2018).

Ministry of Water Resources, Government of India. 'India-China Cooperation'. New Delhi: Ministry of Water Resources, Government of India, n.d. Available at http://www.wrmin.nic.in/printmain3.asp?sslid=372&subsublinkid=290&langid=1 (accessed on 23 April 2018).

Moramudali, Umesh. 'Sri Lanka's Debt and China's Money'. *The Diplomat*, 16 August 2017. Available at https://thediplomat.com/2017/08/sri-lankas-debt-and-chinas-money/ (accessed on 26 August 2021).

National Reform Development Reform Commission. *China's National Climate Change*. Beijing: National Reform Development Reform Commission, 2007. Available at http://www.ccchina.gov.cn/WebSite/CCChina/UpFile/File188.pdf (accessed on 7 June 2017).

Office of the Historian. 'Telegram from the Embassy in India to the Department of State'. Foreign Relations of the United States [FRUS]: 1961–1963. Washington, DC: US Government Printing Office, [1963]2000), Vol. 19, item 307. Available at http://history.state.gov/historicaldocuments/frus1961-63v19/d307 (accessed on 26 August 2021).

Office of the President, Republic of China. 'Eight Years of Reform Create a Better Taiwan' (President's Notes). Taipei: Office of the President, Republic of China, 2016. Available at http://english.president.gov.tw/Default.aspx?tabid=1124&itemid=36480&rmid=3048 (Accessed on 14 December 2020).

Office of the United States Trade Representative, Executive Office of the President. *U.S.–India Trade Facts*. Washington, DC: Office of the United States Trade Representative, 2020. Available at https://ustr.gov/countries-regions/south-central-asia/india (accessed on 3 December 2020).

Press Information Bureau, Government of India. Text of *Agreement on Cooperation on Addressing Climate Change between the Government of the People's Republic of China and the Government of the Republic of India*. New Delhi: Press Information Bureau, Government of India, 2009. Available at http://pib.nic.in/newsite/erelease.aspx?relid=53517 and https://mea.gov.in/bilateral-documents.htm?dtl/25238/ (accessed on 14 June 2018).

Radhakrishnan, R. K. 'Hidden in History'. *The Hindu*, 2012. Available at http://www.thehindu.com/todays-paper/tp-features/tp-sundaymagazine/hidden-in-history/article2764986.ece (accessed on 26 August 2021).

Rapp, Tobias, Christian Schwagerl, and Gerald Traufetter. 'The Copenhagen Protocol – How China and India Sabotaged the UN Climate Summit'. *Spiegel Online International*, 2010. Available at http://www.spiegel.de/international/world/the-copenagen-protocol-how-china-and-india-sabotaged-the-un-climate-summit-a-692861.html (accessed on 26 August 2021).

Reuters. 'China's Xi Offers Fresh $295 Million Grant to Sri Lanka',. 2018. Available at https://www.reuters.com/article/us-sri-lanka-china-grant/chinas-xi-offers-fresh-295-million-grant-to-sri- lanka-idUSKBN1KC0D8 (accessed on 26 August 2021).

Sanderatne, Nimal. 'Sri Lanka's Massive Foreign Debt Generates a Debt Trap'. *The Sunday Times*, 2017. Available at http://www.sundaytimes.lk/170423/columns/sri-lankas-massive- foreign-debt-generates-a-debt-trap-238010.html (accessed on 26 August 2021).

Sehgal, R. 'Delhi's Skewed Sex Ratio: 24000 Girls Go Missing Every Year'. Accessed 31 January 2006. http://www.infochangeindia.org/features290.jsp

Sethi, Nitin. 'Climate Talks: Jayanthi Natarajan Applauded for Stirring Speech at Durban'. *The Times of India*, 2011. Available at http://articles.timesofindia.indiatimes.com/2011-12-10/global-warming/30501920_1_climate-talks-climate-change-small-island-countries (accessed on 1 February 2018).

Stone, Diane. 'Think Tanks and Policy Advice in Countries in Transition', Paper prepared for the Asian Development Bank Institute Symposium: 'How to Strengthen Policy-Oriented Research and Training in Vietnam'. 31 August 2005. Available at www.adbi.org/discussion-paper/2005/09/09/1356.think.tanks/ (accessed on 23 June 2018).

Thakur, Ramesh. 'Beyond Commonwealth, Cricket & Curry'. *The Hindu* (Chennai), 2013. Available at http://www.thehindu.com/opinion/lead/beyond-common-wealth-cricket- curry/article4449477.ece (accessed on 26 August 2021).

The Tribune. Promise of B. G. Verghese, 'Political Fuss over the Indus – 1', 'Peace Indus – 2', *The Tribune* (Chandigarh) 24–25 May 2005; 'New Charter for Water' *Hindustan Times* (New Delhi) July 2009. Available at http://www.bgverghese.com/articles.htm#water (accessed on 26 August 2021).

Third World Network. 'India and China Maintain Primacy of UN-two Track Negotiations'. Info Service on Climate Change, 2010. Available at http://www.twnside.org.sg/title2/climate/info.service/2010/climate20100301.htm (accessed on 12 July 2021).

Times of India. 'No Binding Pacts Inked in Durban Climate Meet: Jayanthi Natarajan', 2012. Available at http://articles.timesofindia.indiatimes.com/2011-12-22/developmental-issues/30546288_1_binding-commitments-kyoto-protocol-climate-negotiations (accessed on 1 February 2018).

UNFCCC. 'Establishment of an Ad Hoc Working Group on the Durban Platform for Enhanced Action', paragraph no. 4 of Decision 1/CP 17. New York, NY: UNFCCC, 2012a. Available at http://unfccc.int/resource/docs/2011/cop17/eng/09a01.pdf (accessed on 1 February 2018).

UNFCCC. CDM Reaches Milestone: 4000th Registered Project (Press Release), 2012b. Available at http://cdm.unfccc.int/CDMNews/issues/issues/I_L9HTDCWQC5OT5N0A7U0L9Q97XSZB7Q/viewnewsitem.html (accessed on 11 June 2018).

UNFCC. 'Increasing Ambition Level under Durban Platform for Enhanced Actions' (Submission by Government of India). New York, NY: UNFCC, 2012c. Available at http://unfccc.int/files/documentation/submissions_from_parties/adp/application/pdf/adp_india_28022012.pdf (accessed on 11 June 2018).

UNFCC. 'China's Submission on Options and Ways for Further Increasing the Level of Ambition'. New York, NY: UNFCC, 2012d. Available at http://unfccc.int/files/documentation/submissions_from_parties/adp/application/pdf/adp_china_08032012.pdf (accessed on 11 June 2018).

United Nations. 'Join Hands to Address Climate Change', Statement by H. E. Hu Jintao, President of the People's Republic of China at the Opening Plenary Session of the United Nations Summit on Climate Change, 22 September 2009, New York. Available at http://www.fmprc.gov.cn/eng/wjdt/zyjh/t606275.htm (accessed on 3 February 2019).

Varadarajan, Siddharth. 'NSG Ends India's "Clean" Waiver'. *The Hindu*, 2011. Available at http://www.thehindu.com/news/national/nsg-ends-indias-clean-waiver/article2132457.ece (accessed on 26 August 2021).

Wijesiriwardane, Panini. 'Sri Lankan President Signs "Strategic Cooperative Partnership" with China'. Oak Park, MI: World Socialist Web, 2013. Available at http://www.wsws.org/en/articles/2013/06/11/sril-j11.html (accessed on 26 August 2021).

Xinhua. 'China Urges Developed Countries to Take Serious Actions at Durban Climate Conference'. Xinhua, 2011. Available at http://news.xinhuanet.com/english/china/2011-12/07/c_122391570.htm (accessed on 26 August 2021).

Yan Xuetong. 'The Problem of "Mutual Trust"'. *The New York Times*, 2012. Available at http://www.nytimes.com/2012/11/16/opinion/the-problem-of-china-and-u-s-mutual-trust.html?_r=0 (accessed on 26 August 2021).

Zhaokun, Wang. 'China-built Port Terminal Opens in Sri Lanka Capital'. *Global Times*, 2013. Available at http://www.globaltimes.cn/content/801743.shtml (accessed on 26 August 2021).

About the Author

Raviprasad Narayanan has been with Jawaharlal Nehru University (JNU) since October 2015. His teaching and research interests focus on China, its foreign policy, economic reforms, and pedagogies explaining China. International Relations and theories explaining state behaviour motivate his research and publications.

At JNU, he has taught four courses for M.Phil. and MA students—*Research Methods in International Relations*—a primer to understand methods of/for writing dissertations and conducting research, relevant to a research university like JNU; *Strategies of Economic Development in China* explaining the deep history and processes that have led to China becoming the global destination for investment and internal economic transformation now expanding outwards—in economic and strategic terms, and the course titled, *The State in Modern China* detailing the modern nation state putting on a veneer over a civilizational state with the CPC presiding over every segment of politics, economy and society. He has taught a new course titled *China and Taiwan Cross Strait Relations* for M.Phil. this semester.

He was earlier Associate Research Fellow/Associate Professor with the Institute of International Relations (IIR), National Chengchi University (NCCU), Taipei, Taiwan from 2009 to 2015. Before IIR/NCCU, he was with the Institute for Defence Studies & Analyses (IDSA), New Delhi from 2003 to 2009.

His CV can be accessed at https://www.jnu.ac.in/Faculty/raviprasad/cv.pdf

Index

Academia Sinica, 226
academic vacuum, 231
Act East Policy of India, 185
actor linkages, 121
Advisory Group on Greenhouse
  Gases (AGGG), 110
Air India aircraft, crashed, 186
Alliance of Small Island States
  (AOSIS), 115
American corporate sector, 159
American Studies Center (ASC), 39
anti-communist alliance, 163
Anti-Communist Bill, 163
arbiter model, 74
arena model, 74

Bay of Bengal Initiative for Multi-
  Sectoral Technical and Economic
  Cooperation (BIMSTEC), 84
Beijing
  decision-makers, 47
  FPDM, 91–93
  Open Door Policy, 47
  policy outcomes, 47
Bharatiya Janata Party (BJP), 78
bilateral 'notes of dissonance'
  analysing, 87
bilateral relations
  gravitas impetum concitati, 162
bilateral trade, 167, 187
  Sri Lanka and China, 210
BJP, 164
boundary dispute, India and China,
  87–88
business process outsourcing (BPO), 85

Center for International Studies
  (CIS), 37
Central Military Commission
  (CMC), 89
Central Military Commission
  General Office (CMCGO), 26
Central Water Commission (CWC),
  138
Chen Mumin, 41
China
  Climate Change, guidelines, 126
  commonality, 165–68
  concept of peaceful development in
    foreign policy, 91
  contemporary foreign policies, 1
  decision-makers, 48
  disputed boundary with India, 87
  economic modernization, 169
  environment bureaucracy, 131–34
  establishment intellectual, 27–30
  foreign policy decisions, 63
  FPDM, 66
  geopolitical perspective, 94
  India bilateral and Taiwan, analysis,
    188–97
  Indian Ocean Rim, influence, 192
  Indian political system, 94
  India, permanent stasis, 180, 181
  India relations, gradations, 188
  intellectual, 46
  MFA, 78
  national interests, 169
  negotiating for Climate Change, 127
  new security concept, 34
  political culture, 30

political elites, 46
Sikkim and Ladakh, border transgressions, 193
strategic developments, 190
strategic policymaking think tanks, functions, 30–39
Taiwan, ideology and economics, 182–85
Tibet Autonomous Region, 90
weltanschauung, 179
China Arms Control and Disarmament Association (CACDA), 39
China–India relations, 109
China–Pakistan Economic Corridor (CPEC), 93
Chinese Academy of Sciences (CAS), 36
Chinese Academy of Social Sciences (CASS), 36, 44
statement by Dr Manmohan Singh, 82
Chinese foreign policy framework, 6–7
Chinese policymaking influenced by think tanks, 44
Chinese Premier Zhu Rongji NDA tenure, 81
Chinese Strategic Culture and Foreign Policy Decision-Making, 70
civilizational states, 178
Civil war between Kuomintang (KMT), 182
Clean Development Mechanism (CDM), 115
projects, 115
Climate Change, 230
China's approach, 133
China's guidelines on negotiations, 126
defined by UNFCCC, 111
dual challenges, 118
India–China cooperation, 113–18
negotiation, 124–31, 140

outcome of China–India cooperation, 121
security impact, 111
theoretical approach and hypotheses, 112–13
closed door model, 49
Cold War, end, 166
Colombo, conflicts, 215
Commission for the Protection of Environmental and Natural Resources (CPENR), 131
Common Minimum Program (CMP) statement on foreign policy, 80
Communist Party of China (CPC), 23, 89, 157, 160, 180–82
Confucius Institutes (CI), 180
constructivists, 153, 165
gained theoretical acceptance, 153
contemporary foreign policies
China, 1
India, 1
cooperation, 118
position, 137
Copenhagen Conference, 117
Countering America's Adversaries Through Sanctions Act (CAATSA), 168
Covid-19 pandemic, 171, 180
Cross-Strait Relations Research Centre (CSRRC), 39
Cultural Realism
Strategic Culture and Grand Strategy in Chinese History, 69

decision, 63
decision-making, 66
defence diplomacy with India, 167
Democratic People's Party (DPP), 185
Deng Xiaoping's policy, 183
Development Research Center (DRC), 37
diplomatic freeze, 159
domestic reform, 231

Index 257

Dravida Munnetra Kazhagam (DMK), 213
Durban Conference, 130

East Asia Summit (EAS), 84
Economic Cooperation Framework Agreement (ECFA), 184
economic development, 119
economic diplomacy, 167
economic incentive
  bilateral trade, new vector, 84–86
Economic Research Center (ERC), 37
Economic, Technical and Social Development Research Center (ETSDRC), 37
education, 230
Election Commission of India, 171
Environmental Protection Bureaus (EPBs), 132
environment cooperation, 118
  diplomacy, 118–19
  explanation, 119
EU–China Think Tank Round Table, 40

Foreign Affairs Leading Study Group (FALSG), 23–25
  characteristics and values, 25
foreign policy decision-making (FPDM), 23
Foreign Policy Decision Making (FPDM)
  classical theories, 2–3
FPDM, 62, 226, 232
  China – India, 230
  IR discourse, 1, 2
  review of literature, 67–70
  Sino-Indian relations, 91
functional linkages, 121

global climate, 153
Graduate Aptitude Test in Engineering (GATE), 172

Graduate Record Examinations (GRE), 172
greenhouse gases (GHGs)
  emission cut, 116
Guomindang (GMD) government, 7

harakiri, 170
hydro-cooperation, 134–38

India
  Act East Policy, 193
  contemporary foreign policies, 1
  disputed boundary with China, 87
  Doklam and Galwan crises, 189
  foreign policy, 190
  relations with China, 94
  Taiwan, past and contemporary, 185–87
  Taiwan relations, 180, 188
  United States, 162–65
India–China cooperation
  environmental sustainability, 123
  explanation, 119
  positive spillovers, 122
Indian foreign policy, 215
  China, Beijing's limitation, 190
Indian FPDM, 189
India's Act East policy, 186
India Sri Lanka Free Trade Agreement, 214
India–Taipei Association (ITA), 186
India–US bilateral trade, 167
Indo-Pacific power, 194
Indus Water Commission (IWC)., 137
inside access model, 50
Institutional School, 5
intellectuals
  China, 27
  Chinese history, 27
  studies, 28
intelligence agencies, 169
intermediate zone, 7, 8
internally displaced people (IDP), 213
International Container Terminal, 211

International Monetary Fund (IMF), 228
international relations (IR), 37
IR, 71, 152
  Chinese approaches, 9–14

Kuomintang (KMT), 157, 184
Kyoto Protocol, 122
  objectives, 111

least developed country (LDC), 227
Liberation Tigers of Tamil Eelam (LTTE), 209
Line of Actual Control (LAC), 216
linkage politics model, 73–74
Look East policy, 185–86

Maoist/communist ideology, 6
Maritime Silk Route Initiative (MSRI), 179
Marshall Plan, 157
MFA, 169
  role, 65
military–industrial complex, 167
Ministry of Commerce (MoCOM), 169
Ministry of Environmental Protection (MEP), 131
Ministry of Environment and Forests (MoEF), 116
Ministry of External Affairs (MEA), 228
Ministry of Foreign Affairs (MFA), 33
mobilization model, 50
modern state, 61
modus vivendi, 151
most favoured nation (MFN), 159

NAM, 227
National CDM Authority (NCDMA), 116
National Coordination Committee on Climate Change (NCCC), 116
National Defence University (NDU), 26
National Democratic Alliance (NDA), 78
National Development and Reform Commission (NDRC), 116, 131
National People's Congress (NPC), 131
National Security Leading Group, 25
Nelum Kuluna, 212
New Delhi, foreign policy establishment, 217
New Delhi's policy of engagement, 195
Non Aligned Movement (NAM), 194
Non-Aligned Movement (NAM), 164
Northern Province, 212
Nuclear Suppliers Group (NSG), 167
nuclear tests of 1998
  impact on Sino-Indian Relations, 78–80

One Belt One Road (OBOR), 179
Open Door policy, 27, 158, 183
organisational process model, 5
organizational model, 72
Organization of the Petroleum Exporting Countries (OPEC), 114
Outside Access Model, 50

peace and development, 8–9
People's Liberation Army (PLA)
  role in decision-making process, 75
People's Liberation Army (PLA), 26
  examples of think tanks, 26
People's Republic, history, 44
pluralist model, 74–76
  fifth belief, 74
  first belief, 74
  fourth belief, 74
  second belief, 74
  third belief, 74
political elites
  China, 46

Politically Rational Foreign Policy Decision-Making, 69
Popular-Pressure Model, 50
post-conflict Sri Lanka–India relations, 212
public sector units (PSUs), 228

rational actor model, 71–72
Reach-Out model, 50
realist/rational actor, 4
Republic of China (ROC), 186

SAARC, 213
SCO, 231
security, 230
Seventh Schedule of the Indian Constitution, 232
Shanghai Communique, 156
Shanghai Cooperation Organisation (SCO), 84
Sikkim and Ladakh
　border transgressions, 193
Sino-Indian relations, 77, 159–62
　FPDM, 91
　impact of nuclear tests of 1998, 78–80
　perceptions influencing decision-making process, 93–94
social structures, defined, 153
South Asia
　arguments, 179, 204
　China, long-term strategic gains, 217
　geopolitical transition, 209
　methodology adopted, 206
South Asian Association for Regional Cooperation (SAARC), 190
South China Sea under Annexure VII of UNCLOS, 191
Special Economic Zones (SEZ's)
　Four Modernisations, policy, 183
Special Representatives (SR), 195
Sri Lanka
　China and India, 215

Chinese infrastructure investments, 210
Indian investments, 214
UN Human Rights Council, 215
Sri Lanka Podujana Peramuna (SLPP), 214
standard operating procedure (SOP), 217
State Environmental Protection Agency (SEPA), 131
Stockholm Conference, 113
Strategic Cooperative Partnership, 210
String of Pearls, 212
structural changes, 231
studies
　Chinese state, 28
　intellectuals, 28
　think tanks and the Chinese state, 28

Taipei Economic and Cultural Center (TECC), 186
Taiwan Relations Act of 1979, 186
Taiwan's Go South policy, 185
Technical Economic Research Center (TERC), 37
terrorism, China and India, 231
think tanks
　development of horizontal linkages, 38–39
　information filters, 35–36
　introducers of new ideas', 36–38
　policy advocates', 30–32
　policy control, 34–35
　policy interpretation', 33–34
Tiananmen 1989 movement, failure, 31
Tianxia, 179
Tibet, 89–90
traditional/historical school of scholarship, 3
Trans-Pacific Partnership (TPP), 168
trilateral, theoretical frame, 152

UNFCCC, 153, 168
Union of Soviet Socialist Republics (USSR), 152, 159
United Nations Conference on the Human Environment (UNCHE), 110, 113
United Nations Convention of the Law of the Sea (UNCLOS), 172, 191
United Nations General Assembly (UNGA), 111
United Nations (UN)
structural expressions, 227
United Progressive Alliance (UPA), 213
United States and China
historical issues, 154–56
institutional convergences, 172
Open Door policy, 156–59

value linkages, 121
Vision Statement, 86
global content, 85
political connective content, 83

weltanschauung, 170
Westphalian interpretation, 178
White House, 167
World Bank, 228
world, description Hobbesian terms, 38
World Trade Organization (WTO), 86